TWO KINGDOMS OF UGANDA

Snakes and ladders in the Scramble for Africa

To
In

```
CW01044417
```

one old Africa hand
to another ...

Cedric
November 2010

www.pulfordmedia.co.uk/ituri

Also from Cedric Pulford and Ituri

Casualty of Empire (history)

Eating Uganda (history/religion)

Air Madness: Road's Mistakes Repeated (environment)

Siren Society (politics)

JournoLISTS: 201 Ways to Improve Your Journalism

Byliners: 101 Ways to be a Freelance Journalist

Our Vanishing Freedoms (politics) *pamphlet*

About the author

Cedric Pulford is a British journalist and author with more than 25 years' experience of Anglophone Africa, working mainly on training projects across the continent. He has had a long association with the Guardian newspaper in London. For 10 years he was the UK correspondent of Ecumenical News International news agency, an associate of the World Council of Churches. He has an MA degree in philosophy, politics and economics from Oxford University and an MA in political science from Case Western Reserve University (USA), where he did research into East African business elites.

TWO KINGDOMS OF UGANDA

Snakes and ladders in the Scramble for Africa

Cedric Pulford

ITURI

© Cedric Pulford: 1999, 2007, 2011

The moral rights of the author have been asserted

Two Kingdoms of Uganda published 2011 by Ituri Publications
4 Chestnut Close
Woodford Halse
Northants NN11 3NB (UK)

ISBN **978 0 9567222 0 1**

Text set in Century Schoolbook 10.5/12 point
with headings in Bliss
by Book Production Services, London

Printed and bound in the UK by 4edge Ltd
www.4edge.co.uk

A CIP catalogue record for this book is available from the British
Library

www.pulfordmedia.co.uk/ituri

*This book uses environmentally friendly papers certified by the Forest
Stewardship Council*

FSC Mixed Sources
SA-COC-001695
© 1996 FSC A.C.

CONTENTS

DIAGRAMMATIC MAPS

ACKNOWLEDGEMENTS

This book is a conflation of my two previous titles, *Eating Uganda* (1999) and *Casualty of Empire* (2007), updated and with added material. The new material particularly involves Dr David Livingstone as well as two traditional kingdoms elsewhere in Africa, Barotseland and Asante. I hope that bringing the experiences of Buganda and Bunyoro "under one roof" will give a sharper focus to their contrasting experiences under colonialism. The chapters on Barotseland and Asante illustrate the fact that Britain's impact on Africa took different forms from place to place, yet in another sense was everywhere the same.

Grateful thanks are due to the following for help variously with *Eating Uganda, Casualty of Empire* or material in the present volume:

Paul Barrett, Andrew Boyd, David Brummell, Breege Cameron (who drew most of the maps), Brenda Ellison, Tommy Gee and Eric Norris (both veterans of Bunyoro), Paul Hopkins, Richard Ibreck, Sheelagh Killeen, the Rev Michael Meech, Martin Revis, Georgina Rhodes and Richard Proctor (Rhodes and Proctor), Dr Helen Szamuely, Liz Tayfun, Roderick Thomson, Professor P.K. Tibenderana (Makerere University, Uganda), the chief librarians and staff of the London Library and Rhodes House, Oxford.

I gladly acknowledge a debt to Thomas Pakenham, whose magnificent *Scramble for Africa*, combining scholarship with colour and pace over a huge canvas, first made me aware of the fascinating Uganda Question.

The present title is a salute to the Rev R.P. Ashe, author of *Two Kings of Uganda*. This pioneer missionary was one of those writers who have given us invaluable insights into advanced African states before the European conquest.

FRONT COVER and page xi: The mystical Nile as depicted in Sir Samuel Baker's *Ismailia*, 2nd edition 1879

BACK COVER: In snakes and ladders players who land on a snake fall backwards; those who reach a ladder climb nearer to the winning square. Picture by permission of the Early Learning Centre

NAMES AND PLACES

The spelling of names and places in Uganda can be confusing, particularly with differences between Victorian and modern texts. The following is a modest guide through the forest:

I have kept the original spelling of names and places in direct quotes, with a bracketed explanation if needed, but otherwise use the modern forms.

Many names include "r" in their older forms and "l" in their current forms: Kabalega, the king of Bunyoro, one of the constituents of modern Uganda, is now preferred to Kabarega, for example.

Bunyoro in older texts is described as Unyoro, while Uganda originally referred to the rival kingdom of Buganda, not the entire colony created by the British.

The people of Buganda are the Baganda. An individual man, woman or child is a Muganda. The language is Luganda. The preferred adjectival form is Ganda – eg Ganda culture.

Similarly, the people of Bunyoro are the Banyoro. An individual man, woman or child is a Munyoro. The language is Runyoro. The preferred adjectival form is Nyoro – eg Nyoro culture.

In older texts "w" may be used instead of "b" – eg the Wanyoro, the people of Bunyoro; the Waganda, the people of Buganda. wa- is the coastal (Swahili) form, and ba- is the form used by the Banyoro and the Baganda. The early European travellers used wa-. I have not changed these references in quotations, but otherwise I use the ba-style. That modern tribe of African leaders who measure their success in Mercedes-Benz cars are universally known as the wa-Benzi, however!

The varying use down the decades of Buganda and Uganda requires explanation. The kingdom was and is Buganda, but at the coast it was called Uganda. The early explorers and writers, coming to the country from the coast, naturally continued to call it Uganda. Early in the colonial period, however, the two words ceased to be interchangeable. Buganda came to mean the original kingdom while Uganda referred to the larger colonial protectorate, which took in Bunyoro, Ankole, Toro, Busoga and other areas.

In the interests of the book's wider appeal, I have kept non-English words to an absolute minimum. I generally use English translations rather than original terms: eg, county instead of saza. Where an original word is used, like barusura (Kabalega's elite troops), I immediately explain it. A very few original words appear repeatedly and are not explained each time.

Thus it is worth remembering that mukama and kabaka are words for king, in Bunyoro and Buganda respectively. Katikiro means chief minister and saza (which creeps in from time to time) means county.

For names, I have used the current forms except in quotations. The River Zambezi, for instance, was for Dr David Livingstone the Zambesi.

Explorers gaze on the fabled Nile (detail from illustration in Sir Samuel Baker's Ismailia). Missionaries and conquerors used both the Nile and the African east coast routes to reach Buganda and Bunyoro

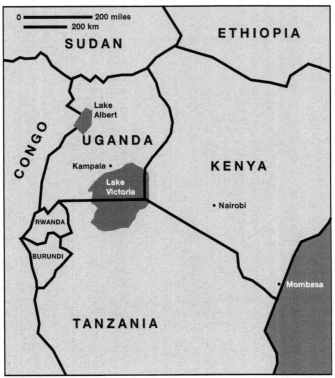

Map 1: East African political boundaries, present day

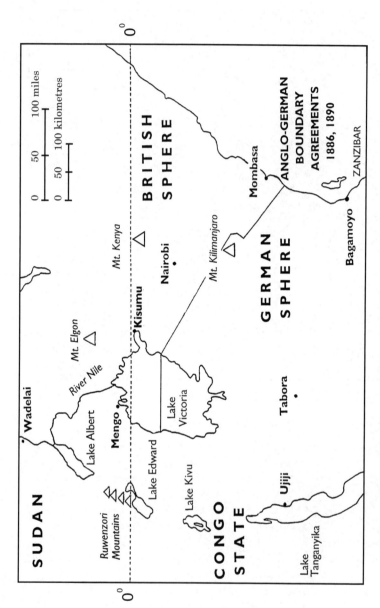

Map 2: The Great Lakes region in the latter 19th century

1 Introduction

Mention Uganda and most people know little. Older folk remember Idi Amin, the monstrous (in every sense of the word) dictator whose tyranny put the country in the world's headlines for a few years; younger ones know him in fictionalised form through the film *The Last King of Scotland*. Yet once upon a time, the country was well known to most Britons. Sir Winston Churchill famously, and the explorer Henry Morton Stanley before him, called Uganda the "Pearl of Africa".

In the 1890s, the Uganda Question gripped the British nation in the way that more recently the great African famines have done. The issues are worth revisiting because of what they can tell us about Africa now. The issues were varied: the abolition of slavery, the protection of Christian missionaries and converts, the expansion of commerce. In two months of 1892, the Foreign Office in London received 174 "resolutions", mostly with many signatures. Religious organisations, particularly the Church Missionary Society, were prominent. Slavery was mentioned in 104 resolutions, commerce in 75 resolutions. Christianity and commerce were never far apart in 19th century Africa.

The question stirring up so much commotion was whether Britain should annexe Uganda, a country or properly a series of kingdoms with which it had become progressively involved through the activities of explorers, missionaries and administrators of the private Imperial British East Africa Company. It was a question on which the public, filled with images of David Livingstone's missionary travels and General Gordon's violent death in Khartoum at the hands of Islamic zealots, felt free to have an opinion.

There was plenty to be said on either side of the case. William Gladstone's government was itself divided, with the foreign secretary, Lord Rosebery, in favour of annexation while the prime minister – whose delay in sending relief had probably cost Gordon his life – was against further colonial escapades.

Uganda was well known because two of the heroes of African exploration, John Hanning Speke (1862) and Henry Morton Stanley (1875), had been there and told the world. Buganda, the principal kingdom, was the most sophisticated country in the whole of eastern and southern Africa, yet it lay mysterious and exotic deep in the interior, north of the Great Lake, the Victoria Nyanza, more an inland sea than a lake. Another great kingdom, Bunyoro, lay along the shores of Lake Albert. On top of all that, Uganda was the source of the Nile, for so long the preoccupation of geographers and explorers.

After the explorers had come the missionaries, and after the missionaries the soldiers in a seemingly inevitable sequence. Buganda was unusual in Britain's imperial story. First, the missionary presence in the remote kingdom had been brought about by one man – Stanley, whose trumpet call for evangelists brought a rapid response from the Church Missionary Society in London. Secondly, the annexation issue was precipitated as much by the need to protect those missionaries and their converts as by the prospects of trade.

What drove the missionaries over much of Africa was the continuing spectre of slavery. Their inspiration was Dr David Livingstone, who had travelled in Africa for more than three decades and publicised the evil traffic in human beings.

This book is not an attempt to rival professional historians over ground already covered. In fact, it is not a history at all in the usual sense. It is a study of two dichotomies. First is the contrasting fates of Buganda and Bunyoro with the coming of the colonisers. Buganda co-operated with the British and reaped the rewards; Bunyoro resisted the British and paid the price for years to come. The second theme is the "missionary wars" between Catholicism and Protestantism, symbolised by their respective cathedrals on opposing hills in what became Kampala. For me, there is something bizarre in these two wings of Christianity bringing theological disputes into the African bush. They fought each other when they should have been spreading the message they shared.

The Uganda story is a clash of two advanced cultures, the African and the European. It is an astonishing pageant of kings and chiefs, explorers, missionaries, soldiers, porters – the literal beasts of burden. If ever the expression "a cast of thousands" fitted, it is in this story.

Now that Kenya is the powerhouse of East Africa, it is strange to realise that in the 19th century it was simply somewhere one passed through on the way to Buganda. Much of it was barren and peopled by tribes perceived as backward. The souls to be won were to be found in Buganda and in the other kingdoms and territories of what became Uganda. The beginning of the city of Nairobi, Kenya's capital, was accidental. The existing tiny settlement was picked as the headquarters for the Uganda Railway administration because it was more or less half way between the coast and Lake Victoria, from where steamers completed the journey to Buganda. A town began forming and the Kenya colonial administration at Machakos felt it had to shift so as to be on the railway line.

We naturally think of Uganda as part of East Africa along with Kenya and Tanzania; yet with a different roll of history's dice it might have been an extension of North Africa, an Egyptian, Islamic province instead of a British, Christian colony. It might have looked not eastwards to Mombasa for its route to the world but northwards along the Nile to Khartoum and Cairo. Early European contacts with Buganda came as readily from the north as from the east. Samuel Baker, the first governor of Egypt's Equatorial Province (part of the Sudan) in the 1870s, tried but failed to absorb Bunyoro to the south. His successor in Equatoria, Charles Gordon – later the hero of Khartoum – sent emissaries to both Bunyoro and Buganda. He even tried to garrison Buganda but the ruler, Mutesa, captured his troops and they were extricated with difficulty. In 1879, soon after the missionary Alexander Mackay reached Buganda by the east coast route, a Church Missionary Society party of three arrived from the north along the Nile.

The rise of the Mahdi in the 1880s removed the prospect of Egyptian administration extending south to Bunyoro and Buganda by cutting off the farthest provinces from Cairo and eventually Khartoum. It also blocked the access of European travellers via the Nile. The Mahdi's Islamic fundamentalist movement conquered much of southern

Sudan before it took the capital Khartoum in 1885; for a while, it looked poised to reach even Bunyoro and Buganda. In fact, the high tide of Mahdism reached only as far as Equatoria, covering some but not all of that province.

In what remained of the province the governor, Emin Pasha, was stranded along with his several hundred Egyptian and northern Sudanese officials, clerks and soldiers. With the blocking of the Nile route and then the fall of Khartoum, he had no source of supplies and had to subsist on whatever could be procured or made locally.

Emin hoped that Equatoria could become a British territory along with Buganda. If this wish had been realised, the tragic history of Sudan in our own time, arising from the domination of the Muslim north over the Christian and animist south, would surely not have happened. The capital of Equatoria before Emin, under pressure from the Mahdists, removed it south to Wadelai was Lado, near modern Juba, the present southern Sudanese capital. If Equatoria had become British, a smaller, Muslim Sudan would have faced a larger, Christian Uganda, or perhaps the Commonwealth country of Equatoria, which would also have taken in other parts of the non-Arab southern Sudan.

The governor was visited by the occasional traveller; he was also able to get letters out to the east coast via Mackay in Buganda. In these ways his plight became known. A relief expedition was organised in London under Stanley. The failure of this expedition (1887-89) was a cause célèbre in its day. It managed not the relief of Emin but his removal, with many of his followers. A couple of years later the soldier Frederick Lugard began the making of Uganda as a British colonial possession, but by then there could be no question of including Equatoria because there was no Equatoria to include.

The British government's eventual answer to the question should Britain annexe Uganda was yes, and Buganda was joined with adjacent kingdoms into a protectorate, declared in 1894. The country spent the next seven decades under British rule, although protectorate status – based on treaties with the indigenous rulers – provided somewhat more local autonomy than a colony would have done.

At the heart of the Uganda story are the great lakes. The Victoria Nyanza is the largest lake in Africa – 26,000 square miles (67,000 sq km) in size, almost as big as Scotland. Nowadays it is bordered by three countries: Uganda, Kenya and Tanzania. In Victorian times it found glory as the long-sought source of the Nile. This flows out the lake and makes its way via Lake Kyoga into Lake Albert at the top (northern) end.

Lake Albert has a most distinctive shape: it is 100 miles (160 km) long and around 20 miles (32 km) wide. On one side is Uganda and on the other side the Republic of Congo (the former Zaire). This formidable body of water is still less than $1/12^{th}$ the size of Lake Victoria.

From Lake Albert the Nile flows northwards through the heartland of the one-time Egyptian province of Equatoria. At Khartoum this White Nile is joined by the Blue Nile from the Ethiopian highlands, to form one of the world's mightiest rivers.

Uganda's other great lake is Lake Edward, which again it shares with Congo. The lake is linked to the smaller Lake George by the Kazinga Channel. To the south, beyond the Uganda border, lie Lake Kivu and Lake Tanganyika; beyond those again is Lake Malawi (formerly Lake Nyasa).

Uganda is a country of a stunning beauty made up of rivers, forests and hills. Part of its western boundary runs along the Ruwenzori Mountains, which haunted Victorian writers under their ancient name, the Mountains of the Moon. The Ruwenzori reach 16,765 ft (5,110 m). The whole country is high up although with a big variation in height: Lake Albert is at 2,030 ft (619 m), Lake Edward 2,991 ft (912 m) and Lake Victoria 3,717 ft (1,133 m) – a fact that the builders of the Uganda Railway from the coast knew too well.

From the beginning the Victoria Nyanza, or Lake Victoria, was an obsession with European travellers. Ronald Hardy, in *The Iron Snake*, pictures how the railway builders in the 1890s were at one with earlier travellers in their feelings:

The Lake was much more than the terminus for a railroad. It had long had a mystical place in the imagination, exciting many of the Great Explorers and those that sent them on their strange and wonderful journeys. An aura of cruelty lay on its southern shore: to these beaches the early Arab slavers had come from Kazeh. It was romantic: only forty years had passed since Speke came to Mwanza and saw for the first time this vastness of water. It was beautiful: behind the tawny beaches the land was exuberant with palms, mangoes and flamboyants. It was malignant: the northern shore was infested by the mosquito, the spirillum tick and the tsetse, and in the groves and islands lived death and desolation. It was unpredictable: it oppressed with its gloom and sullenness and turbidity, it enticed with its colour, it disturbed with its scent of barbarism, it beguiled with its serenity, it frightened with its sudden moods of violence and the electric storms that charged the water with power and turned it black as pitchblende. And, of course, it was the fountain of the Nile ... The Lake was no docile basin of water. It was a force: a secret and a mystery: the source of life and fertility.

The lake was also a barrier for Buganda-bound travellers in the sense that a straight line from either Bagamoyo (near Dar es Salaam in present-day Tanzania) or Mombasa (Kenya), which were the main points of departure, runs through the middle of it. Alexander Mackay sailed across the lake from the Church Missionary Society base at Kagei to reach Buganda for the first time, but most travellers went round it. Earlier travellers followed the routes of most of the explorers, leaving from Bagamoyo and entering Buganda through Karagwe, at the southwest end of the lake. The other way was from Mombasa through Masailand and into Busoga, at the north-east end of the lake.

The choice of the Bagamoyo route was based partly on fear of the Masai, across whose lands the route from Mombasa ran. The fierceness of the nomadic and pastoralist Masai had been much exaggerated by the explorer Joseph Thomson, who may himself have been given a false impression by traders wanting to discourage outsiders. The Masai's seemingly gruesome habit of feeding on their animals' blood helped build a myth that has lasted to this day.

Busoga, the territory next to Buganda on the approach through Masailand, was highly sensitive. The Baganda had a belief that a conqueror would emerge from the east (as he did in the form of Captain Lugard of the Imperial British East Africa Company) so they were extremely suspicious of strangers entering Busoga. When this route became safe for European travellers, it was the shorter and better way. Eventually, the Uganda Railway followed close to the caravan route.

To reach Buganda from the coast a trek of about three months was needed for the journey of approaching 700 miles (1,150 km) through the tribal lands of what are now mainland Tanzania and Kenya. Travellers moved in caravans at a surprisingly slow pace: seven or eight miles (11-13 km) a day was usual. Water, food and fuel-wood were constant preoccupations. Parties picked their routes by the availability of water, and had to stop early to scour the area for food and fuel.

Provisions were paid for with trade goods, of which cloth, wire and beads were especially popular. An eye had to be kept on fashions, however. Frederick Jackson recorded how a vast stock of blue beads, which had accumulated at the Mumia's staging post, became valueless because of a sudden change in fashion. (*Early Days in East Africa*)

Journeys relied on human porterage. Many experiments were made with pack animals, especially donkeys, but these did not cope well with the climate, the tsetse fly or the fevers that abounded. Illness was common among the porters, whose standard load was 65 lb, or 30 kg – half as heavy again as a suitcase filled to airline maximum weight, which most modern travellers can manage from the trolley as far as the check-in belt. Another reason for the slowness of marches was that sick men travel slowly – except where they were treated like useless pack animals and discarded by the roadside.

It is not easy for modern people to imagine the constant illness that was the experience of the early Europeans in Africa. Fevers were commonplace and frequent, as they still are for many millions of Africans even in the cities. Illness affected not only European travellers but also those in a settled situation. Often it was brought on by hard work. Both Lugard and Père Lourdel, one of the first Roman Catholic missionaries at the Buganda capital, make interesting comments (quoted later) about the connection between fatigue or stress and illness. It is an insight easily missed in modern urban life, but one that could save millions of pounds in doctors' fees and prescriptions.

2 Livingstone's legacy

The story of modern Uganda begins many hundreds of miles to the south with the man who more than any other brought home to the English-speaking world the evils of the slave trade throughout Africa. David Livingstone was the inspiration for the first missionary involvement in the country.

He was born to poor parents in Blantyre, Scotland (now on the edge of Glasgow), in 1813. After starting working life in a cotton mill, he eventually qualified as a medical doctor and became ordained. He arrived in Africa in 1840, aged 26, marrying the daughter of the famous missionary, Robert Moffat. With only two visits to Britain, Livingstone was to spend the rest of his life – more than three decades – there.

He worked at first for the London Missionary Society, a Protestant group whose resolute non-denominationalism he keenly supported. He wrote that he joined the LMS because it "sends neither episcopacy nor presbyterianism, nor independency (congregationalism), but the gospel of Christ to the heathen. This exactly agreed with my ideas of what a Missionary Society ought to do."

When Livingstone started in southern Africa, it was just one generation since the world had taken the first tentative steps in the abolition of slavery. A British MP, William Wilberforce, in 1807 persuaded parliament to abolish the transatlantic slave trade that had laid waste to communities in West Africa.

It was seven years since Wilberforce's successor as leader of the abolitionist movement, Thomas Buxton, convinced parliament (in 1833) to declare the end of slavery throughout the empire. It remained rampant beyond Britain's reach, however.

On various travels Livingstone came face to face with the ghastly reality of slavery, of captured Africans, many of them young boys, wrenched from their homes and put into yokes as they were marched towards the coast, of villages burnt and deserted after a visit by slave raiders.

These searing experiences caused him to turn away from the life of a settled missionary to take up travel and exploration. Livingstone's vision was to find viable routes into the interior for legitimate commerce and Christianity. He believed that slavery would only be ended through the commercial development of Africa, which would put in place alternative, honest means of making a living.

What remains inspirational about Livingstone's journeys is that for much of the time he travelled solely with African companions and, at least in his early years, with very little money. He enjoyed such good relations with chiefs that they gave him porters for no payment. This style of travel differed sharply from that of most Europeans at the time.

He wrote in 1852: "There is not a native in the country but knows now for certain whose side I am on."

With his family back in Britain, Livingstone set out for Barotseland (now part of Zambia). The Barotse had been conquered by the Makololo, a branch of the Sotho from southern Africa. It was the Makololo overlords with their ruler Sebituane and after him his son, Sekeletu, whom Livingstone encountered.

He was much impressed by Sebituane, describing him as "decidedly the best specimen of a native chief I ever met". (*Missionary Travels and Researches in South Africa*) The king was fleet of foot and led warriors into battle himself.

In an illustration of the cheapness of human life (or alternatively of the value of firearms), Livingstone recorded that eight boys, the children of captive tribes, were exchanged for eight guns.

Meanwhile, Sekeletu proved an apt pupil in learning to read:

> Seeing I was anxious that he should learn to read, he subjected his father-in-law to learn first, as some men like to see the effect of medicines on other people before they imbibe them themselves; and finding that it did him no harm, Sekeletu was taught long enough to gain the ability to read.*

---

* Address at the Town Hall, Cambridge, December 5, 1857

Livingstone, with 27 Makololo, left from the Makolo capital, Linyanti, to seek a route to the west coast. This was a journey by river and land of more than 1,000 miles (1,600 km). They reached Luanda and got back, but the route did not seem promising, and soon Livingstone – this time with more than 100 Makololo in support – was heading over a similar distance for the east coast.

The route lay along the River Zambezi. In November 1855 he became the first European to see the Victoria Falls, or Mosi-oa-Tunya (the Smoke that Thunders) as the local people called it. This expedition ended at Quilimane on the coast of Angola, so he had successfully crossed the continent from west to east.

He returned to Britain in 1856 to a hero's welcome. During this visit of about 15 months he wrote *Missionary Travels and Researches in South Africa*, which was published in 1857. At the end of the year (December 4), Livingstone made his famous challenge to well-wishers crowding the Senate House, Cambridge: "I go back to Africa to try to make an open path for commerce and Christianity; do you carry on the work which I have begun. I leave it with you!"

Livingstone opened the speech with an image of the people of the Kalahari desert in southern Africa with a pre-scientific state of understanding. They sent to the mountains for rain-makers. "They say the people in those mountains have plenty of rain, and therefore must possess a medicine for making it." They would not be persuaded otherwise.

Sechele, chief of the Bakwains tribe, however, put what Livingstone acknowledged was "rather a poser". It was a question that would not have been out of place in a theological college. The ruler asked how it was that if Livingstone's forefathers had known about the terrors of the Last Judgement they had allowed his forefathers to pass away into darkness without knowing anything of what was to befall then.

In answer, Livingstone relied on the difficulties of geography, and explained that the word had to spread upwards from Cape Colony. The time would come, he added, when the whole world would receive the knowledge of Christ because that was Christ's promise.

The chief pointed to the Kalahari desert, and said, "Will you ever get beyond that with your Gospel? We, who are more accustomed to thirst than you are, cannot cross that desert; how can you?" I stated my belief in the promise of Christ; and in a few years afterwards that chief was the man who enabled me to cross that desert; and not only so, but he himself preached the gospel to tribes beyond it.

Livingstone turned to his travels. He explained that his cross-continental journey arose from the need to find a path to the sea for the purposes of commerce. "Civilisation and Christianity must go on together," he declared.

As the Doctor and his party of Makololo entered Portuguese territory, heading for Luanda, payment was demanded for everything. But he had nothing to pay with. He refused the offer to trade one of his men for supplies. On another occasion, a chief offered him a slave-girl. Upon Livingstone explaining that "I had a little girl of my own, whom I should not like my own chief to give to a black man, the chief thought I was displeased with the size of the girl, and sent me one a head taller".

As they neared the coast, however, "the name of England was recognised". At Luanda the party went on board a British anti-slaving vessel.

The route to the west coast proved unsuitable because of dense forests and boggy streams. Livingstone returned to Linyanti, and from there set out for the east coast. This time the chief equipped him with 114 men rather than the 27 of the previous expedition. The party reached the coast at Quilimane.

There followed a digression on the appearance of African women, whom Livingstone thought would be "much handsomer than they are if they would only let themselves alone; though unfortunately that is a failing by no means peculiar to African ladies". One tribe knocked out all their front teeth, producing a "perfectly hideous" effect; another filed all their front teeth to a point so they looked like alligators; others variously widened the nose by piercing the cartilage and inserting a reed, tied the hair into "basket-work" and dressed their hair with a hoop around it "so as to resemble the Gloria around the head of the Virgin".

The people of Central Africa had stronger religious views than those to the south. One tribe (unnamed) could read and write, which Livingstone traced to the work of Portuguese Jesuits.

> Their only books are, however, histories of saints, and miracles effected by the parings of saintly toe-nails, and suchlike nonsense. But, surely, if such an impression has once been produced, it might be hoped that the efforts of other missionaries, who would leave the Bible with these poor people, would not be less abiding.

Livingstone was excited by the development possibilities of the highlands surrounding the Zambezi.

> My desire is to open a path to this district, that civilization, commerce, and Christianity might find their way there. I consider that we made a great mistake, when we carried commerce into India, in being ashamed of our Christianity; as a matter of common sense and good policy it is always best to appear in one's true character.

The natives of Central Africa were very desirous of trading but their only traffic was in slaves, of which the poor had "an unmitigated horror". They were not, Livingstone admitted, "absolutely anxious to receive the gospel" but were open to Christian influences. "Those two pioneers of civilization – Christianity and commerce – should ever be inseparable."

The sort of men who were wanted for missionaries Livingstone saw before him in the Senate House – men of education, standing, enterprise, zeal and piety. It was not enough to be pious – one had to be practical. In the early ages, monks were not ashamed to hold the plough.

> The missionaries now take the place of those noble men, and we should not hesitate to give up the small luxuries of life in order to carry knowledge and truth to them that are in darkness ...
> Education has been given us from above for the purpose of bringing to the benighted the knowledge of a Saviour. If you knew the satisfaction of performing such a duty, as well as the gratitude to God which the missionary must always feel, in being chosen for so noble, so sacred a calling, you would have no hesitation in embracing it.

Livingstone emphatically denied that he made a sacrifice to become a missionary.

> Can that be called a sacrifice which is simply paid back as a small part of a great debt owing to our god, which we can never repay? ... Say rather it is a privilege. Anxiety, sickness, suffering, or danger, now and then, with a foregoing of the common conveniences and charities of this life, may make us pause, and cause the spirit to waver and the soul to sink, but let this only be for a moment.

He would rather be a poor missionary than a poor curate!

For the missionary, there were also the pleasures of the welcome home. He heartily thanked his audience for their welcome, and he expressed the hope of an eventual welcome from the Lord: "Well done, good and faithful servant."

He ended, rousingly, with the passage for which the speech is remembered:

> I beg to direct your attention to Africa; I know that in a few years I shall be cut off in that country, which is now open; do not let it be shut again! I go back to Africa to try to make an open path for commerce and Christianity; do you carry out the work which I have begun. I LEAVE IT WITH YOU!
> *The full text of the speech is reprinted here as an appendix (starting on p 287)*

This speech proved to be one of the most influential ever in the history of Christian mission and, through the missionary societies, the development of Africa. It was the direct inspiration for the foundation of the Universities' Mission to Central Africa and later, through Henry Stanley, the Church Missionary Society entry into Uganda.

Livingstone thus inspired two distinctive and opposing strands of Anglicanism in Africa – the Anglo-Catholicism ("high church") of the UMCA and the evangelicalism ("low church") of the CMS.*

---

* Anglo-Catholics accept many of the distinctive doctrines of the Roman Catholic church (see pp 58), but not the universal jurisdiction of the Pope or his infallibility; evangelicals are more strictly Protestant, finding their ultimate authority in the bible and what is understood to be the practices of the early Christian church

The Doctor found himself drawn to the Anglo-Catholics, which Andrew C. Ross (*David Livingstone, Mission and Empire*) sees as a sign of his developing views on Christian mission. Livingstone admired the work of the (Roman Catholic) Jesuits in nearby Angola, and he was taken with St Boniface's 8th century mission to Germany.

Boniface planted monasteries among the then-pagan Germans, which over time changed the surrounding communities culturally and economically as well as religiously. For Livingstone in the 19th century, the approach contrasted with the typical missionary emphasis on individual conversions. Ross describes it as "the eighth-century version of Christianity, commerce and civilisation" – Livingstone's own approach.

Livingstone made a further visit to Barotseland, this time with his brother, Charles. Also on the expedition was a young doctor, John Kirk. He was later the British consul-general in Zanzibar, a diplomatic figure of consequence and a major force behind the final suppression of the slave trade in East Africa. The Makololo, the Livingstones commented, were "by far" the most intelligent and enterprising of the tribes the brothers had met – a judgement that later observers applied to the Barotse when they regained the ascendancy.

Sekeletu and his subordinate chiefs expressed a wish for English settlers in the Batoka highlands.

He said he would cut off a section of the country for the special use of the English [wrote the Livingstones in their account of the expedition]; and on being told that in all probability their descendants would cause disturbance in his country, he replied, "These would be only domestic feuds, and of no importance".

Livingstone now explored the Zambezi and Shiré rivers, using a portable boat, the Ma-Robert (an African name for Livingstone's wife). During this five-year expedition, he explored Lake Nyasa (now Lake Malawi), and led the Makololo whom he had left near the coast after the crossing of the continent back to their homes at Linyanti. Sometimes the tragedies of the slave trade could be forgotten: this was an Africa of primeval beauty. He counted a herd of 800 elephants. With primeval beauty went primeval tragedy: fever was ever-present, and in 1862 Mrs Livingstone died from a fever at Shupanga on the Zambezi.

Around this time the world took another significant step in the abolition of slavery. In 1863, during the American Civil War, President Abraham Lincoln proclaimed slaves in the Confederate South to be free.

Livingstone was back in Britain in 1864, staying for just over a year and writing (with his brother) *Narrative of an Expediton to the Zambesi and its Tributaries*. When he sailed to Africa for the third and final time, it was at the request of the Royal Geographical Society to explore the watershed around Lakes Nyasa and Tanganyika and to try to unravel the continuing mystery of the source of the Nile.

Livingstone was already 52, even today an advanced age for expeditions and perhaps unwise in the conditions then. His supply of quinine was stolen – a devastating loss in the malarial climate. Nevertheless, he walked doggedly on, exploring Lake Mweru (now shared by Zambia and Congo) and Lake Bangweulu (in modern Zambia). Even his faithful followers became restive at the Doctor's desire to see yet another lake, but Livingstone knew that he was by the headwaters of either the Congo or the Nile, and would not be deterred.

Slavery was all about. He confided to his journal: "I am heartsore, and sick of human blood." He travelled into the country of the Manyema, a tribe much feared by those around them. At that time they were cannibals, and were also used by the Arabs in slave raids. By now more than six years had passed since his return to Africa. He was fever-racked and a living skeleton when he made for Ujiji, an Arab settlement on Lake Tanganyika. He had ordered supplies to be sent there, but they had been stolen.

Livingstone was ill and destitute when Henry Stanley, on an assignment for the New York Herald, found him in Ujiji on October 28, 1871. With Stanley's resupply and his company, Livingstone rallied. They sailed together in a canoe on the lake, then travelled to Unyanyembe. Stanley left with the promise to send supplies and equipment to allow Livingstone to carry out a final task: he wanted to ascertain whether the River Lualaba fed into the Congo or the Nile (it was the Congo). The supplies arrived, but by now he was too ill to continue the work and died at Chitambo's village in Ulala on May 1, 1873. He was 60.

The world rightly saw as his finest epitaph the fact that six of his followers brought the body through many difficulties and obstructions to Zanzibar, from where it was returned to Britain for interment in Westminster Abbey. Livingstone's heart, meanwhile, had been cut out and buried at Chitambo's. The memorial stone in the abbey quotes Livingstone's words about slavery to the New York Herald, the newspaper that sent Stanley to find him: "All I can add in my solitude is, may Heaven's rich blessing come down on every one, American, English, or Turk, who will help to heal this open sore of the world."

The quotation shows that Livingstone was under no illusions about the work still to be done. Progress remained grindingly slow. Even into the 1890s slavery was a reality in much of Africa. Slaves made the short crossing from the east coast to the Arabian peninsula, while men, women and children were taken as slaves in inter-tribal warfare.

Britain suppressed the slave trade, internal and external, in Uganda from 1890, although imperialism's many critics claim that the common practices of indentured labour and forced labour were not far short of slavery.

Worldwide, slavery today has gone underground but it has not gone away. Forced labour and human trafficking are forms of slavery.

After the lionising of Livingstone, it was inevitable that a reaction would follow in later years. His achievements in exploration have been questioned; it has been said he made few converts, that he exposed his wife to the hazards which killed her, that travel in the end became travel for travel's sake. Even if it were all true, Livingstone's enduring achievement is one of witness: of dramatising the evil of the slave trade, of humanity and forbearance, of non-violence and doggedness unto death. Africa certainly says so. Three decades after independence, when other European names had been consigned to history, there was still a town called Livingstone in Zambia and a city called Blantyre in Malawi.

Four disparate forces have laid claim to Livingstone, elevating him to "mythic status" in Ross's appraisal:

(A)s a saintly hero of Protestantism, as an icon of imperialism, as a leading embodiment of resurgent self-consciousness, and lastly, in the 1960s, as the patron saint of African nationalism ... David Livingstone was a more complex person than can be captured by any of these myths, but Livingstone as patron saint of African nationalism is closer to who he was than the others. (*David Livingstone, Mission and Empire*)

In Blantyre, Scotland, Livingstone's birthplace has been a museum since 1929. The tenement block was once home to 24 families including the Livingstones. Set in 20 acres (8 ha) of gardens overlooking the River Clyde, the museum contains a variety of personal objects including diaries, educational certificates and medical, scientific and navigational equipment.

The continuing potency of Livingstone's name is shown in the small Essex town of Ongar. He spent just six months there, training for the ministry with the Rev Richard Cecil, the Congregational minister. It was enough to call into being a plaque at the Congregational (later United Reformed) church, a memorial window in the parish church and a row of cottages named after the explorer. The plaque declared: "In this room David Livingstone lived in 1838 just before proceeding to his great work in central Africa." The nearby towns of Epping and Harlow also remembered Livingstone, Epping with a room in the United Reformed church named after him and Harlow with a David Livingstone Church.

Livingstone also called into being the career of one the giants of African exploration − Henry Stanley. When Stanley met Livingstone he was a journalist who had knocked about here and there, and for whom the expedition was ultimately just another assignment; after what Stanley recognised as a defining experience of his life, he saw himself as an explorer and gave the rest of his life to work in Africa.

When Basil Mathews's *Livingstone the Pathfinder* was published in 1912, a living voice emerged from history: Sir John Kirk. Livingstone's companion on the Zambezi expedition added his recollection to later editions of the book. He spoke of Livingstone's "absolute lack of any sense of fear" (adding that it "amounted almost to a weakness").

This quality, which probably cannot be learnt or willed, allowed Livingstone many times to face down hostile tribesmen and to die in God's time, not man's.

Kirk told how Christ Church Cathedral was built on the site of the old slave market in Zanzibar. He said of his old chief: "How happy he would be to see it! ... Perhaps he does."

3 Rhodes strikes north

Livingstone's hosts in Barotseland in the 1850s and 1860s, the Makololo, were eventually overthrown. They left behind the legacy of their language, which became the tongue of the Barotse themselves (now known as Lozi). The Barotse in their turn maintained the dominion of Sebituane and Sekeletu over the less advanced peoples surrounding them.

The story of the Barotse empire and its encounters with the incoming British has many parallels with the experiences of Buganda and Bunyoro, which are the subject of this book.

From the turmoil of the end of the Makololo period emerged the man who became the most famous litunga (king) of Barotseland, Lewanika. He ruled for almost four decades until his death in 1916.

Lewanika was drawn to Britain because he wanted British protection from three forces that threatened him: the nearby Matabele (originally from Zululand) under their leader Lobengula, from the Portuguese in Angola and from some of his own dissident subjects.

Cecil Rhodes, the visionary-adventurer and South African mining magnate, one of the most contentious figures in African history, seized the moment. Frank Lochner, representing Rhodes's Chartered Company, secured a far-reaching concession from Lewanika in 1890, the year in which the Company planted the flag in Lobengula's domains at what became Salisbury (now Harare) and also the year in which Uganda began its decisive encounter with British arms.

The concession covered all Lewanika's country, allowing the Company to engage in manufacturing, mining, banking, the provision of infrastructure works and the importation of arms and ammunition.

Whatever Lewanika's fears of Lobengula, it is impossible to imagine that the Barotse king realised the full implications of such a one-sided deal.

Within a few years his arch-rival was dead. The 1893 Matabele war started over a small incident when the telegraph link was cut and wire stolen. The Chartered Company seized the opportunity and treated this as a casus belli. Maxim guns made short work of Lobengula's impis (regiments). The king fled his capital, Gubulawayo (close to today's Bulawayo), and soon died, probably of smallpox.

However, the process of assimilation was by now unstoppable. Barotseland was absorbed into Northern Rhodesia at first under the Company and, from 1924, as a British protectorate. Northern Rhodesia became independent in 1964 as Zambia, with Barotseland later renamed the Eastern Province.

The Lochner concession was followed by more treaties up to 1909. The Lawley concession of 1898 reduced Lewanika's annual subsidy from £2,000 to £850 and gave the Company judicial powers in disputes between whites or whites and blacks. It was the blueprint for the Lewanika concession of 1900. This affirmed the Company's administrative authority over the king's domains. It excluded prospecting in the Barotse heartland – and yet an astonishing postscript provided that if gold in worthwhile quantities was not found outside the reserved area, it could be sought inside the reserved area!

Colonel Colin Harding, who was a witness to the signatures on the treaty, wrote (in *Far Bugles*) that "on more mature consideration [Lewanika] realised that it carried him further than he had meant to go". In a curious addition that may have been an attempt to distance himself from the deed, Harding went on:

> I would like to say here that although I was present when this Ratifying Treaty was signed and my name was appended as a witness to the other signatures, the full contents of the document were not divulged to me.

There were more concessions to come. By a simple exchange of letters in 1904, Lewanika gave the Company farming and settlement rights throughout his kingdom except the Barotse valley and near Sesheke. The 1909 Wallace concession reiterated these farming and settlement rights except in areas where prospecting was prohibited (including the heartland). Villages and gardens were specifically allowed to be uprooted, albeit with consent and compensation. The consent need not be that of the people affected, however. It could also be given by the high commissioner of the territory – ie a Briton.

This was a massive land grab, even if the worst of it never materialised by comparison with Southern Rhodesia. Nor were these deals made solely by rapacious commercial opportunists in Rhodes's name; they involved British imperial officials. It is hard now to understand how these people could bless such unequal treaties. It is equally hard to imagine why Lewanika and his advisers gave away so much.

The Baganda were fortunate that they were not exposed to the same pressures. Uganda did not have the same interest for settlers and prospectors.

Two points may be made in support of Lewanika, who remains a hero to the Lozi. He kept the Barotse heartland intact and the British came to his country by treaty, not conquest. Thus Barotseland differed from Lobengula's kingdom, and merited different treatment in Lozi eyes and also to a degree in those of colonial officials.

The situation is paralleled in what is now Uganda. There, Buganda reached an accommodation with the incoming British and for ever after was treated better than the rival kingdom of Bunyoro, which had to be subdued by force of arms.

In Barotseland as in much of the empire, the British style was to rule without overt displays of power. Norman Knight recounts how as a young district officer he was borne home in state by bearers, to the anger of the provincial commissioner, who happened to see the incident. There was a good reason – Knight had been injured – but he had some explaining to do. (*Memories of a District Officer in Northern Rhodesia and of the War Years*)

The indifference of colonialism to traditional boundaries was illustrated by the King of Italy's boundary award of 1905. This sliced a huge chunk from Lewanika's domains, allocating it to Portugal. However, Catherine Winkworth Mackintosh claimed (in *Coillard of the Zambesi*) that the king was probably left with as much territory as he had ever occupied effectively.

He lost more than a quarter of his land but still had 181,947 square miles (471,243 sq km), not greatly short of Germany's 208,947 square miles (541,173 sq km). Another loss of territory occurred in 1941 when Balovale district, where the Lozi had long claimed overlordship, was excised from Barotseland.

Colin Harding, who travelled up the Zambezi from Victoria Falls into Barotseland, gave an account (*In Remotest Barotseland*) of Lewanika's daily routine. He sat in the courthouse between 9 am and 10 am, hearing complaints, promulgating laws and attending to other government business. The indunas, or senior officials, representing the people, sat on his right. They alone had the right to criticise the king.

An early European resident, R.H. Palmer, declared in his reminscences that Lewanika was a natural ruler. (*Lewanika's Country: Reminiscences of a Pioneer*)

In *Far Bugles*, Colin Harding praised Lewanika's "charming personality", his "loyalty and other inherent virtues". When the litunga visited London for the coronation of King Edward VII, with Harding in attendance, the king and his retinue were found not to touch alcohol.

"Lewanika's whole and consistent attitude was befitting a gentleman and a great native ruler," Harding wrote.

More than 60 years later Lewanika was still winning praise. A 1968 biography by Gervas Clay, *Your Friend, Lewanika*, could not speak too highly of the litunga:

> He died full of honour, loved and respected by his people as a great chief, leaving the heart of his country reserved to the Barotse by treaty rights and his own family secure on the throne. No African ruler of his time achieved more, and none was more regretted by all who had known him.

Barotseland, like Buganda, enjoyed a large degree of autonomy under the British. However, this once leading state, afflicted by its remoteness, slipped into backwardness. Development in Northern Rhodesia became focused on the mining areas and along the line of rail from Livingstone through Lusaka to the Copperbelt. Furthermore, in more recent times, as Gerald L. Caplan points out in *The Elites of Barotseland 1878-1969,* the country became an underpopulated labour reserve with 1/6th of the land mass but less than 1/10th of the population of Zambia. Both developments have similarities with the experience of Bunyoro.

Although David Livingstone "discovered" Barotseland, Francois Coillard was the missionary who exerted the greatest influence in the early years of European contact. Lewanika said:

> There are three sorts of whites, those of the government, the traders and missionaries. Fear those of the government, they have power; prey on the traders, for they have come to prey on you. As for the missionaries, a missionary is one of us. (Quoted by Clay, above)

Coillard (1834-1904), a French Protestant of the Paris Evangelical Mission, stayed in the country for many years and was close to Lewanika. *On the Threshold of Central Africa* is his account of the experience.

The missionary had worked for 20 years among the Sotho in Basutoland (now Lesotho). When he came north his first plan was to work among the Banyai, who were under the Matabele. But Lobengula said no, and Coillard went to Barotseland instead.

At that point, 1877, the Makololo (who were Sotho) had not long been overthrown. They had treated the Barotse well, hence Coillard and his fellow evangelists were accepted by Lewanika and much of the country.

Coillard settled in Barotseland in 1880, remaining there (apart from two years' leave in Europe in the late-Nineties) until his death in 1904, aged 69. His dominance in the mission field was threatened for a time by a movement known as the Ethiopian church. It flickered out relatively soon but remained a beacon for the later emergence of indigenous African associations.

The French missionary instinctively favoured the Chartered Company as the agent of "civilising" European influence – a nexus that was also to be seen in Uganda. "Coillard ... gave Lochner (see above) all the support he could. Coillard viewed with distrust the whole structure of the Barotse state as it was imbued with paganism," Lewis

Gann writes in *The Birth of a Plural Society*.

Barotse chiefs vetoed Lewanika's conversion to Christianity for political reasons, although his son and successor, Letia, was a Christian. The king read his bible almost daily but was said (by Catherine Mackintosh in *Lewanika of the Barotse*) also to sacrifice to his ancestors.

The 1911 edition of the Encyclopaedia Britannica described the Barotse, in language that would not be acceptable today, as "the intellectual and physical superiors of the vast majority of the negro races of Africa".

Like Buganda and Bunyoro and other advanced African kingdoms, pre-colonial Barotseland had an economic reach beyond local or tribal groups. Gann, in *The Birth of a Plural Society*, says the country had some regional economic specialisation with the different parts interdependent.

The constitutional arrangements were unusual, however. The litunga reigned jointly with a queen, the mokwai, who was his eldest sister. The mokwai had a separate capital, Nalolo, to the south of the litunga's seat, Lealui.

Life was dominated by the River Zambezi. The heart of Barotseland is the flood plain up-river of the Victoria Falls in Zambia. The plain stretches for 120 miles (193 km) and is 25 miles (40 km) across at its widest. The annual flooding, between February and July, gave rise to a migratory, river culture whose symbol was the Kuomboka. The royal court led the move in the royal barge Nalikwanda to higher, drier ground at the plain edge, from Lealui to Limulunga.

In modern times, the Kuomboka has been re-enacted as a cultural affirmation and as an important regional tourist attraction.

A detailed account of the river culture in traditional times was given by the anthropologist Max Gluckman in *Economy of the Central Barotse Plain*. The Barotse typically spent three months at the plain margin because of flooding. On the plain itself high spots of land (mounds) were preferred for settlement because they rose above the water level.

In later times, the margin became the most densely populated part of Barotseland.

Barotseland's religio-social arrangements were also

curious, at least to European eyes. V.W. Turner (*The Lozi Peoples of North-Western Rhodesia*) describes a religion in which the supreme god was not omnipotent. His name was Nyambe, and his wife was Nasilele. He was driven from earth into heaven by man.

D.W. Stirke, who spent eight years among the Barotse and whose book proclaimed exactly that (*Eight Years Among the Barotse*), claimed that children of similar ages started sexual relations almost as soon as they could walk. The not surprising result was that virginity was unknown.

The mwalianzo ceremony marked a girl's first menstruation, after which she was married. There was no offence of rape. On the other hand, according to Stirke, there was no known case of a girl needing coercion – a conclusion that feminists today would certainly challenge.

Catherine Mackintosh quoted her uncle on the impermanence of marriage among the Barotse. This was because of the ease of divorce. "There are no unhappy couples here; they part," said Coillard.

A visitor to the kingdom, Reginald Arthur Luck, stressed the dominance of the Barotse over other peoples. In his 1902 book, *A Visit to Lewanika, King of the Barotse*, he said: "Slave trading is supposed to be at an end, but as a matter of fact, all the surrounding tribes are slaves to the Barotse."

In 1906, under British encouragement, Lewanika proclaimed the abolition of slavery in his kingdom. He had been struck on a visit to England by the sight of people working for themselves. Everybody seemed to be at work, but in his country "people just sit about".

Hindsight, both positive and negative, has its limitations. *Twilight on the Zambesi* by Eugenia W. Herbert (2002) is one of the few recent books to touch on Barotseland. She cautions us to

> ... resist the temptation simply to see "colonialism" and "nationalism" as so many abstractions ... [it is] much easier to divide the actors willy-nilly into good guys and bad guys and move on. Everyone acknowledges that their own lives are a lot more complicated than that, but we often fail to grant the same complexity to the past.

Herbert points out that the Zambian government has behaved just as stingily towards Barotseland as the colonial treasury.

It was Barotseland's misfortune to be caught up in wider imperial politics in one of its most sensitive areas, southern Africa. Cecil Rhodes dreamt of an "all red" route from the Cape to Cairo. Gladstone's administration, according to John Marlowe's *Cecil Rhodes: The Anatomy of Empire*, went along with Rhodes's Chartered Company, preferring its "unscrupulous and insubordinate methods" to the weakness of the counterpart company in east Africa. This was the Imperial British East Africa Company, which as later chapters will show started the colonisation of Uganda and then dumped it in the British government's lap.

Rhodes's dream of all-red territory the length of Africa materialised in 1918, long after his death, when Britain obtained the United Nations mandate over the former German colony of Tanganyika. However, the "iron spine", a railway to connect all the territory, was never built.

As a kingdom within a country, Barotseland since independence has sometimes had a troubled relationship with the centre. In this it is like Buganda. But the parallel ends there. Buganda has a dominant place in Uganda, but Barotseland is at the periphery of Zambia. In this it is more like Bunyoro.

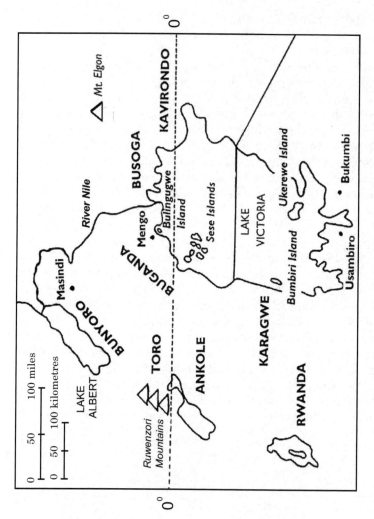

Map 3: Environs of Lake Victoria

4 Explorers come calling

The kingdoms of Bunyoro-Kitara and Buganda can be traced through the chronology of their kings at least to the 14th century. M.S.M. Kiwanuka explains how this is reliably established in the absence of written records.*

Taking the case of Buganda, he explains that substantial material remains were to be found in royal shrines featuring jawbones, umbilical cords and tombs. These made it "extremely difficult to doubt the existence of any king so commemorated". The office of keepers of these shrines was mostly hereditary, facilitating memories coming down through generations.

The social and political stability of Buganda, and the involvement of the various clans in the history of the royal family (Buganda did not have a separate royal clan), were other factors that contributed to the dependability of the accounts.

The missionary-anthropologist J. Roscoe came to a similar conclusion two generations earlier:

> (T)aking into consideration the remarkably accurate memories of the people in recounting events long past and their conservatism in religious ceremonies and social customs, the reader will recognise that it is possible to obtain from them a fairly accurate account of the past." (*The Baganda*, 1911, quoted by Kiwanuka)

Nevertheless, the several chronologies of the Ganda kings differ substantially. The one compiled by Sir Apolo Kaggwa, katikiro both before and after the coming of the British, has been preferred by historians. It was based on extensive research among the clans, and lists 30 babaka down to Mutesa in the later 19th century.

The Bunyoro list is slightly shorter (22 bakama) but, given that Ganda kings were frequently succeeded by brothers rather than sons, the number of generations is similar.

---

* in his edited edition of Sir Apolo Kaggwa's *The Kings of Buganda*

Beyond the kings whose existence can be established with reasonable certainty lies the land of myths and legend. The Banyoro recognise the Batembuzi rulers, descended from the mythological Kakama. They were followed by the almost equally shadowy Bachwezi. They in turn were followed by the undeniably historical Babito dynasty, starting with Isingoma Mpuga Rukidi.

A.R. Dunbar (in *A History of Bunyoro Kitara*) suggests that something factual must lie behind the Batembuzi and the Bachwezi, presumbly a folk memory of incoming tribes.

The Baganda count their kings as starting with Kintu and Chwa I, whose existence is uncertain. In some accounts, Kintu is part of a creation myth, descending from the gods. History begins with the third kabaka, Kimera.

The Nyoro and Ganda accounts of the beginning of the royal lines differ radically, in fact irreconciliably. Nyoro tradition holds that Rukidi and Kimera, the rulers of Bunyoro-Kitara and Buganda respectively, were the twin sons of Kyomya of the Bachwezi clan. The effect of this is to establish the deeper roots of the Banyoro (Rukidi was only the first Babito mukama, not the first mukama).

The Baganda, naturally, prefer to see their kingdom starting independently of Bunyoro, and trace the kingship beyond Kimera to Chwa I and Kintu. Furthermore, the claim that Kimera was a contemporary of Rukidi is disputed. Kiwanuka refers to evidence suggesting that Rukidi's more likely contemporary was Kiggala, the fifth kabaka. This, of course, pushes the origin of the kabakaship back further in time.

What can be said with some confidence is that the historical record for both countries begins around the 14th century. For most of the centuries Bunyoro-Kitara was by far the more powerful state. Many of the kingdoms and territories of modern Uganda were once under its sway: Ankole, Busoga, Karagwe, Koki, Toro, even Buganda (if one accepts the Nyoro account) and also Rwanda.

In John Hanning Speke's mid-19th century map of the region, Buganda is shown as a narrow strip of land on the northern shore of Lake Victoria.

This imperial legacy must have left its mark on Nyoro bakama. John Beattie makes the interesting suggestion (*The Nyoro State*) that Samuel Baker's difficulties with Bunyoro – which were to echo down the years with such terrible consequences – arose because Mukama Kamurasi was so different from the minor chiefs he had previously encountered:

> Baker's violent antipathy to the Nyoro ruler may perhaps be more understandable if it is remembered that until he reached Bunyoro his experience of African rulers had been confined to the comparatively minor headmen of the segmentary Nilotic societies to the north ... (H)e may well have been disconcerted that Kamurasi did not conform to his idea of a petty African chief. Had he come to Bunyoro by way of the very much more autocratic Ganda court, as Speke and Grant did, his reactions (and in consequence Bunyoro's future) might have been very different.

The 19th century saw the expansion of Buganda, much of it at the expense of Bunyoro. One reason for this was the cohesiveness of Ganda society: it was "double knit", in D.A. Low's phrase.* The country was organised around clan chiefs (the bataka) and territorial chiefs (the bakungu). Overlapping the latter were chiefs of royal estates (the batongole).

Although this created tensions among the various elements, it also in Low's view promoted social cohesion. The ordinary people, the bakopi, were subject both to the bataka and the bakungu, and through them to the kabaka. Nor were there tensions between the bakopi and the kabaka.

Bunyoro was historically much more loosely organised. It was cattle country, and the interests of its Babito kings lay "in raiding and not in ruling". (A.R. Dunbar: *A History of Bunyoro-Kitara*) Buganda offered better prospects for missionising – a process that Henry Morton Stanley now set in motion.

For us more than a century later, Stanley's words seem to crash through every racial and ethnic taboo in sight. The Ganda – the inhabitants of Buganda – were "an

---

* *Buganda in Modern History*

extraordinary people, as different from the barbarous
pirates of Uvuma, and the wild, mop-headed men of
Eastern Usukuma, as the British in India are from their
Afridi fellow-subjects, or the white Americans of Arkansas
from the semi-civilized Choctaws", he told readers of
Through the Dark Continent. Fine if you are a Briton, a
white American or a Ganda; not so hot if you happen to be
an Afridi, a Choctaw or from Uvuma and Usukuma.

At the time of publication in 1878, however, Stanley's
readers would have been untroubled by such language.
Here was confirmation that in this near-legendary kingdom of Buganda, in the African interior, were foundations
that could be built upon for Christianity, commerce and
civilisation. Few doubted that the three belonged together,
or that the people of the world were strung out in levels of
social evolution, with the goal for all to become like the
great industrial nations of Europe and North America.

When Stanley met Mutesa, the kabaka (king) of
Buganda, beside Lake Victoria on April 5, 1875, he quickly formed a favourable view of the ruler. The explorer John
Hanning Speke, visiting more than a decade earlier, had
found Mutesa wallowing in blood, but for Stanley he was
"an extraordinary monarch", "an intelligent and distinguished prince". In the evening of their first meeting,
Stanley confided to his diary: "In this man I see the possible fruition of Livingstone's hopes." Mutesa was "the light
that shall lighten the darkness of this benighted region".

Stanley clearly had no doubts about deciding what was
right for Africa and, misplaced as such self-confidence may
seem to us, his attitude then was commonplace. He wrote
of the kabaka: "My impression of him was that ... I should
make a convert of him, and make him useful to Africa."
Perhaps Stanley saw what he wanted to see: he needed a
charismatic figure as the climax to this stage of his expedition, and he found one. Missionaries later spoke of
Mutesa's continued blood orgies, but for Stanley a change
of character had been wrought by a visiting Muslim called
Muley bin Salim. Unfortunately, this meant Mutesa's conversion to Islam, but Stanley was not deterred. "I shall
begin building on the foundation stones laid by Muley bin
Salim. I shall destroy his belief in Islam, and teach the doctrines of Jesus of Nazareth."

This was Stanley's second African expedition, following his journey to find Livingstone. He was the prototype explorer-journalist, generating press copy as abundantly as he made discoveries. For this trip the New York Herald, sponsors of the Livingstone expedition, had been joined by the Daily Telegraph of London. One of Stanley's tasks was to establish the shape and proportions of the great inland sea of the Victoria Nyanza (lake). Along the northern side of the lake lay Buganda.

Mutesa's scouts found Stanley aboard his big rowing boat, the Lady Alice, named after one of his unsuccessful loves, so that when the expedition was ready to land in Buganda the kabaka and his nobles were waiting in full ceremonial order beside the lake at Usavara. Two to three hundred guns, as Stanley estimated it, were fired in welcome with much drumming and shouting.

It was nearly another mangled meeting for the explorer. He had greeted Livingstone with a banality born of unnecessary precision; now he strode up to a short young man standing beside a great standard, but was told in time that this was not Mutesa but the katikiro. Not knowing what a katikiro was, Stanley bowed and the young man bowed back. Later, Stanley learnt that the katikiro was the title of the first minister. He met the ruler after being given the opportunity to bathe, brush up and prepare externally and mentally for the Foremost Person of Equatorial Africa (Stanley's capitals).

Mutesa must have made a very striking figure. He wore a tarboosh (fez) and a black robe, with a white shirt belted with gold. Approaching middle age, he was slender and about 6ft 1in (1.85 m) tall. Stanley explains that among the Baganda this was not an unusual height. The explorer was just 5ft 5in (1.65 m), although heavily built. Stanley described the king as dark red brown in colour, with a "general expression of amiability combined with dignity". When not in council, he gave rein to hearty peals of laughter. He seemed to be interested in the manners and customs of European courts, and wanted to hear about "the wonders of civilization".

Out of this meeting, and those that followed, Stanley became convinced that the intelligent and agreeable Mutesa was the ideal person to fulfil David Livingstone's dream of planting Christianity and commerce in Africa. The explorer wrote in his diary: "In this man I see the possible fruition of Livingstone's hopes." So too was the advanced nation of Buganda the ideal setting for missionary work.

Mutesa, as well as some of his chiefs, could read and write Arabic. The king had learnt well from a Muley bin Salim. He understood Swahili, the coastal lingua franca, as well as the indigenous Luganda language. (Luganda had yet to be produced in written form.)

Yet Stanley was seeing only one side of Mutesa's chameleon personality. The benign and literate prince, who enjoyed intellectual debates, was also a bloody tyrant who on several occasions engaged in mass executions.

The Ganda author, Apolo Kaggwa – who was katikiro (chief minister) of Buganda both before and after the coming of the British – in *Basekabaka be Buganda* (The Kings of Buganda) lists Mutesa's enormities.He began his reign by executing many chiefs and princes (his brothers) on the grounds that they disputed his succession. In the Nnalongo massacre about 700 commoners, 216 slaves, 500 royal wives and about 35 chiefs died.

"It was a terrible and most dreadful thing to execute so many people," commented Kaggwa.

On another occasion Mutesa executed about 100 pages and royal wives, on the grounds that they had been seeing each other. Court politics led about 10 of his mother's chiefs to the executioner.

In 1875, around the time of Stanley's visit, there were mass arrests and executions of non-Muslims, Mutesa having converted to Islam.

Kaggwa's editor* adds that Mutesa's capital of Kabojja was nicknamed "Ndabiraako ddala" (see me for the last time) because when two men met they never knew whether they would see each other again.

The cruelties of Kabalega in Bunyoro were a constant theme of European commentators, used as a justification for acting against him. However, Mutesa's record, and that of his son and successor, Mwanga, who "imbrued (stained

---

* 1971 edition

or saturated) his hands with innocent blood ... until he had filled the cup of his crimes to overflowing"*, suggest that Kabalega was not exceptional.

If Stanley was impressed with Mutesa, the feeling was probably mutual. Stanley shot a crocodile at 100 yards (90 m). The party soon transferred to the nearby capital, which Stanley in his book introduces in breathless tones. The hill Rubaga! The imperial capital! This was journalistic licence. Although Rubaga was on a large scale, it was a town of straw huts and vegetable gardens set among plantain groves.

The country was described as crescent-shaped beside the lake, 300 miles (480 km) long and 60 miles (95 km) wide. Including Sese and other islands in the lake, the size was 30,000 square miles (77,700 sq km) with tributaries adding another 10,000 square miles (25,900 sq km). Stanley estimated the population of Buganda proper at 750,000 and the total population including the tributary states as 2,775,000. These figures can be nothing more than "best guesses" by the traveller (and the density of population in the tributary states is curiously higher), although Buganda's allocation of the country into feudal estates must have helped the accuracy of the guesstimates.

At the royal court, Stanley found another European visitor. This was Colonel Linant de Bellefonds, a member of General Gordon's staff in the Equatorial Province (Equatoria) of the Sudan. Much of the conversation at court was about Christianity. Fortunately for the future of Christian mission in Buganda, the French de Bellefonds was a Protestant. The first missionaries might not have found a footing if Protestants and Roman Catholics had contradicted each other at the start, as happened commonly later on. As it was, Stanley records Mutesa's astonishment that the Frenchman "employed nearly the same words, and delivered the same responses" as Stanley had.

The king learnt about Christian doctrines including the Ten Commandments. Stanley prudently added an 11th commandment: "Honour and respect the Kings, for they

---

* R.P. Ashe: *Two Kings of Uganda*

are the envoys of God." His evangelical fervour was rewarded when Mutesa ordered Christian prayers every Sunday. Mutesa was still a Muslim, but before Stanley finally left Buganda he converted to Christianity – which the explorer acknowledged was "only nominal".

It was a start. but Stanley, as we have seen, had plans for Mutesa. Before he left the court after a visit of 11 days, he wrote his famous letter to his sponsors, the New York Herald and the Daily Telegraph, appealing for missionaries. It was entrusted to Col Linant de Bellefonds, who would send it on after his return to Equatoria. De Bellefonds was ambushed and killed on the journey back. The letter was found concealed in one of his boots. Seven months after Stanley wrote it, the letter reached England, where its publication in November 1875 caused a sensation.

The appeal, written hurriedly as Stanley acknowledged, was couched in the most high-flown language:

> What a field and harvest ripe for the sickle of civilization! Mtesa would give [the missionary] anything he desired – houses, lands, cattle, ivory, &c.; he might call a province his own in one day. It is not the mere preacher, however, that is wanted here. The bishops of Great Britain collected, with all the classic youth of Oxford and Cambridge, would effect nothing by mere talk with the intelligent people of Uganda. It is the practical Christian tutor, who can teach people how to become Christians, cure their diseases, construct dwellings, understand and exemplify agriculture, and turn his hand to anything, like a sailor – this is the man who is wanted. Such an one, if he can be found, would become the saviour of Africa. He must be tied to no church or sect, but profess God and His Son and the moral law ...

> I speak to the Universities Mission at Zanzibar and to the Free Methodists at Mombasa, to the leading philanthropists, and the pious people of England. 'Here, gentlemen, is your opportunity – embrace it!' The people on the shores of the Nyanza call upon you. Obey your own generous instincts, and listen to them ...

With its echoes of Livingstone's Senate House speech, what a stirring call to evangelism and adventure! Stanley was writing the job description of an angel rather than a human being, but thousands of young men must have felt they could fill the bill.

The author, meanwhile, continued the exploration of the lake. There were his customary scrapes, including an escape from the dastardly chief of Bumbireh Island, whom he later attacked in revenge. In Ukerewe, he was impressed by King Lukongeh, whom he described as "quite as much influenced by conversations about Europe as Mtesa" and "as eligible a convert to Christianity". The route took the party near what became the Ripon Falls, the boundary between Buganda and Busoga. Here Stanley met Mutesa again.

This time the kabaka was in battle mode. He was about to make war on Uvuma. Stanley put Mutesa's army at 150,000 spears, plus 50,000 women followers and 50,000 children and slaves. Scholars have challenged the figure of 150,000 troops as inconceivably high, just as Stanley years later gave an even less credible figure of 200,000 Wanyankori (Ankori [Ankole] was claimed by Buganda as a dependency) brandishing spears. All agree that the numbers were large. The time needed to assemble the army left plenty of opportunity for talk. At one of these meetings in the camp at Nakaranga, Mutesa remarked that if you wanted knowledge you must talk to the white men to get it, then lobbed in: "Now, Stamlee, tell me and my chiefs what you know of the angels." Stanley was not flummoxed, at least not for long: he described the angels of Michelangelo and Gustav Doré, then, sending for his bible, translated passages about angels from Ezekiel and St John. He knew his bible and pressed it to his aid.

There is no reason to doubt the genuineness of Stanley's Christianity. Nor was it simply an expedient to open Buganda to a European presence. Stanley was, however, a man of the deepest paradoxes, whose personality and actions have puzzled and divided biographers ever since. He was an evangelical Christian who stomped through Africa in shoot-'em-up style. He claimed to fight for food only when he could not trade for it, yet he fought far more than most other explorers, some of whom did not find it necessary to fight at all. He was a Welsh poor-house boy who became a knight of the realm. He was British, then American, then British again. In his later activities directed at Equatoria and Buganda he may have been serving two masters and playing the highest politics, or he may have been rescuing a trapped man for humanity's sake. He was self-taught, yet wrote with the erudition and style of an Oxford scholar. He has been called a suppressed homosexual, but he could look back on heterosexual amours and married for the first time when he was over 50.

At least until his final expedition into Equatoria, Stanley could rightly claim to be the most successful African explorer. He was also one of the most brutal. He was Bula Matari (the "Breaker of Rocks"), a nickname that referred to his road-building exploits in the Congo and also describes his character. Whether he was successful because he was brutal, maintaining discipline, securing provisions, forcing the way through, is a question that still divides commentators. To present-day readers (and to many contemporaries) Stanley's readiness to execute members of his own expeditions for disciplinary offences is shocking. So too are revenge attacks like the one he made on the chief of Bumbireh Island. Stanley saw these actions as setting examples and sending signals. His writings do not suggest that he had any doubts about his actions. A certain sort of evangelical has the happy knack of knowing that God invariably agrees with his own preferences.

Frederick Jackson summed up in *Early Days in East Africa* Stanley's reputation as he found it in Zanzibar:

> There, he was regarded as a man of undoubtedly great courage and determination, but self-centred, overbearing, ruthless and a man who would stick at nothing; not quite the hero he was in Europe and America.

Stanley is full of paradoxes, yet in another sense he seems transparent. It is easy, and not necessarily wrong, to see the seeds of the man in his monumentally disadvantaged beginnings. Born illegitimate in 1841, he was named John Rowland. He was abandoned by his mother to the poorhouse, and again rejected by her a few years later. In his mid-teens he went to America as a ship's boy and stayed. He took the name Henry Morton Stanley from a great benefactor he found in New Orleans. The benefactor soon died, leaving him friendless again. With Stanley's lack of height, and with this background, you either learn to stick up for yourself or you go under.

Stanley got caught up in the American Civil War, enlisting on the Confederate side. After capture, he "turned" and served with the Union forces – evidence of opportunism for his critics. He landed on his feet at the New York Herald, where with the most rudimentary education his resourcefulness and a willingness to be away from home (which he hardly had) for months at a time soon took him to the post of a top foreign correspondent. Then he was picked for the choicest assignment of all: to find Livingstone.

Stanley's background seems the perfect crucible for the man he became: self-reliant, serious and tough. All commentators, contemporary and current, agree that Stanley had a will of iron that nothing could break. This gave him the edge on his rivals.

Frank McLynn, in *Hearts of Darkness: The European Exploration of Africa*, finds both practical and psychological motives for African exploration in the 19th century. It was a means of rising socially and financially; it could also be an expression of an "action neurosis" – the need to keep moving. Many explorers had a distaste for urban life and the burgeoning industrialisation of the period. Stanley manifests a "Prospero complex" – seeking a world where one can ignore the personalities of others. Leading expeditions across the expanses of Africa was obviously an inviting activity for a 19th century Prospero, and McLynn points out that Stanley could not accommodate equals. All five Europeans on his first two expeditions died, for instance. Excessive aggression directed to the external world, McLynn notes, is a classic sign of a death drive. (It is not suggested that Stanley brought about the deaths of his companions.) Stanley did not get his wish, if that is what it was, to leave his young bones in Africa, but he was several times on the point of death there. He died in England in his early sixties, racked to the last by the fevers that had been his constant companions in Africa.

Mutesa's prime motive in accepting a European presence that eventually "ate" his country was to obtain goods and, above all, weapons. These he needed to withstand the attacks he feared from the Mahdists to the north. Moreover, the kabaka seems to have had a love of ideas and learning. Buganda combined complex political and social structures with a very low technological base. What was needed for life above the village subsistence level had to come from outside. The Europeans were an even better source of goods than the Arabs, whose presence they balanced. In time the Europeans ceased to be an opportunity and became a threat, but the failure to see a fledgling cuckoo is only too common. In the modern world, there are plenty of present-day countries that have found great powers easier to invite in than to get out.

Stanley's *Through the Dark Continent* gives us a detailed sketch of Buganda before the coming of the Europeans. His aim was to awaken Great Britain and beyond to the opportunities for trade and Christianity in Buganda. He drew for his readers a picture of an advanced state, under a civilised prince, lacking only the redeeming moral base of religion. Even with these rose-coloured lenses, the information is valuable reportage from one of the first whites to see the country.

Social organisation was evidenced in the scale of the kabaka's dramatically sited hilltop palace at Rubaga. The audience chamber, which was made of a wooden frame and supports covered with straw, was 60 ft (18 m) long by 18 ft (5.5 m) wide. It had a gabled roof which at its highest reached to 25 ft (7.6 m) . The king's compound consisted of many huts, and the whole was surrounded by palisades. The palace was approached by wide avenues cut through the plantain groves.

Construction techniques were of the simplest. Alexander Mackay, who arrived in Buganda in 1878, remarked that wood was fixed together by lashing, not nailing or pegging, while the principle of the lever was unknown. However, the principle of the wheel was understood: banana trees were used as rollers to move logs or canoes, and Stanley noted that Mutesa was planning a wagon or carriage.

Much of the country was of "inexhaustible fertility" with a landscape dotted with hills giving way to higher land of treeless savannah. Stanley, with his reporter's eye for detail, listed the crops: plantain, banana, pawpaw (papaya), yams, sweet potato, peas, beans, melons, cucumber, vegetable marrow, manioc (the unattractive root, dangerous unless properly cooked, that was both life and death for African expeditions), tomato, wheat, rice, maize, sesamum, millets and vetches. Not only was the food various but it was also plentiful. So too was pombé (beer) and maramba (banana wine). The great staple in the area was plantains.

The people were elaborately clothed compared with most surrounding tribes. The universal dress was bark cloth, made from strips of tree bark beaten time after time until the required thinness was achieved. This was worn as a clay-coloured robe reaching to the feet. The nobles wore woven cloths obtained from the Arab traders. Many Baganda were tall, as Mutesa was: they often stood more than 6 ft 2 in (1.88 m). The language, Luganda, was not put into written form until the coming of the missionaries, but Stanley noted that the kabaka and many of the nobles could read and write Arabic.

Buganda society is presented in three layers: the kabaka, chiefs and peasants. The treatment is inevitably superficial; the writer spent just days in the country. Even the term "peasant" belongs more to the toilsome lands of Europe than to favoured Buganda where crops virtually leapt fully formed out of the ground. Stanley's archetypal peasant, contentedly at home in his hut surrounded by simple but sufficient household effects, has a decided feel of Merrie England!

Either Stanley was puzzled by the ordinary people of Buganda, or he bent his comments to support his theme of an estimable nation awaiting only the arrival of Christianity: they are said to love cleanliness, neatness and modesty; also to be crafty, fraudful, deceiving, lying and thievish knaves – a range of qualities not usually found together.

Stanley's writing is characterised by enormous energy and range, and when he forgets to be portentous in the high Victorian manner, great clarity. The range of subjects is especially striking: no sooner have we learnt in detail about the rank structure of the Buganda royal family than we are offered a list of the various uses of the banana plant, which "in the eyes of the untaught civilized man ... seems to be of no other use than to bear fruit after its kind".

However, the different varieties of banana give the Baganda

(1) their main food,
(2) a "honey-sweet, cider-flavoured" wine and, mixed with millet, beer,
(3) fronds for thatch, bedding, wrappers and covers of everything from a table to a pudding,
(4) stems for fences and as rollers to move heavy logs or canoes,
(5) stalks from which can be made both shields and sun-hats,
(6) pith to be turned into toilet sponges,
(7) cord from the fibres.

Stanley concludes that

> ... besides its cool agreeable shade, the banana-plant will supply a peasant of Uganda with bread, potatoes, dessert, wine, beer, medicine, house and fence, bed, cloth, cooking-pot, table-cloth, parcel-wrapper, thread, cord, rope, sponge, bath, shield, sun-hat, even a canoe – in fact almost everything except meat and iron.

Stanley did not conceal the arbitrary power of life and death wielded by Mutesa. For the peasants, despotic power was the serpent in paradise, but paradise was a big place where they might hope to avoid the kabaka. For the chiefs, though, insecurity was a fact of everyday life. A young man called Magassa rises through the feudal system (Stanley relates). He is given the title of the pokino and the estates that go with it. He rises higher still, becoming the katikiro. But he is still subject to Mutesa's arbitrary power. He never knows when the "lords of the cord" (the official stranglers) will visit him, and of course in the end they do.

Unsurprisingly, everybody wanted to please Mutesa. His retinue was considerable – about two score of drummers, a score of fifers, half a score of guitar-players, several mountebanks, clowns, dwarfs and albinoes, a multitude of errand boys, pages, messengers, courtiers and claimants, besides bodyguards and two standard-bearers, "either following or preceding him wherever he goes, to declare his state and quality". On a smaller scale the chiefs repeat this display, and so on down to the peasant or cowherd, "who makes an infantile slave trot after him to carry his shield and spears".

As presented by Stanley, the kabaka was a bundle of contradictions. Besides Mutesa's obvious civilised attributes there were "strong evil propensities", as Speke had mentioned already and Mackay was to do later. One of those civilised attributes was a liking for ideas, as when he asked Stanley about angels. Mutesa was no savage chieftain simply gouging goods out of travellers. Every visitor had to give something: arms were especially welcome; goods were acceptable; the fortunate traveller might get away with sharing some of his intellectual property. "Mtesa is the most interesting man in Africa," Stanley wrote, "... through him only can Central Africa be Christianized and civilized."

Buganda's great rival was Bunyoro, which the explorer Samuel White Baker brought to European consciousness. Unfortunately for generations of Banyoro, his perceptions were deeply negative whereas Stanley's were highly optimistic about Buganda.

Perhaps it is not surprising that Baker was jaundiced. His first Bunyoro adventure almost cost him his mistress, Florence; his next adventure almost cost him his life.

The kingdom in the late 19th century was past its glory days, for all that its mukama, Kabalega, tried to restore it. It was 4,700 square miles (12,170 sq km) in area. That is about one third the size of Holland and not much more than half that of Wales. This was the remnant of the far larger country of Kitara, hence the Banyoro call their country Bunyoro-Kitara.

The ancient kingdom included the later states of Ankole and Toro to the west. It reached into Rwanda and Congo. To the east its influence extended to Teso, Busoga, Lango, Acholi, Madi and West Nile.

As the 19th century progressed, land was lost to secession and to conquest by Buganda in the south; in the north territory was nibbled at by the Egyptian empire; more land was taken away by the British, and before the century was out the whole country was ruled by the colonial masters.

The traditional enmity between Bunyoro and Buganda

reflected two very different societies: Bunyoro where the cattle of the elite ranged over the savannas, and Buganda whose swamps, hills and abundant fertility were more suited to agricultural cultivation.

The explorer Speke reached Bunyoro in the early 1860s during the expedition that established Lake Victoria as the source of the Nile. He formed a poor opinion of the mukama (king), Kamurasi, complaining of his alleged deviousness and childishness. The snobbish Speke particularly disliked being mistaken for a trader, although this was an understandable mistake. Kamurasi had encountered many Arab traders, and Speke with his travelling companion, James Augustus Grant, brought many goods (intended as presents for the rulers whose territories they passed through).

Kamurasi's palace, on a tongue of land where the River Kafu runs into the Nile, pleased no more than the ruler. It was "a dumpy, large hut, surrounded by a host of smaller ones, and the worst royal residence we had seen since leaving Uzinza". (*Journal of the Discovery of the Source of the Nile*)

Kamurasi returned the compliment. Speke and Grant were tracing the river that flowed out of Lake Victoria to confirm that it was the Nile, beginning its 4,000-mile (6,400-km) journey to the sea. The mukama's hostility forced them to travel overland.

Rejoining the Nile, they reached Gondokoro – near modern Juba, in Sudan. There they met Sam Baker, and his partner, Florence, who were travelling along the Nile in the opposite direction

What the travellers told Baker fired him with enthusiasm for the prospect of a major discovery. To the northwest of Lake Victoria there was known to be another great lake. This Baker was to reach and name Lake Albert.

Doubtless, Speke also passed on to the Bakers* his negative views of Kamurasi. Baker added many of his own, and these were to prove a damaging legacy for Bunyoro down the years.

---

* This is shorthand: they married later, in 1865

To reach the mysterious lake meant entering Kamurasi's kingdom, which the Bakers did in 1864. They found the Banyoro far more developed than the tribes to the north. Baker was struck by their skill at pottery. In contrast to the nakedness of northern tribes, the men wore gowns of bark cloth and the women, bare-breasted, wore short double petticoats.

Kamurasi was eager for Baker's gifts. They were not, though, thought to be enough. The king set out 24 pieces of straw to signify what Speke had brought, and complained that Baker offered only 10. Kamurasi also persistently demanded his watch. Baker called the king "this miserable, grasping, lying coward".

Baker's mood was not improved when Kamurasi expressed interest in Florence. Baker pulled a gun on him, but the king replied emolliently: "Don't be angry!" He explained that it was customary to give visitors pretty girls as wives and he thought Baker might like to exchange.

Kamurasi provided the Bakers with an escort on their journey to the lake. The journey, although successful, was hazardous. Food was often short. The pair were constantly ill. They had run out of quinine to treat their malaria.

On their return from the lake, according to Baker's book, *The Albert Nyanza, Great Basin of the Nile*, they had a huge surprise. They met Kamurasi again and found he was really M'Gambi, a younger brother who was impersonating the king for security reasons.

The real Kamurasi, whom Sam and Florence now met, was no better in Baker's eyes. He was described as "cowardly". He demanded Baker's watch, compass, double Fletcher rifle and Highland costume.

Bunyoro was under attack from a slave-raiding army from the north. Baker's guns helped to see off the attack. It was many months before he and Florence could get away and back to Gondokoro.

Seven years later, in 1872, the pair were back in Bunyoro. This time Baker came not as an explorer but a would-be colonial administrator. He was at the head of a column of troops and intended to stay. He had been appointed governor of Equatoria by the khedive of Egypt, whose country was nominally part of the Turkish empire but was under strong British influence. Equatoria was the most distant of the khedive's provinces, with a boundary abutting Bunyoro. It was now intended to add Bunyoro to the province.

The declared reason for this push south was the suppression of the slave trade, which was flourishing at this time. Arab traders exported slaves as well as ivory, while slaves were taken as prizes in inter-tribal warfare.

Slavery must have had a special resonance for Florence because she had been a slave intended for a Turkish harem. Baker bought her at an auction in the Balkans when she was 17 and he was twice her age. Although they later married, the relationship scandalised Queen Victoria. The monarch refused to receive Florence because she had lived in sin.

Florence was from Transylvania, at that time ruled by Turkey. She survived the massacre of her family in the year of revolutions, 1848, only to fall into the hands of slave masters. Richard Hall, in *Lovers on the Nile*, explains that although Turkey made a show of forbidding slavery the practice remained widespread. Wealthy Turks liked the cachet of having white girls in their harems.

Baker no doubt was moved by more than pity when he made the winning bid for Florence. She was slim and small, her hair loosely braided at the back of her head.

> The gulf in years between Florence and himself [writes Hall], the complete disparity of their backgrounds, the sheer inability to talk to one another except in German (which Sam had rarely used since he was twenty)* – all this leaves little room for doubt as to the mainspring of their liaison.

> Florence could have been, at first, only the servant to his repressed instincts. However, events would soon prove her more self-assertive than that. As she would reveal again and again in Africa, she was not by nature timid. She would also be able to display, even in the tightest corners, a sense of humour that matched his own.

---

* Original parenthesis

In Bunyoro, the Bakers found that Kamurasi had died and his son ruled as Mukama Cwa II Kabalega. He had been his father's choice for king because, according to the later Nyoro historian and politician, John Nyakatura, even as a child he had been full of "self-will and high spirits". (*Aspects of Bunyoro Customs and Tradition*)

These were felt to be valuable qualities for safeguarding the kingdom. Others disagreed, and Kabalega had to fight Kabigumire, his elder half-brother with a gentler temperament, for the throne.

Baker had no higher view of Kabalega than he had of Kamurasi. In *Ismailia: a narrative of the expedition to Central Africa for the suppression of the slave trade* he described the new mukama as "a gauche, awkward, undignified lout of twenty years of age, who thought himself a great monarch. He was cowardly, cruel, cunning, and treacherous to the last degree."

He was, however, physically striking. He was about 5 ft 10 in (1.78 m) tall with a light complexion. Baker found the ruler well clad in beautifully made bark cloth striped with black, but every virtue became a vice in Baker's eyes: Kabalega's teeth were "exceedingly white" while his large eyes "projected disagreeably"; he was "excessively neat".

A more sympathetic portrayal came from Florence. She said of the king:

> He is a very clean-looking young man of about 18 or 19 years old, he keeps the nails of his feet and hands beautifully clean and wears a very nice bark cloth of a light brown colour, and a neck-lace of pretty small different coloured beads. His skin is dark brown, his eyes are large, but they always have a frightened look." (Richard Hall: *Lovers on the Nile*)

Kabalega's light complexion proclaimed his Nilotic ancestry, the Nyoro royal family tracing its origins to an invasion probably in the 16th century by the Lwo people.

To modern sensibilities it may seem weird that someone should march into a country and announce he had taken it over. That is what Baker did in the name of the anti-slavery movement, with a trading sub-text.

Yet not a lot has changed in more than a century: in 2003 George W. Bush and Tony Blair, the leaders of the

United States and Britain respectively, marched into Iraq and took it over in the name of democracy, with a trading sub-text.

Baker told Kabalega that Bunyoro was now a dependency of Egypt, and would share in the benefits of trade. He drove home the point with an array of cutlery, crockery, watches and cloth as well as spinning tops, tambourines and whistles.

Richard Hall's *Lovers on the Nile* tells how the Bakers built a house designed to impress the king. When he saw "a great number of Kabba Regas" in looking glasses at opposite ends of the room, he pronounced it magic. He made all his entourage try the electric shock machine, but did not have a go himself.

A portrait of the Princess of Wales, Queen Victoria's daughter-in-law, was shown three-quarter face. Visitors asked why she had only one ear. While this may have seemed proof of the primitive savage to Baker's readers at the time, all it shows is a problem with the perception of European art by someone with no experience of it.

There was a strong element of distorting mirrors in Baker's proposition that from now on Bunyoro would enjoy the benefits of trade. Where were these goods to come from? Gondokoro, which was itself an outstation, was a long and difficult journey of about 400 miles (640 km), with cataracts in the Nile offering a formidable barrier. The route to the east coast of Africa had not been established, while a river route from the west coast was unimaginable.

The Banyoro were not persuaded. Baker, with 100 men armed mainly with primitive rifles, had overreached himself. The party found itself under siege in Masindi as Kabalega's regiments camped all around. Two threats were thwarted, the first by striking up the band and distracting the warriors, the second by torching the grass huts of the town.

Lovers on the Nile describes the bizarre musical bluff by which Baker bought himself a week's grace to fortify his camp:

> Baker and his officers were looking for some way out of the trap, knowing that if fighting did begin, they would be destroyed by the weight of numbers; the soldiers carried only

muzzle-loading muskets for drilling and after one volley would have no time to reload. At that moment, Baker spotted several senior chiefs of Bunyoro among the warriors, with an interpreter. He strolled casually over and called out: 'Well done! Let us all have a dance!' When this was translated, the chiefs looked momentarily bewildered, and Baker seized his chance. He told the band to strike up a lively tune, and announced that his men would perform a dance of their own. He asked for the crowd to stand away, then told his men to advance on every side with their bayonets. Baffled by these manoeuvres, the warriors fell back from the parade ground, and to Baker's relief one of the chiefs told them to sit. The band played on and the troops re-formed their square.

The attack a week later was beaten off, aided by setting the town on fire, but the position was unsustainable. Baker's party made a fighting retreat from Masindi, under constant harassment, to beyond Bunyoro and safety.

Thwarted, Baker gave his support to Ruyonga, a cousin of Kabalega and claimant to the throne, who was in rebellion in the north of the country. To Kabalega this was a betrayal, an act of "apostasy", which "determined Bunyoro's hostility towards Baker and his successors in a number of encounters that followed". (D.A. Low in Oliver and Mathew's *History of East Africa*, Vol 1)

> This hostility was fully reciprocated [Low writes], and until the end of the century, Bunyoro, in European circles, was invariably reckoned to be implacably hostile. For this there was little warrant, but, later on, the consequences for Bunyoro were to be disastrous.

Baker's view of Kabalega is of critical importance because it pervaded the thinking of later British administrators in Uganda and hence colonial policy towards Bunyoro. Here is the source of many of that country's troubles.

A further attempt was made to colonise Bunyoro from the north. General Charles Gordon – later the hero of Khartoum – who followed Baker as governor of Equatoria, established a military post in the Nyoro heartland, near Masindi, but this was soon abandoned.

5 Enter missionaries

If the "the people on the shores of the Nyanza" were calling upon "the pious people of England", in the words of Stanley's 1875 appeal, they were quickly answered from London by the Church Missionary Society. Two days after the appeal appeared in the Daily Telegraph, the society's lay secretary received this letter:

November 17th, 1875

Dear Mr Hutchinson, – My eyes have often been strained wistfully towards the interior of Africa, west of Mombasa, and I have longed and prayed for the time when the Lord would, by His Providence, open there a door of entrance to the heralds of the Gospel.

The appeal of the energetic explorer Stanley to the Christian Church from Mtesa's capital, Uganda, taken in connexion with Colonel Gordon's occupation of the upper territories of the Nile, seems to me to indicate that the time has come for the soldiers of the Cross to make an advance into that region.

If the Committee of the Church Missionary Society are prepared at once and with energy to organize a Mission to the Victoria Nyanza, I shall account it a high privilege to place £5000 at their disposal as a nucleus for the expenses of the undertaking.

I am not so sanguine as to look for the rapidity of success contemplated by Mr Stanley; but if the Mission be undertaken in simple and trustful dependence upon the Lord of the Harvest, surely no insurmountable difficulty need be anticipated, but His presence and blessing be confidently expected, as we go forward in obedience to the indications of His providence and the command of His Word.

I only desire to be known in this matter as AN UNPROFITABLE SERVANT" (The signature refers to Luke 17, v 10: "We are unprofitable servants: we have done that which was our duty to do.")

It was an enormous gift. A further £10,000 was soon found, and within less than half a year a party of eight volunteers were on their way to Buganda. Among them was Alexander Mackay, the man whom Stanley was to judge "the best missionary since Livingstone".

The Church Missionary Society was (and is, under its revamped name, the Church Mission Society) a voluntary organisation within the Anglican Communion. It was founded in 1799 in London by a small group of Church of England members who felt there was both room and need for another missionary body alongside the Society for the Propagation of the Gospel and the Society for Promoting Christian Knowledge.

The later 18th century had been a bad time for organised religion. As Britain's empire grew a parallel need was felt to minister to the overseas settlers and to the indigenous peoples they lived among; yet the scientific rationalism of the Enlightenment had for many made God deeply unfashionable, an outdated idea that could be consigned to history. This was the time when Bishop Butler declined to be made Archbishop of Canterbury, the spiritual head of the Church of England, because he saw no future for a "falling church". Then in reaction came the "Great Awakening". The founders of the CMS were moved by the same evangelising impulses that moved the Methodists in England and the Moravians in Germany. Evangelicals to this day are a major strand in the Church of England.

Like the Roman Catholic White Fathers – soon to be its rival in Buganda – the CMS could take pride in a major church figure within its ranks. With the White Fathers it was their founder, Cardinal Lavigerie, a leader in the fight to suppress slavery. With the Church Missionary Society it was Henry Venn, who was the London-based clerical secretary and effective leader of the society from 1841 to 1872. Venn kept the society on its evangelical rails, echoing his clergyman father's dictum of "the church-principle but not the high-church principle". He was a pioneer in elaborating the proper relationship of missionaries to the communities they serve. The missionary brings the gospel to those outside the church and the pastor ministers to those within the church. For Venn it was dangerous for missionaries to become tied down in, for example, education and medical work because they then lacked time for evangelising.

Venn became famous as the advocate of the Triple Autonomy principle for indigenous churches – that they should become, as soon as possible, self-supporting, self-governing and self-extending. Jocelyn Murray comments in *Proclaim the Good News* (a history of the CMS, published in 1985):

> This teaching is now seen as almost an axiom of the missionary movement, but we do well to remember that this was not always the case, and how much we owe to Venn for his insight. He logically associated it with a high view of the ability of African, Indian and other new Christians to receive a theological education, to take responsibility, and to exercise leadership.

The aim of Triple Autonomy was, in a delightful phrase, the "euthanasia of mission", when local Christians were able to run their own churches. Murray explains how, following Venn's principles, a Christian community steadily grows until there is the basis for forming an Anglican diocese under an indigenous leader – a position, of course, long since reached throughout the Majority World. Venn urged the formation of "Christian companies" under an elder. These would become congregations, which in turn would form into conferences, which would support an episcopal structure.

In an age when travel to distant places was measured in weeks rather than hours, Venn never saw any of his ideas being worked out on the ground. His ideas were forged in England and he never visited any overseas mission field.

Venn was a visionary before his time. Canon Timothy Yates said in a sermon to mark the 200th anniversary of the CMS (1999):

> In Venn's view, the way was not to impose a top-down model by hierarchical method, with leadership imposed from outside by, for example, a European bishop, taking with him a whole lot of European assumptions and culturally-inherited forms. Rather, the aim was to give local Christians and local churches freedom to develop and a sense of self-worth, by releasing

them from dependency and control by either missionary societies or western missionaries.*

However, while claiming to continue Venn's legacy, his successors in the heyday of colonialism watered it down:

> A central plank of Vann's mission strategy (the aim to create independent and culturally sensitive native churches) was gradually undermined by other aims and objectives that seemed more relevant to an age of colonialism, given the leading role of European culture and personnel.†

Enlightened in other ways, Bishop Tucker – the third bishop of Eastern Equatorial Africa and the first to reach Uganda – found it hard to envisage a Ugandan following him, and his successor, Bishop Willis "was even more dismissive of the idea".‡

The last word was with Venn. His legacy gradually reasserted itself, leading to today's flourishing indigenous churches.

It was to a society alive with Venn's ideas that Alexander Mackay offered himself. He was the son of a presbyterian minister in Aberdeenshire, Scotland. He trained as an engineer at Edinburgh University and at a locomotive works in Germany. He had a wonderfully practical disposition. In Africa he contrived a magic lantern out of some lenses and a biscuit tin. His workshop included a forge, lathe, grindstone and printing press. These practical skills must have commended him to the CMS for Stanley had stressed that "the practical Christian tutor" not "the mere preacher" was needed for Buganda. Mackay also struck the right note when he wrote to the society from his German lodgings, where he had chanced to see an advertisement asking for volunteers.

> My heart burns [wrote Mackay] for the deliverance of Africa, and if you can send me to any of those regions which

---

* Reprinted in Anvil, vol 17 no 1 (2000)
† Kevin Ward in the International Bulletin of Missionary Research, April 1999
‡ Ward, see above

Livingstone and Stanley have found to be groaning under the
curse of the slave-hunter I shall be very glad.

The leader of the CMS party was Lieutenant Shergold
Smith, whose Royal Navy career was ended by losing sight
in one eye after an attack of fever. Smith had known
enough of Africa and its troubles to want to stay there in
another role. Like Mackay, he was moved by the spectre of
slavery. He also struck the right note, telling the society:
"Send me out in any capacity, I am willing to take the lowest place." Aware of his capabilities, the recruiters sensibly
decided otherwise.

The march up-country was about 600 miles (970 km),
from the starting point opposite Zanzibar island to the
south side of Lake Victoria, from where the missionaries'
own boat, carried in parts, would take them across to
Buganda. The CMS party went off in sections. Mackay left
on August 27, 1876, in the company of two (unrelated)
Smiths – his great friend, Dr John Smith, and the expedition leader. Ahead of them was a trek of about three
months. It must have been a bitter disappointment to
Mackay that after 73 days he had to turn back. Seriously
ill with fever, he returned to the coast helped, and often
carried, by faithful bearers.

The party found it necessary to split into several parts.
Shergold Smith and an ordained man, C.T. Wilson, had
the honour of being the first missionaries in Buganda.
Crossing the lake, Smith had met with a personal tragedy.
They were stoned by the inhabitants of an island en route.
Broken glass from his spectacles went into his one sighted
eye, and blinded him. The horror of being so handicapped
in such a situation is almost unimaginable. Nevertheless,
they continued, reaching Rubaga on June 30, 1877. The
next day, the Sabbath, was passed in retirement. They
called on Mutesa on the Monday. This is Smith's account
of the meeting:

Rubaga, Uganda, July 8th, 1877

This was our reception. I could not see, so my report is that of
ear.

The king rose as we entered, and advanced to the edge of his carpet, and shook hands. A fine fellow, over six feet (1.83 m), broad shoulders, and well made; grace, dignity, and an absence of affectation in his manner. He motioned us to seats. Then five minutes were allowed for drum-beating and looking round. I longed for sight to see.

Calling one of our guides, I heard his animated report. Then the Sultan of Zanzibar's letter was read, after which the C.M.S.'s.

It was read in Swahili by a young fellow named Mufta*, one of the boys Stanley had brought with him, and left with the king, at his request, to teach him to read the Bible. At the first pause, the king ordered a *feu de joie* to be fired, and a general rejoicing for the letter; but at the end, where it was said that it was the religion of Jesus Christ which was the foundation of England's greatness and happiness, and would be of his kingdom also, he half rose from his seat, called his head musician, Tolé, to him, and ordered a more vigorous rejoicing to be made ...

The following day we went twice. In the morning it was a full court as before, and from some cause he seemed suspicious of us, and questioned us about Gordon, and rather wanted to bully us into making powder and shot, saying "Now my heart is not good." We said we came to do as the letter told him, not to make powder and shot; and if he wished it, we would not stay. He paused for some time, and then said, "What have you come for – to teach my people to read and write?" We said, "Yes, and whatever useful arts we and those coming may know." Then he said, "Now my heart is good: England is my friend. I have one hand in Uganda, and the other in England."

He asked after Queen Victoria, and asked to know which was greatest, she or the Khedive of Egypt. The relative size of their dominions was explained to him, and referring him to our letter, I said how desirous England was that his kingdom should be prosperous ...

Shergold Smith was soon to die. He and another mission member, T. O'Neill, were massacred with most of their

---

* Also called Dallington

party on Ukerewe island, on the south side of Lake
Victoria, after gallantly refusing to give up an Arab fugi-
tive they were sheltering. Mackay's great friend, Dr John
Smith, died from fever.

Mackay, after convalescing on the coast, reached the
south side of the lake at his second attempt. It was June
13, 1878. The CMS missionaries had established a lake-
side base at Kagei. From here he commented in a letter on
the lack of technology he found around him:

> Among the natives a sail is unknown ... It is a strange fact,
> and one which I believe is true of every tribe in Central Africa,
> that the natives are absolutely unacquainted with the art of
> fastening two pieces of wood together, except by lashing. As a
> rule, therefore, they prefer the laborious task of hewing every-
> thing out of the solid. Oars are unknown. Propulsion is by
> short paddles like large wooden spoons. Much toil is therefore
> entailed, but only what one might expect; for no negro knows
> the use of the lever, or of any other simple mechanical appli-
> ance by which to save labour. In all operations, work is done
> by the application of sheer brute force; hence the people are
> everywhere worn out at an early age, merely for want of con-
> trivances. It is really astonishing that an old man or old
> woman is scarcely ever to be found. All are done up, or worked
> out, in middle life, and then they die.

A knowledge of "contrivances" was why Mackay lasted so
long in Buganda. He soon had an opportunity to use his
remarkable practical skills and ingenuity. Wilson came
across the lake in the portable boat, the Daisy, and they
set out together for Buganda. In a storm the boat was
forced back to the shore, with Wilson, Mackay and the
crew being lucky to escape with their lives. The damaged
boat needed repairs, but where to find suitable timber?
Mackay cut out the boat's middle section to use the wood
for the fore and aft sections. The resulting Daisy was stub-
bier but seaworthy again.

They reached Buganda on November 1, 1878. Mackay,
the man who was "burning" for the deliverance of Africa,
had already spent more than two years on the continent
without even seeing his mission field, but at last the work
could begin. With Wilson and Mackay together the work of
bringing souls to Christ could be doubled. Soon there was

an unseemly competition in salvation. The White Fathers arrived the following year (1879). The two sets of missionaries squared up to each other as well as to heathendom and vice.

Even the physical location of the missions in the capital underlined the competition, the Catholics on Rubaga hill and the Protestants facing them across a valley from another hill, Namirembe. The sin of Christian disunity had already reached Buganda. The respective cathedrals remain there to this day.

The French-speaking White Fathers – the Society of Missionaries of Africa – were founded in Algiers in 1868 by Cardinal Charles Lavigerie. They were so called because they wore an Arab-style white robe and burnous (a hooded cloak), with a rosary around the neck like a Moslem chaplet. Three of the fathers found martyrdom in 1875 on the way to Timbuktu. Their leader in Buganda was Père Lourdel, a man who like Mackay stayed in Africa for many years without a break and left his bones there.

Among the Protestants, great anguish was caused by the Catholic habit of "shadowing" their missions by setting up rivals nearby. This seemed particularly indefensible when so much of Africa was an unsown field. The Catholics, however, felt it their duty to counter the heretics. The Protestants felt a parallel duty to correct the errors of the Church of Rome.

Language was often extreme on both sides, although the comment by the Vatican's *Annals of the Propagation of the Faith* (1828) about Protestant bible societies takes some beating: "Let us hope that the zeal of the children of light becomes as ardent as that of the children of darkness." After such a comment the Annals' observation that the Protestant bibles are "poisoned with the venom of error" seems almost mild!

The White Fathers for their part (says Alyward Shorter in *Cross and Flag in Africa*) were shocked by the "palpable hatred" of Catholic teaching that they encountered from Protestant evangelicals in Buganda and elsewhere. This was "fuelled by the violence that characterised the Reformation in Britain and by three centuries of anti-Catholic propaganda".

Both Mackay in letters and a CMS colleague, Robert Ashe, in his book *Two Kings of Uganda*, recorded examples of the Catholic fathers dropping in on Protestant services at the Buganda court, and ostentatiously declining to take part. Mackay vividly describes an incident when the Catholics refused to kneel in prayer. When the Baganda asked why, Lourdel became excited and said: "We do not join in that religion, because it is not true; we do not know that book, because it is a book of lies."

The difficulties were rooted in conflicting understandings of Christianity arising from the Reformation. Partly the dispute was about the relative importance of sacraments and the word of God expressed in scripture. Many Protestants loathed the veneration of the Virgin Mary, which they saw as "Mariolatry" and tantamount to worship. Praying to the saints for intercession with the deity was seen to contradict the biblical assurance of Christ as the only mediator between God and man. For many Catholics, the Protestants' rejection of the heir of St Peter (the Pope), who spoke with the voice of Christ, and "the One True Church" was part of a trail of heresies. Protestants despised the control that Catholic priests wielded over their flocks through the power to grant or withhold absolution from sins. While Catholics believed that each and every mass was a further sacrifice by Christ for our salvation, Protestants held that this denied the sufficiency of the sacrifice on Calvary.

None of the doctrinal issues has gone away in the present day, but the heart of Africa in the 19th century was not the place to fight them out. Nor were tensions limited to the two Christian communities. When the Mill Hill Fathers, another Catholic group, arrived to make a third missionary presence, there were often tensions between them and the White Fathers.

Both Protestant and Roman Catholic missionaries were driven by a desire to see the end of enslavement in Africa – warring tribes who made slaves of their neighbours or the organised traffic in human beings for export. In Buganda's wars with surrounding countries no quarter was given to the defeated soldiers. Thus large numbers of women and children became available to be made slaves. The countries of Bunyoro and Busoga were the main source of slaves. The missionaries redeemed as many as they could. There were many small boys at the CMS mission. Some had been given by chiefs and others had been bought. A boy called Lwanga cost a padlock and four yards (3.7 m) of calico.

The 1885 Treaty of Berlin, which triggered the scramble for Africa, agreed powers for European nations to suppress slaving, while Cardinal Lavigerie was a prime mover behind the 1890 Brussels conference for the abolition of the slave trade.

Lavigerie's Armed Brethren of the Sahara, founded in 1890, favoured a robust way for winning converts. The publication Truth satirised this approach:

Take this Banner, and if e'er
Arabs will not bow in prayer,
Chant a psalm their shrieks to drown,
Shrive and Bible in your hands
Teach the truth through heathen lands
Preach, convert, baptise, anoint,
Even at the bayonet's point.
Far and wide, without surcease,
Spread the Gospel's news of peace
Far and wide, in Heaven's name,
Spread the news with steel and flame
Brethren! Oh! be not afraid
Heaven your Christian work will aid;
Banish all your doubts and tears,
Rifles cannot fail 'gainst spears.
Take your banner! Onward go!
Christian soldiers, seek your foe,
And the devil to refute,
Do not hesitate to shoot

Roman Catholic mission work, which had tended to lag behind that of Protestantism, was reanimated during the pontificate of Leo XIII, 1878-1903. Much of the effort went into creating villages to develop a sense of work and community. Many of the inhabitants were children ransomed from slave traders. These Christian converts, boys and girls, were encouraged to marry each other when they grew up, creating the nub of an enduring Christian community.

Protestants too sheltered ex-slave children and orphans – Stanley commented that at Mackay's last mission station, Usambiro, there were boys everywhere – but they also emphasised the growth of commerce as a way to check the slave trade. Another perceived evil was polygamy. The Protestant missionaries often came as married couples. This was partly to offer an example of successful monogamous families in the face of polygamy.

Mackay, who was evidently a skilled debater, recorded this exchange on the subject with Muslims:

Sunday, October 5th (1879). – The subject of polygamy was talked on for some time. I told them that I fully recognized the difficulty of the case, but said that we should also go in for many wives were it not that the plain command of God was against it. I said that they could still keep their households of women as servants. The Mussulmans had again much to say. They declared that polygamy had nothing to do with religion. I asked their chief advocate, "How many wives have you?" "Four." "Why not five?" This they knew to be an injunction of their creed, and could not answer. They then maintained that religion was a thing of pure belief, and had nothing to do with matter of life. I asked, "Then why did you not join the chiefs and me in the food which the king sent out to us just now?" They were floored again, and Mtesa and the whole court laughed heartily at them.

The difficulty is this. At present a man's status is reckoned by his establishment, which depends on the number of his wives. These cook the food, and do all the work.

"How is a man to get on with one wife and several children alone in his house?" asked the king. "Who will look after the goats, cook the food?" &c. I said that we in Europe had women servants always in the house; but they were not our wives, and need not be necessarily wives here either.

Both Catholics and Protestants emphasised the ability to read as the way to obtain access to the joys of Christianity. Both have been accused of destroying local cultures but, according to Jean Comby, in *How to Understand the History of Christian Mission*, this was partly accidental:

This emphasis on the written word rather than the oral word, combined with the struggle against pagan literature, meant a certain destructuring of local cultures, though this was not necessarily sought.

The missions were very western in their style and approach, however. Stephen Neill, in *A History of Christian Missions*, finds that the association of missions with western governments was "far closer than was wise or right", while "the duty of the convert is clear – to trust in the superior wisdom of the white man". Neither approach would have appeared so outrageous at the time as it does today. Then, commerce and Christianity were seen as elements of the same package so it was considered natural for governments and churches to work together. It was expected that indigenous people should be evangelised into the whites' mode of Christianity.

The missionaries found that much traditional spirituality was incompatible with Christianity. Propitiating numerous earth spirits could not be reconciled with worshipping a single God. Present-day efforts to fuse Christianity and animism also express the ethos of a period, our own. No doubt history will decide. Moreover, numerous tribal customs were a problem for the missionaries – for example, slaves buried with their chiefly masters or wives of the dead passed to the husband's brother.

Both Catholics and Protestants stressed sexual continence outside marriage. For the Catholics there appeared to be a further obstacle to the creation of an indigenous African priesthood: the rule of celibacy of the clergy. Neill points out: "Celibacy, entirely unknown in a continent in which early and universal marriage was the rule, seemed to present an insuperable obstacle." This assumption, however, proved to be too pessimistic.

Looking at the general picture around the world, Neill found that the Roman Catholics – after a late start – often "with government support, with apparently inexhaustible supplies of recruits, with a very flexible policy in regard to baptism, were able to rival, and in a number of cases to surpass, the Protestants". Opposition between the two sides was the rule. "Protestant and Roman Catholic missionaries could live for years in the same town and never exchange a word. It was taken for granted by the majority of Roman Catholics that the Protestants were the enemy." The Vatican was supposed to have sent a directive calling for "the heretics" to be "followed up and their efforts harassed and destroyed".

The basic institutions of African missions were catechists and schools, with a medical dispensary not far behind. Catechists were local people who had learnt the elements of the religion and were able to pass it on. Mackay realised that all native gods were cure workers, hence "the great influence in favour of Christianity that a medical mission can exert, if prudently conducted".

It was an obvious breakthrough when Africans were able to go into the villages as evangelists. Ganda teachers spread Christianity to Bunyoro, Toro and Koki. Apolo Kivebulaya, an Anglican of simple and profound piety, proclaimed the faith in Mboga, on the far side of the River Semliki in what became part of the Congo. He was a canon of the Church of Uganda and, as a bachelor, an exception to the rule of universal marriage referred to above. Apolo ran a famous mission to the pigmies of the great Congo equatorial forest.

The early missionaries in Africa survived entirely at the sufferance of the king or chief. Wilson took the earliest opportunity to take Mackay to meet Mutesa – Stanley's "intelligent and distinguished prince", "the light that shall lighten the darkness of this benighted region". Mutesa was courteous as he usually was to visitors, but he did not feel well that day. Mackay gave the kabaka a present of a musical box. He was not certain how the audience had gone, but a present in return of some cows indicated that it had been successful.

Mackay was delighted by Buganda. The climate he found "like an ever-English summer". In an early letter he wrote:

> The people are not savages, nor even barbarians. They are out of sight far in advance of any race I have met with or even heard of in Central Africa.

He was not starry-eyed about the task ahead, however. He wrote on another occasion:

(T)he heathen do not, by nature, wish the gospel, although we know they sorely need it; that in every land people are jealous for their faith, which came down from their ancestors of long-lost memory; that they are greedy of gain, and jealous for their land, which they fancy we have come to possess, or rather spy out with a view to our nation possessing. They understand only material gain at first, and are generally disappointed that we do not aid them more in that way; but it takes time to win their confidence and convince them that we mean to be their true friends. When we have gained that point, but not till then, we can build upon it.

Wilson and Mackay were not long on their own at the CMS mission. In February 1879 a party of three arrived from the north along the Nile route. This was a rival to the East Coast route until it was closed a few years later by the fall of Khartoum to the Mahdi. The party included Robert Felkin, later to be influential in persuading the Imperial British East Africa Company to take on Uganda. In April two more travellers arrived from the south. One of them was Charles Stokes, who later gave up mission and adopted Mammon. He was eventually captured in the Congo Free State by a strategem and summarily executed for gun-running. This quite substantial band in time dispersed, leaving three missionaries including Mackay in Mengo. In April 1881 Philip O'Flaherty, an ordained man, arrived and carried out the first of the CMS baptisms, five in number, the following year. The first communion with African Christians followed in 1883.

As Mackay got to know Mutesa, he was unable to recognise the "enlightened and intelligent king of Uganda" hailed in Europe. Mackay wrote to his father:

Some have blamed Mr Stanley for giving far too glowing an account of Mtesa and the kingdom which he rules over ... But I cannot blame Stanley. He and Speke, and every traveller, resided only a few months, at most, at Mtesa's court. They had opportunity of seeing only the outside, and that in many respects is fair enough.

A year later he wrote far more strongly about the kabaka:

Mtesa is a pagan – a heathen – out and out. All the faculties of lying, low cunning, hatred, pride and conceit, jealousy, cruelty and complete ignorance of the value of human life, combined with extreme vanity, a desire for notoriety, greed, and absolute want of control of his animal propensities, – all these seem not only to be combined, but even concentrated in him. All is self, self, self.

Robert Ashe, who arrived in Mengo for his first tour of duty in May 1883, produced a rounded assessment of Mutesa in *Two Kings of Uganda* while insisting how difficult it was to give an accurate judgment. Ashe summed up the king as "easy-going" – not the first quality expected of an African absolute ruler, which may explain why he made a favourable impression on so many travellers.

However, it was with deeply blood-stained hands that Mutesa donned his fine robes. The life of bakopi (peasants) was of little account, and slaughter underlined the monarch's power. An episode earlier in the reign went beyond expected levels of violence. Mutesa had been flirting with Islam, but some of the chiefs at court took the new religion further than the kabaka did, undergoing circumcision and refusing to eat meat from the king's butcher because it had not been killed in the halal manner. A furious Mutesa retaliated by slaughtering the chiefs.

No doubt Ashe was aware of the episode when he spoke about Mutesa's cruelty:

To say he was great would hardly be true [wrote Ashe], but to say that he showed some fine qualities, and that he was, in spite of his clogging surroundings, a man who sought after better things, is to give him no more than his due ...

His generally courteous treatment of all Europeans, and his forbearance, with myself for example, showed a generous spirit. I knew he disliked my intruding religion on him; I did not know the language well enough to put it in a humorous or amusing manner, even if I had possessed the wit to do so; and as Mutesa looked upon religion as an amusement and a recreation, my readings about a great White Throne of Judgment, before which even kings were to stand, must have been most distasteful to the easy-going potentate ...

(H)is education had been a training in cruelty, brutality, and lust.

Ashe complained that men and women might be killed for trivial offences like a breach of court etiquette. "Daily went up the terrible cries of unhappy victims, as they were deliberately hacked to pieces, with strips of reed, sharp enough to be used as knives ..." Brutalities and "such vile obscenities as make daylight ashamed" showed that his "training in these vices had born a plenteous crop of fearful crimes". However, "what was frequent and notorious in his unhappy successor (referring to sodomy by Mwanga), was seldom practised by himself".

Ashe finished with a true Victorian flourish:

> But yet, in judging of these things, it is well to remember that there are none to whom the fearfullest crimes are not more than possibilities, for in every human heart are all these things, and out of every human heart they may proceed at any time, as He well knew, who bade His people pray, "Lead us not into temptation."

Ashe was concerned to treat the freed slaves well. He must have been quite put out by the lad called (for a reason not given) James Greenway, or Jimmy. He cost a gun, a white box, a looking glass and some other things. When they got back to the mission, Jimmy promptly said he wanted to return to the slave owner. The rueful Ashe told him that if he still wanted to go back after seven days, he could. When the week was up, Jimmy had changed his mind and stayed.

Both Catholics and Protestants enjoyed access to Mutesa's court, and he did not impede the work of evangelism in and around the court. The early missionaries were largely restricted to the court, but exposing the leaders to the Christian message had the unintended effect of speeding the evangelisation of the Baganda. Mutesa committed himself to neither group, although he was ready enough to debate theology and to order Sunday services. Maybe it was intellectual curiosity and mental sport. But Mutesa also had good reason to balance the factions represented by the two emerging Christian groups as well as the

Muslims and the traditionalists.

The CMS missionaries were keen for Mutesa or senior chiefs to visit Queen Victoria. This would cement the relationship with England and Anglicanism. It was also a trump card over the French missionaries. Mackay and his colleagues were in Buganda with the knowledge and informal support of the British government. England was the heartland of the Anglican church. The French had no comparable advantages. French governments had a long history of anti-clericalism. No doubt Cardinal Lavigerie could have arranged a visit to the Pope, but a post-Risorgimento Vatican, its temporal authority reduced to a pocket handkerchief of land, might have compared badly with the world's largest empire.

Mutesa was tempted to visit England but was persuaded by the chiefs that his dignity required visitors to come to him. The chiefs also passed up on the trip. Malamba Kiwanuka suggests in his *History of Buganda* that the reason a trio of ordinary subjects went was the belief that they would not come back. People who went on trips with the Arabs seldom returned.

The three Baganda went to England by the Nile route with the missionaries Wilson and Felkin. The visit was a resounding success. In London they were taken to see the Horse Guards, the Zoo and St Paul's Cathedral – "rather similar to the modern British Council course", Kiwanuka comments. They must have seemed as exotic to the British – when, for example, they sat in on a meeting of the Royal Geographical Society – as London seemed to them.

They got to meet the queen, presenting her with presents including sandals with leopard skin straps, traditionally reserved for royalty in Buganda, bark cloth and other examples of Ganda handicraft. In return, Queen Victoria sent Mutesa two bird rifles, ammunition, a sword, jackets and overcoats, fezzes and iron boxes. This was a formidable list. There was no doubt that Victoria was a great queen indeed.

Although Stanley liked to depict Mutesa as lord of all he surveyed, the kabaka of Buganda like any other absolute ruler was absolute only so long as he could contain the centrifugal forces that were ready to tear him apart. Ashe saw the kabaka's work as playing off one chief against another. He did the same with foreigners. Although writing after Mutesa's death, Ashe apparently had him in mind and not his successor when he wrote: "How shrewdly he guesses that it is the devoir (duty) of one party (the Roman Catholics) to counteract the teaching of heresy by the other, and of the latter party (the Protestants) to protest against errors [of the Church of Rome]."

This passage is typical of Ashe's generous approach to the rival faith, equally balancing the "heresy" of one party – even though it was his own – with the "errors" of the other. His approach, regrettably, was all too rare at the time.

In Buganda, the tiny bands of missionaries could not avoid encountering each other. Ashe recorded that relations with Père Lourdel and his confrère, Père Jeraud, were cordial:

> We were always on very good terms with them, and I think by that time we all recognised that there was room for both parties, and that they had learnt the lesson that however much they objected to our doctrine, public denunciation of it was of no earthly use.

When Mackay was ill in 1881 the French fathers sent a note and some wine containing the restoratives of iron and quinine. They also offered to send a cow. Lourdel was repeatedly ill with lumbago, neuralgia and rheumatism, and Mackay visited him.

Mackay, the Scottish Presbyterian, was very much the hard-line Protestant. Ashe wrote of him that he "looked upon the teachings of the Church of Rome with the deepest abhorrence. Their evasions, windings, mysteries, and their hocus-pocus mock-miracle-working formula he could not bear, though he saw clearly that formulas expressing great truths, when properly used, might be of value." Ashe, on the other hand, wrote emolliently after a visit to the Catholics at their Bukumbi mission station south of the lake: "Unable as I am to reverence the system which they support, or many of the doctrines which they believe, I can at least reverence the simple devotion of their lives."

Both Protestant and Catholic missionaries were up

against Islam as well as traditional Ganda beliefs. Mackay
recorded in his journal one such encounter in 1883:

> Mtesa then began with his usual excuses. "There are these
> two religions," he said. "When Masudi reads his book, the
> Koran, you call it lies; when you read your book, Masudi calls
> it lies: which is true?"

> I left my seat, and going forward to the mat, I knelt on it, and
> in the most solemn manner, I said, "Oh, Mtesa, my friend, do
> not always repeat that excuse! When you and I stand before
> God at the great day of judgment, will you reply to Almighty
> God that you did not know what to believe because Masudi
> told you one thing and Mackay told you another? No, you have
> the New Testament; read there for yourself. God will judge
> you by that. There never was anyone yet who looked for the
> truth there and did not find it."

Much of Mackay's work centred on the printing press. He
literally did it all, from translating St Matthew's Gospel
into Luganda, the local language, to operating the press
and even cutting the printing types. He had brought a
small stock of lead type with him, but it was not enough
and he made more characters in both wood and lead. On
his 30th birthday – October 13, 1879 – he spent all day
carving wooden types. It was tedious work: at the end of
the day he had made only 10 letters.

Before Mackay could translate St Matthew into the ver-
nacular, he first had to master the language. In an early
comment he was far ahead of his time in advocating the
Direct Method of language learning:

> February 5th, 1879. – Studied the language. Endeavoured to
> reduce the seven classes of nouns to four, to find a rationale of
> concords. I think I see my way pretty clearly. One thing I feel
> strongly on, viz., the absurdity of multiplying minute differ-
> ences into distinct classes, thus confusing new learners.
> Steere's eight classes of nouns in Swahili are a damper to a
> beginner. The small book with exercises and four classes of
> nouns is out of sight better for beginners than his handbook.
> We all learn to speak our mother tongue before we study the
> grammar of it. This should be the order, as far as possible, in
> acquiring a new language also. How many years' hard work
> does it not take to learn Latin by cramming up five declen-

sions? Did Cicero know anything about the declensions? If he did not, and yet knew Latin, how absurd it is to attempt declension before one knows Latin! I learned German first, and afterwards studied German grammar. I never saw any speed by following the inverse order.

Mackay seemed to be equally at home mending a boat, working a printing press, explaining the Christian faith and unravelling the Ganda theological system. The Baganda acknowledged two principal gods: Katonda, the creator, who however stayed out of human affairs and therefore could safely be ignored; and Lubale, the god of providence, who is actively involved in human affairs and to whom sacrifices were made. The Lubale had an incarnation in a human being called Mukasa, at this time an old woman who lived on an island in Lake Victoria and who was uniquely powerful in Ganda society.

The Baganda's system of belief was unveiled to the missionaries only bit by bit. H.P. Gale, in *Uganda and the Mill Hill Fathers*, credits Mackay with discerning for the West the mysteries of Katonda and Lubale. In particular, writes Gale, "the Kabaka's divinity was the heart and centre (of Ganda religion), and in consequence was never clearly revealed to Christian missionaries".

Mutesa's status as a demi-god was based on his descent from Kintu, the first kabaka. Kintu was said to have married a daughter of the Sky Father. Other descendants of Kintu inhabited the Sese Islands, and were therefore also semi-divine. At the time of King Nakibinge, the eighth kabaka – Mutesa being the 30th kabaka, according to the ranking of Sir Apolo Kaggwa, a katikiro of Buganda – the Sese Islanders helped the Baganda in a war against the neighbouring state of Bunyoro. In return the grateful king built temples for the worship of these descendants of Kintu.

This was the origin of the cult of Mukasa. The kabaka was an absolute ruler and in practice the Sese cult was under his control. He was semi-divine himself, and so had two ways to control Ganda religion. Gale comments: "Thus, whichever way we turn, we find the Kingship at the heart of the religion of the Baganda ..."

When Mackay remonstrated with Mutesa about the

worship of Mukasa, the kabaka replied: "What you say, Mackay, is true, and I know all witchcraft is falsehood." This did not mean that Mutesa was ready to convert to Christianity (which he never did). Gale and also J. Roscoe, in *The Baganda*, say the kabaka was merely acknowledging the truth that he knew better than anyone, that spirits were an emanation of his own kingship, the means whereby the blood of his people brought him life and vigour.

The Baganda, it appeared, had once believed in a single supreme being (Katonda) and immortality of the soul. To the missionaries this implied ancient contacts with Christianity, which was previously more widespread over North Africa. Now however, as Mackay recorded, each phenomenon of nature had its own divinity: there were gods of food, famine, rain, war, earthquake and plague. Some living creatures, especially snakes and parrots, were worshipped, as were what he called "monstrosities of nature" like misformed trees and rocks. All of this meant a huge amount of propitiation by the hapless human beings. Charms were seen as a potent way of securing a god's goodwill.

Some grass charms, dipped in blood, were brought into court while Mackay was with Mutesa. The missionary realised that credibility forced him to act. Harm was supposed to await anyone who destroyed the charms, but Mackay announced to the court that the grass was just a "mouthful for a cow". The charms were not supposed to burn, but he put a light to the grass to underline the impotence and worthlessness of the idol. Mackay then explained that it was not possible to mix old and new religions just as new cloth cannot be effectively sewn onto old garments.

Mutesa died in October 1884. Once more Mackay's practical skills were called upon. He was asked to make a coffin for the king. Lead for the lining was not available, but he made a suitable alternative by knocking together old copper and brass trays.

6 Bunyoro as it was

As Stanley did for Buganda, early travellers have left pen portraits of Bunyoro before the British conquest. They were struck by the variety of crops grown by the Banyoro, aided by the equable weather. The country lies just north of the equator, but the tropical climate is moderated by the upland setting – mostly a plateau 3,500 ft (1,070 m) and more above sea level.

Gaetano Casati lived for several years in Kabalega's kingdom in the 1880s as the Egyptian envoy. He left his detailed observations in the book *Ten Years in Equatoria and the Return with Emin Pasha*. The climate, Casati found, was healthy and temperate with abundant rain. Vegetables grew easily, and termites were eaten as a source of protein.

Bushmeat from chimpanzees was taboo. With an insight echoing Darwin's, the Banyoro recognised that ages ago chimps had formed part of the human race. They could not be hunted without royal permission.

Curiously for one who lived so long in the country, Casati appears to be wrong in suggesting that plantains were the Nyoro staple food. Into modern times finger millet has been the main staple, with plantains grown mainly for the production of beer. (John Beattie: *The Nyoro State*) Plantains were the favourite of the Baganda, who frequently caused offence by sneering at other foods.

Beer was a chief attraction for Banyoro menfolk, Casati reported. They loved to feast and dance, celebrating the new moon each month by drinking to excess. Women ran the houses and also attended to the fields.

For wives at the royal court gorging on food was the way to the king's favour. Obese women were desired: some became so fat that they could only move on all fours.

Meanwhile, Kabalega lived on a repetitious diet of veal boiled with bananas, telabun (millet) porridge and banana beer. The varied crop-based diet was eaten only by the common people; for the nobles their food came from cattle products.

Colonel Henry Colvile, who headed the army that invaded Bunyoro in the 1890s, found that the Banyoro did not rely on bananas as the people of neighbouring Buganda did, but planted beans and sweet potatoes.

Major A.B. Thruston, a member of the invading force, spoke of "a very fertile, picturesque, and hilly country, with broad valleys, in which were the pleasant plantations of the Wunyoro, smiling with banana groves, patches of sweet potatoes, Indian corn (maize) and sesame".

"Early on the third morning, on breasting a low hill, we saw before us the ruins of a large town of grass huts, all black and smouldering," Thruston continued. "This was all that was left of Mapala (Mparo), the capital of Unyoro, and the residence of Kabarega." (*African Incidents*) Kabalega had destroyed the town himself ahead of the enemy advance.

Frederick Lugard, another actor prominent in our story, reported that the Banyoro grew millet, maize and wimbi (finger millet), not just the "interminable" bananas and roots of the Baganda.

For nomads, their cattle were both their wealth and their larder. A glimpse of this lifestyle, surviving into modern times, is provided by the childhood memories of Yoweri Museveni, later the president of Uganda. He was born about 1944 into a family of Banyankore Hima nomads. The Banyankore of Ankole are a related people of the Banyoro.

Museveni explains in his book, *Sowing the Mustard Seed,* that his exact date of birth is not known because his parents were illiterate and dated events by reference to external happenings. He was born between the death of a mugabe (king) of Ankole and the installation of his successor.

The family ate almost exclusively cattle products, particularly milk.

The main staple of our diet [Museveni writes] was various types of milk – fresh milk, soured milk, and, once in a while, a kind of thick cream called "eshabwe" which we would eat with steamed bananas. We also ate cattle blood – we would bleed the cattle and bake the blood into a type of cake … We would also eat veal once in a while, especially if the cows produced male calves. The eating of male calves was in effect a method of breeding control as only the best males would be preserved for breeding purposes. Adult cows would only be killed for a big ceremony, never for regular food.

The diet changed dramatically when the family converted to Anglicanism soon after Museveni was born. They started eating beans, sweet potatoes and groundnuts. But his father continued to refuse fish and chicken, and, Christianity or not, later took a second wife, with whom he had eight children.

Food taboos among the nobles produced the curious situation that they were less well nourished than the peasants. Their contempt for vegetable foods meant they were subject to vitamin and calorie deficiencies.* The common people were not restricted by the same taboos. They could consume both cattle produce and vegetables. Their diverse diet contributed to their better physical health.

James Augustus Grant, who travelled with John Hanning Speke in the 1860s, was told by a Nyoro chief that many of his children died. The chief said if one of his wives placed a child with a servant the child usually lived, but any of his own would quickly die. The explanation must be nutrition.

These dietary differences reflected a deep cleavage in Nyoro society. The Bito royal clan and the Hima nobles were cattle-owning pastoralists. Cattle, like sheep in early modern England, were the wealth of the kingdom. The third group – the mass of the population – were peasant cultivators, the Iru.

The distinction remains politically potent to this day in nearby Rwanda and Burundi, where the Hima are known as Tutsi and the Iru as Hutu.

Gaetano Casati said Kabalega had more than 150,000 cattle – and seemed more interested in the cattle than in running the kingdom.

As well as the lifestyle difference – later lost in Bunyoro as the vast herds of cattle disappeared, victims of disease and warfare – there was a marked difference in physical

---

* "Poverty and wealth in traditional African societies: considerations regarding wealth, well-being, and nutrition in the Ganda and Nyoro societies, c 1800 to 1875", Nordic Journal of African Studies, 9 (1) (2000)

appearance. The Hima were taller, lighter-skinned and Caucasoid; the Iru were of the typically African appearance known as Bantu.

To the early western travellers, it meant that the Hima were migrants from the north and ultimately from the Middle East. This "Hamitic hypothesis" has been challenged as a form of racism by Europeans who did not care to accept that "primitive Africans" could produce such refined physical types.

> The Hima and Tutsi groups, whose pastoralism is emphasized, were subjected to intense ideological projection, which must be discarded if the region's historical realities are to be found [writes Jean-Pierre Chretien in *The Great Lakes of Africa* (English edition 2003)] ... The whites wanted to find in the chiefs with whom they aligned themselves lost brothers or at least descendants of pharaohs or Prester John (the legendary ruler of a Christian nation surrounded by savages).

The issue is complicated by the fact that the region straddles two zones of human settlement. The Bantu zone includes Bunyoro but just beyond in modern Uganda lies the zone of Nilo-Hamitic and other northern languages.

Chretien acknowledges that the theory of an invasion from the north remains a possible explanation for the Hima and the Iru. Alternatively, the differences may be wholly internal – with pastoralism and agriculturalism reflecting a socio-economic divide. The Hima and the Iru may simply be different classes of the same racial stock.

Nor does it appear to be in question that the Bito royal clan were originally migrants from the north.

Doubts about the migration theory of the Hima have long been felt. In 1937 Albert Gille, a Belgian in Burundi, said:

> Physical differences: yes, they exist, but they are not general or constant enough to allow us to conclude that there is a neat and always real racial differentiation. (Quoted by Chretien)

Merrick Posnansky, a British archaeologist, declared plainly in 1966:

One may however think of the strongly marked physical differences between the Bairu and the Bahima as due to nutri-
tional and social factors rather than necessarily inferring a
folk movement from the Horn of Africa." (Quoted by Chretien)

What is certain in this ethnographically most complex part
of the world is that no-one knows for certain.

Colvile was able to move his army along well maintained roads and across carefully bridged streams. He
found the roads in better condition than those of Buganda.
John Roscoe, a missionary, also picked up on Bunyoro's
network of roads.

The roads were actually broad paths because the country had no wheeled transport. The wheel was not used in
sub-Saharan Africa until introduced by Arabs and
Europeans. This is less surprising than it seems. While the
ease of moving a log by rolling it must have been noted, a
wheel is only useful if joined to an axle and socket – a far
from obvious connection.*

This wheel-axle combination evolved quite late in the
human story. It was in Mesopotamia in the fifth millenni-
um BCE, or some 150 millennia after the emergence of
modern humans.

Another limiting factor was the lack of effective motive
power needed to pull wheeled transport. Horses could not
be used in places like Bunyoro because African horse sickness has a mortality rate close to 100 per cent (mules 50
per cent, donkeys 10 per cent).

The zebra, a member of the horse family indigenous to
central and southern Africa, rarely displays clinical symp-
toms of African horse sickness, but has not proved a suitable alternative to the horse. It has not been domesticated
as a species. The zebra is a notably fractious animal.
Attempts to put it between the shafts of a cart have usually not succeeded, or at least the rider has not succeeded in
staying in the cart to the end of the journey.

The villages of Bunyoro consisted of conical huts of
bushes and grass, built in the banana woods. The houses
were divided into compartments.

---

* www.wikipedia.org

The biggest settlement, the royal capital, was an imper-
manent affair. A new capital was built at the start of each
reign, and might be moved during the reign. Kabalega
moved his capital several times under the pressures of
war.

Sir Samuel Baker, who visited Bunyoro in the 1860s
and 1870s and whose negative views about the country
and its people coloured the perceptions of generations of
colonial administrators, described the royal enclosure of
Masindi as lacking "any arrangement or plan" and
"exceedingly neglected". It was substantial, however, with
about a thousand large, beehive-shaped straw huts. John
Hanning Speke found the place dirty and farmyard-like.

Baker and Speke misled themselves with the capital's
lack of European character, and failed to grasp its signifi-
cance. Masindi was far removed from a village or a war
camp. It was at the head of an extensive state, carrying out
the functions that this implied.

These included the organisation of trade. The Banyoro
were noted for the quality of their ironwork. They also had
major saltworks, including Kibiro on Lake Albert. Even
while Bunyoro and Buganda were struggling for supremacy in the 19th century, trade continued. Bunyoro exported
iron hoes and salt to Buganda in exchange for bark cloth
and matoke (plantains). (Jan Jelmert Jorgensen: *Uganda,
a Modern History*) Bunyoro's ivory found ready markets,
being taken out by Arab traders even as the outside world
was awakening to the chaos caused by elephant hunting.

Before the importation of merikani (calico) and other
fabrics from the mid-19th century, bark cloth was the
dress of kings and peasants alike. Peasants were still to be
seen wearing it in the early 20th century. In the old days
of Bunyoro-Kitara, according to John Roscoe in *The
Bakitara*, the king wrapped himself in enormous squares
of bark cloth measuring roughly 10 ft (3 m) in each dimen-
sion, knotted on the shoulder. The cloths were white, black
and various shades of brown. Some were decorated with
the blood of favourite wives or princesses.

Kabalega's capital at Mparo, near modern Hoima, was a
substantial place, measured in square kilometres rather
than hectares and with a population of thousands, accord-

ing to Cato Lund.* But Bunyoro's situation beyond the
European pale means that 19th century accounts of its
capitals are limited. Lund had to look to Mengo, the last
capital of pre-colonial Buganda, for a parallel.

Each Ganda chief occupied his own area at the capital,
with part of each site left as cultivable land to be used by
his peasants when they were required to work in town.
With abundant plant life, vegetable gardens, reed fences
and thatched houses, Mengo had a "garden city" feel that
was much remarked on by early Europeans.

Mengo's core was the royal enclosure, or lubiri, on a hilltop. This covered 200-250 acres (80-100 ha) with about 500
houses. The total area of the capital was around seven
square miles (18 sq km), putting the population in many
thousands. Mparo was comparable in size, says Lund.

From the remains of Kabalega's karuzika (palace) a
huge tree was to be seen in the distance. This was said to
be his mother's walking stick, which took root when she
rammed it into the ground at the edge of the royal enclosure.

A word picture of another Ganda capital was painted by
Wilhelm Junker in *Travels in Africa During the Years
1882-86*. Rubaga, he said, was neither a village nor a town.
It was an isolated hilly tract† many miles in circumference,
dotted with enclosures and groups of dwellings. The royal
residence crowned a hill. The market place, Arab quarters
and English and French missions were close by.

John Roscoe, an early Anglican missionary, looking
back from the standpoint of the 1920s, described a typical
Nyoro royal enclosure‡ in his book, *The Bakitara*. He did
not identify a particular place but explained that the
description was based on the current mukama's memories
of the court of his father, Kabalega.

---

* "The royal capitals of the interlacustrine kingdoms: an urban legacy for
Uganda", Uganda Journal, vol 45 (1999)

† Now part of Kampala

‡ Roscoe used the term "royal enclosure" differently from Lund. For Lund
it is part of the town; from the size of Roscoe's royal enclosure we must
infer that he means the whole town

The royal enclosure had a circumference of about two miles (3.2 km) and was surrounded by a fence 6 ft (1.8 m) high made of elephant grass. The court house was the main building in the enclosure and contained within it the throne room, which had a diameter of 120 ft (37 m) and was 80 ft (24.5 m) high at the apex. The many buildings in the enclosure ranged from such grandeur to slave huts with a diameter of a few feet and barely enough to stand up in.

The anthropologist clergyman Roscoe described in some detail the arrangements of the royal palace. Eight drums stood in a row in the throne room. A ninth drum, called Nyalebe, stood beside the throne. All the drums were sacred to the king and only he might beat them.

Two women slept on either side of the throne for it must never be left unattended. They were nominally wives of the king but actually were virgins. Each was on duty for four days at a time. If one was menstruating or ill, another must take her place.

Outside the throne room was the kraal where the sacred herd of cows (nkorogi) were gathered twice daily for milking. Curiously, they trafficked through the queen's reception room to reach the kraal. This room included a pole from which offending princes and princesses were hanged on the king's orders.

The king did not eat any meat except beef. Goats, sheep and fowls were raised for offerings to the spirits or to take auguries. Dogs were kept for hunting.

Roscoe reported the elaborate rituals that surrounded the preparation of the king's meat. Cooks held office for a month at a time. They must live apart from their wives for the month. They were on duty for four consecutive days, two of which were spent in purification and two working. On the two days of service face, arms, hands and chest were smeared with white clay to signify that the person had been purified.

Any meat left over from the king's meal must be eaten by the chief cook, who had to abstain from other meat for 24 hours afterwards.

Life in Bunyoro was permeated with ritual. This included sacrifice up to and including human sacrifice. This fell at random for both nobles and peasants.

Casati, in his book *Ten Years in Equatoria and the Return with Emin Pasha*, vividly described the mpango (axe) ceremony, designed to appease the spirits, especially that of Kabalega's late father, Kamurasi.

A great bass drum boomed out over Kabalega's capital, Casati reported. Numerous villagers were seized and their throats cut. But the great sacrifice was not to be completed until the morning of the next day:

> The King made a sign with his hand [Casati wrote]; the nobles rose and bowing in sign of reverence approached him; he touched the shoulder of one of them with the point of his spear; the chief advanced and extended his neck; the axe descended and the blood was caught in the cup. The King then sprinkled some of the blood on his own forehead and cheeks, then on those of the nobles; then the remainder was poured over the drum and the chair ... At a sign from the King, the sorrowing parents took away the body of Kisa, late chief of the District of Muenghe. The drums called to a feast; oxen were killed and jars of beer brought and the drunken people danced upon the ground bathed with the blood of the late victim.

As described by Casati, human sacrifice was frequent and systematic. It occurred every new moon (monthly) and when members of the royal family were ill. Bulls were sacrificed first, then humans.

Kabalega immolated a boy of 12 with his own hands as a propitiation of his father's spirit, Casati claimed.

The ordinary people of Bunyoro did not like human sacrifice, unsurprisingly since they could find themselves the victims. Yet, Casati implied, they too performed ceremonies in imitation of the royal family.

The blood-letting spared no social classes. The victims of the mpango ceremony included dignitaries holding the order of Condo, who were on the same level as the king's relations.

Casati realised that Kabalega was merely following tradition as he found it. "This custom had been practised from a distant epoch," Casati wrote. At the time Bunyoro had very little contact with Christian missionaries, although these had been established in neighbouring Buganda since 1877. Probably it never occurred to Kabelega not to practise human sacrifice. It was the ultimate way to appease the spirits of ancestors, who otherwise might destroy you.

One of the fullest pictures of Bunyoro and its people was given by the Rev C.T. Wilson and R.W. Felkin in *Uganda and the Egyptian Soudan* (1882). Wilson was one of the first two missionaries in Buganda; Felkin, his fellow member of the (Anglican) Church Missionary Society, arrived two years later.

The book, in a section written by Felkin, drew a striking contrast between the cleanliness of the Banyoro in their persons and the squalor of their dwellings:

> The Wanyoro are not so fine a race as the Waganda, nor are their intellectual powers so fully developed. There are many very light-coloured people among them, their ordinary colour being a dark reddish brown. They are very cleanly in their persons, frequently bathing, and always washing their hands before and after eating. Their huts are dome-shaped; but are not clean, and swarm with vermin. The people are great thieves, and rather treacherous.

The early CMS missionaries were on their own, and Felkin thought this was a handicap in a society where polygamy was universal. Amfina, a cousin of Kabalega, had 10 wives. One of them pulled Wilson's long hair to see if it was genuine. "It is a great disadvantage to be unmarried in Africa," wrote Felkin; "bachelors at once lose caste with the natives, who cannot understand it."

The Banyoro had only a limited incest taboo, Wilson and Felkin found. Brothers might marry sisters, and fathers might marry daughters. However, a son did not marry his mother. Adultery, on the other hand, was not very common.

Perhaps this was not so surprising since penalties were severe in the pre-colonial state. For an unfaithful wife death was the punishment, said J.F. Cunningham in *Uganda and Its Peoples* (1905). The "co-respondent" faced a heavy fine. There is no mention of a penalty for an unfaithful husband.

Adultery with a royal princess meant death, and misconduct with one of the king's wives meant maiming: loss of a hand, or the lips, or an ear, or an eye. "Judging from the number of maimed men formerly met with in Unyoro,

I am afraid it must be admitted that considerable suspicion attached to the royal ladies," Cunningham commented drily.

It is clear from Roscoe's *The Bakitara* that belief in the supernatural was widespread. He placed these beliefs in three groups: superstitions; taboos and omens; fetishes and amulets.

A common superstition was not to hand another anything with the left hand – hardly more fearsome than the modern western reluctance to walk under ladders.

More limiting was when one might cross the Kafu and Muzizi rivers, which were believed to be the abode of sacred snakes. If a man who had had sexual intercourse the night before tried to cross the Muzizi, he risked disaster from the snakes; so did a woman who was menstruating.

Pythons were sacred, and wells contained water spirits. Sickness was thought always to be caused by ghosts or magic. The ghosts of previous occupants of a house were specially menacing. They must be appeased with shrines and offerings of milk.

Taboos and omens existed for the important events of life like marriage, births, work and travelling. It was taboo, for example, for a man to go to work if when setting out he met a woman before another man; he must return to the house for work that day would not succeed. He should also postpone his work if rain fell the previous night, or the fire went out, or a child was born in his kraal, or any relatives died, or a dog had puppies, or a hen hatched chickens, or biting ants entered the house, or an alarm was raised for fire or wild animals.

Fetishes were made of hollowed-out horns or claws, into which was placed powder or other substances dedicated to particular gods. There were large fetishes to protect the house and smaller fetishes for individuals.

Amulets to protect against evil were of all sorts, including bits of tree roots, herbs, sticks, horns with powder, and shells.

Roscoe's work gains authenticity by his use of non-English-speaking interpreters. Where interpretation was needed, he used a local person with whom he shared a third language. "Yet even in these cases [Roscoe wrote] all the information came to me through a native medium, uninfluenced by contact with the western mind."

Writing in the 1920s, Roscoe said he wrote about these customs in the past tense but it should not be assumed that all had necessarily passed away. Indeed, in 2005 a paper from an international research institute observed:

> Contemporary Ugandan communities have been heavily influenced by Christianity, Islam, and foreign cultures to an extent that observance of the traditional taboos and superstitions has weakened, but not died.*

In 1877, Kabalega received a peaceable visit from Emin Pasha, one of the most curious characters on the African scene. He was a myopic German doctor and naturalist named Eduard Schnitzer. He had joined the medical service of the Turkish Empire and taken the name of Emin. By this time he was on Gordon's staff. He later succeeded Gordon as governor of Equatoria.

Emin formed a far better opinion of Kabalega than Sam Baker had:

> He gives one an exceedingly favourable impression, is lively, laughs much, often shaking with mirth, is very talkative, and appears to submit to ceremonial with a certain amount of constraint, greatly differing in this respect from the self-conscious ruler of Uganda (Buganda).

Emin found much less ceremonial at the Bunyoro court than he had at the king of Buganda's. The mukama's nobles disposed themselves quite casually: they either squatted or stretched full length on the ground supported by an elbow. He wrote:

> The next day I was called again to the king whom I found surrounded by ten or twelve persons. Anyone who has seen the strict etiquette in Buganda could not fail to be greatly surprised at the nonchalance and informality of the Wanyoro who lie about the floor chewing coffee in a completely unceremonious manner.

---

* International Food Policy Research Institute, "Who knows, who cares?", CAPRi Working Paper, no 41

Like Baker, Emin noted that Kabalega had an exception-
ally light complexion. Signs of Hima blood, he thought,
were very marked. None of the king's entourage, or the
king himself, could read or write. Kabalega understood
Arabic and a quick intelligence was hinted at by the affair
of the scented soap.

Among a variety of fancy gifts, including a Turkish
dress embroidered with gold, a velvet cushion trimmed
with gold braid, Trebizond linen and yellow glass beads,
Kabalega seemed to be chiefly interested in a few pieces of
scented soap, Emin recorded. These "he repeatedly smelt
and inspected. He understood at once that they were
intended for the face and hands."(Georg Schweitzer: *Emin
Pasha: His Life and Work*, vol 1)

Emin's letters were collected and published by Georg
Schweitzer, a relative. Seeking to cancel out his kinsman's
favourable view of the king, Schweitzer added his own
comment:

> It appears that, towards Emin, Kabalega laid aside the
> despotic demeanour which has otherwise been attributed to
> him. However, the rich presents sent by Gordon may have
> gone a long way to convincing the King as to the power of the
> Government whose ambassador Emin was, while on the other
> hand Emin's comprehensive knowledge could not fail to
> impress him.

It was one of a swell of comments from Europeans that
meant Kabalega could do no right in their eyes. Either he
was behaving badly, or he was behaving well as a mask for
being bad!

Kabalega's reign, like Napoleon's, was defined by his
military exploits. He set out to restore the glories of the
centuries-old empire of Bunyoro-Kitara. In the first part of
the reign he largely succeeded.

He stabilised the country, halted its decline and coun-
tered threats from Equatoria to the north and Buganda to
the south. He expanded into Acholi in the east and recon-
quered Toro in the west. This long-standing part of
Bunyoro-Kitara had been a separate kingdom since 1830,
when a son of the mukama rebelled and established his
own state. Kabalega conquered Toro for the second time in

the 1890s after British protection was temporarily withdrawn.

One reason for Bunyoro's decline was that bakama
(kings) were drawn from the ruling Bito clan, leaving other
clans without a direct stake in the kingship. In Buganda,
by contrast, the kings married into many clans, each of
which therefore might provide the next kabaka.

Nyoro social organisation was traditionally looser than
that of the Baganda. S.R. Karugire sees in this another
reason for Bunyoro's 19th century decline. (*A Political
History of Uganda*) It lacked adequate central machinery
of government.

Some surrounding states looked to Bunyoro for protection, a role she was happy to accept. Yet these extraterri-
torial responsibilities required administrative and military centralisation. "There was thus an inherent contra-
diction in Bunyoro's governmental system and her ambitions," writes Karugire.

The mukama lacked the direct control of his Buganda
counterpart over regional chiefs, and hence their forces.
Kabalega's answer was the barusura, which he transformed from a palace guard into a new model army.

Traditionally, the Nyoro army was drawn mainly from
the peasantry mobilised by the chiefs. The barusura, however, answered directly to the mukama and were stationed
throughout the kingdom. They were the first experiment
with a standing army in the region. (Michael Twaddle:
Kakungulu and the Creation of Uganda 1868-1928)

They were also on the whole the last sort of people one
would want to take tea with. It was no wonder they frightened the civilian population as much as the enemy. They
were supposed to maintain themselves with the goods of
criminals. In practice, many people whom they seized were
simply in the wrong place at the wrong time.

The barusura "were recruited from the deserters of the
Egyptian troops, from runaway slaves, and riotous youths
from the bordering States ... Waganda, Bari, Shooli, Lur,
Walegga, Lango, Madi and Bongo men". (Twaddle, see
above)

Picked for their strength, the barusura formed the effective core of Kabalega's armies. They numbered 3,000-
5,000, consisting of spearmen, archers, musketeers and

riflemen. But their weapons were inferior to those of the British-led forces they faced in the 1890s and ammunition for the muskets was always scarce, according to Kabalega's son, Mukama Tito Winyi IV.* Kabalega usually refused to fight pitched battles with the British: he was wisely recognising this superiority in weapons. In addition, the enemy had the lethal Maxim machine gun. It was a self-powered machine gun that used its recoil to put the next bullet in place, enabling the operator to keep up a rapid and continuous stream of fire.

Kabalega is said to have picked the barusura personally. At every new moon potential recruits gathered at Semwema cave near the present Kakumiro town in Kibale district. The mukama slaughtered cows and served each man with meat. The weak were separated from the strong by the amount of meat they ate. Only those with big appetites were recruited.†

A visiting reporter well brought out the sense of awe that the Semwema cave inspires:

> The cave cuts its way through a gigantic rock mountain via very narrow entrances. In order to explore its interior, you must have a torch. In addition, you must have a long string, which you tie at the entrance and let it unfold as you move through the meandering interior. Short of that, you get lost. As you move through a chain of interconnected chambers you sometimes have to climb up and go down into zigzagging narrow connections ... Local people say stone chairs and animal skin sandals adorn one of the rooms. It was here that Kabalega over the years built a very strong army."‡

The barusura were crucial to Bunyoro's expansionary plans, but for Casati, a hostile witness, the price was too high: "And as if mad, he (Kabalega) deviated farther still from the ancient mode of governing, ruling by oppression and treachery, rather than by reason."

Casati claimed that Bunyoro under Kabalega had become a military state, replacing the old ways when the

---

* Quoted by A.R. Dunbar: *A History of Bunyoro-Kitara*
† Sunday Vision, Uganda, June 18, 2006
‡ Sunday Vision, see above

country was governed by district chiefs (magnoro) with sub-divisions ruled by lesser chiefs (matungoli) under them. The magnoro supplied soldiers to the king and also paid tribute of ivory, animals, iron and food. If this analysis is even half right, opposition to Kabalega must have weakened the king when the British came calling.

7 Turmoil in Buganda

Mutesa's death in 1884 meant a period of potential anarchy in Buganda. There was no automatic succession – "the king is dead, long live the king" – therefore no continuing fount of authority. It was a hazardous time for the missionaries, surrounded by hostile forces – the Arabs and their Ganda co-religionists, including the mujasi (chief of soldiers), and the traditionalists, who simply resented the foreigners.

The new kabaka was to be chosen by the council of chiefs. Buganda had a highly evolved constitutional system. At the apex was the immensely powerful katikiro, who was both the chief minister and the chief judge. The country was split into 10 principal divisions, with each governing chief having a distinctive title:*

Busiro – the mugema
Busujju – the kasujju
Butambala – the katambala
Gomba – the kitunzi
Mawokota – the kaima
Kyadondo – the kago
Kyagwe – the sekibobo
Bulemezi – the kangawo
Buddu – the pokino
Singo – the mukwenda

These great offices of state were bestowed by the king, but below these earldoms was an hereditary class of landed gentry, known as the bataka. Both the lords and the gentry had the power of life and death in their domains, while anyone could kill his slave at will. A slave was killed for dropping a gourd, for which Mackay remonstrated with the chief and managed to shame him.

Titles attached to offices abounded. For instance, the gabunga was the keeper of the king's war canoes and the

---

* Richard Reid: *Political Power in Pre-colonial Buganda*

kimbugwe was the keeper of the palace. Three royal persons were recognised constitutionally: the kabaka himself;
the namasole, or queen mother; and the nalinya, or king's
sister. The occupant of this last office might be a true sister or a cousin. The missionary, Robert Ashe, observed (in
Two Kings of Uganda) that cousin marriage was forbidden
among the Baganda; it was seen as the same as marrying
one's sister, and therefore incestuous.

Ashe was a keen student of Buganda's (unwritten) history, picking up information where he could.

> The historiography of Buganda ... really begins with Robert
> Ashe [writes Richard Reid in *Political Power in Pre-colonial
> Buganda*], a CMS missionary who observed at first hand the
> events of the late 1880s and early 1890s, and his work repre-
> sented the earliest attempt to place these events in a histori-
> cal context.

The interregnum passed off without bloodshed, which
Mackay ascribed to the moderating influence of
Christianity. The council's deliberations were of the highest moment: the kabaka once chosen was not only an
absolute ruler but also a demi-god at the head of traditional religion. The choice fell upon Mutesa's son, Mwanga, a
boy of 18. He had the strongest facial resemblance to his
father, but was shorter and more negroid in appearance.

The Protestant mission was the only one in Buganda at
this time, the White Fathers having withdrawn south of
the lake in October 1882. The reason they gave was the
corruption of their converts by the court – "giving them
presents and practising sodomy on them" – although court
intrigues at that time also meant the fathers feared for
their lives.

Mackay, Ashe and O'Flaherty, the CMS missionaries at
Mengo, soon had reason to doubt that the new king would
be well disposed towards Christianity. He received them
wearing Arab dress, and was under the influence at court
of the Muslims and the traditional animists, headed by the
katikiro.

In January 1885, when Mwanga had been on the throne
less than three months, there came a foretaste of tragedies
ahead for the Christian community. Three young boy

Protestants at court were burnt to death on the king's instructions. These readers, as those learning Christianity were called, had refused to be sodomised by the kabaka. Sodomy was widespread at the court, but from the missionaries the boys – Kakumba, Seruwanga and Lugulama – learnt that it was wrong. Lugulama had a terror of being mutilated before death, and piteously asked (without success) not to have his arms cut off but to be "just thrown onto the fire". The boys went to their deaths singing the moving hymn, Daily, Daily, Sing the Praises.

This stirring hymn, then quite new, was the work of the prolific English hymn writer and novelist, Sabine Baring-Gould. Its opening lines are beautifully clear and confident:

Daily, daily, sing the praises
Of the city God hath made;
In the beauteous fields of Eden
Its foundation stones are laid.

The martyrs were referred to by the Archbishop of Canterbury, Rowan Williams, addressing the Church of Ireland in 2004. He told the story of how the night after their deaths a young man made his way in secret to the devastated and grieving Mackay. The young man asked for baptism because he wanted to know how to die like that.

In July at Mwanga's request the Roman Catholic mission returned in the persons of Pères Lourdel and Girault and Frère Amans. This, however, was nothing to do with any particular love for Catholicism. Mwanga feared that the English missionaries were opening the way for a British military invasion, and wanted to offset their influence.

For both Christian communities it was a very hazardous time. To attend church, receive instruction or even talk with the missionaries courted death; yet on July 26, for instance, there were 173 at the Protestant service and 35 at holy communion. Mackay and Ashe were both seized, then released. The persecution was spasmodic, however, and the Christian community held its own.

Into this unsettled situation marched Bishop James Hannington. He was a young Anglican clergyman making his second attempt to reach Buganda. He had led a missionary party towards the country three years earlier but had to turn back through illness while still south of the lake. When well enough to return to Africa, he was consecrated as the first bishop of Eastern Equatorial Africa.

There were urgent practical reasons for the Anglican Church to have a bishop on the spot. The CMS had revived East Africa as a mission field. In 1875 a station had been started on the mainland opposite Mombasa. It was named Frere Town after Sir Bartle Frere, a British official who fought the slave trade. Ten years later, there were several inland missions as well as Buganda. Only a bishop was able to make lay missionaries into clergymen, through ordination. Even more importantly, a bishop was needed to administer the rite of confirmation. In this rite, the grace of the Holy Spirit is conveyed in a new or fuller way to those who have already received it in some degree or fashion at baptism. *(The Oxford Dictionary of the Christian Church)* Unless confirmed, the African converts could not properly be admitted to holy communion – although this requirement was waived in the special circumstances of East Africa. The position had to be regularised, however.

Hence the need throughout the mission field for Bishop Hannington. He spent several months at Frere Town and at Taita, a new CMS station inland near Mount Kilimanjaro. By mid-1885 he was on his way to Buganda with another clergyman, Ernest Jones, and about 220 porters. He decided to take the eastern route around the lake, via Kavirondo and Busoga. Despite the Masai, whose hostile character the explorer Joseph Thomson had exaggerated, it was much shorter than the western route, via Karagwe.

Mackay warned the bishop not to continue via Busoga because the Baganda had a taboo on strangers entering the country by this route: the conqueror of the country was expected to come this way. Mackay and Ashe told the kabaka that a boat had been arranged so that Hannington could enter by a usual route. Mwanga's fear and anger were understandable when he heard that the bishop had crossed Busoga and was at Lubwa's on the Nile – on the doorstep of Buganda, in fact.

Hannington decided to split the caravan when it was near the lake, taking about 50 men himself and heading for Mengo, leaving the rest to wait with Ernest Jones. Hannington's party was seized by men he took to be robbers. During his captivity the bishop kept a diary, which later came into the hands of the CMS missionaries at Namirembe. Here Hannington describes his feelings at being put on display for the local chief's wives:

> About thirty-three more of the chief's wives came and disported themselves with gazing at the prisoner. I was very poorly and utterly disinclined to pay any attention to them, and said, in English, "Oh, ladies, if you only knew how ill I feel, you would go." When my food arrived in the middle of the day I was unable to eat – the first time, I think, since leaving the coast I have refused a meal ... Another party of wives coming, I retired into the hut and declined to see them. A third party came later on, and being a little better, I came out and lay upon my bed. It is not pleasant to be examined as a caged lion in the Zoo, and yet that is exactly my state at the present time.

Hannington found that "Mackay's name seems quite a household word. I constantly hear it." A further sentence "But of the others I scarce ever hear a word" was in the diary when it reached Mengo, but did not appear in the biography produced soon afterwards by E.C. Dawson, omitted presumably for diplomatic reasons.

As a captive, the bishop found himself "refreshed" by Matthew 5:44-45: "But I say unto you, Love your enemies, bless them that curse you, do good to them that hate you, and pray for them which despitefully use you, and persecute you; That ye may be the children of your Father which is in heaven: for he maketh his sun to rise on the evil and on the good, and sendeth rain on the just and on the unjust." He was "much comforted" by Psalm 28: "Unto thee will I cry, O lord my rock; be not silent to me ... The Lord is my strength and my shield ..." He was "held up" by Psalm 30: "I will extol thee, O Lord; for thou hast lifted me up, and hast not made my foes to rejoice over me ... Thou hast turned for me my mourning into dancing: thou hast put off my sackcloth, and girded me with gladness ..."

Hannington's choice of the eastern route cost his life and those of most of the party, because Mwanga now ordered them killed. Hannington's end has all the character of a nightmare. His captors kept him apart from the men. Only in the final moments, on October 29, 1885, as he was taken to join them did he realise that they were in a place of execution. His last words were: "Tell the king that I die for Buganda. I have bought this road with my life." Then a horde fell on the men, spearing and hacking them to death.

In the chaos one man escaped and brought the news to Ernest Jones. He could hardly believe it although the proof was inescapable. Eventually, he led the party back to Frere Town with a banner – made up with material from the expedition's trade goods – inscribed ICHABOD, the Old Testament exclamation of regret. The glory has departed. At that moment it seemed never more appropriate than for Bishop James Hannington.

Frederick Jackson (*Early Days in East Africa*) knew Hannington in Zanzibar as the bishop was preparing for his final trek.

> Bishop Hannington struck me as inclined to be domineering [wrote Jackson], very impetuous, and intolerant of opposition; but, as subsequent events proved, quite fearless, and a great believer in his own judgment.

Jackson described a lunch party where Hannington frequently made mistakes about the history of the Holy Land, which he had just visited. When corrected by another clergyman at the table, W.E. Taylor, Hannington appealed to his chaplain for support, which was dutifully given. But Taylor "stuck stoutly to his guns, and was certainly the more convincing".

Hannington's death caused dismay in England, although it was not realised at first that Mwanga was behind it. Many African travellers fell victim to robbers or feuding tribes. Mwanga's action was not without reason, however. Even Frederick Lugard, the later conqueror of Buganda, who was no friend of the kabaka, acknowledged it:

> Dastardly as this murder was [Lugard wrote in *The Rise of Our East African Empire*], it must be admitted that Mwanga looked on Hannington's arrival as the precursor of war; and it

was most unfortunate that the bishop should have adopted
the route *via* Usoga (Busoga).

Hannington could hardly have picked a worse time to
arrive in Busoga. Mwanga, who was only a youth, had not
yet consolidated his power in Buganda. Behind the missionaries and their converts lay (earthly) powers that, he
assumed, wanted to eat his country. Germany was annex-
ing part of the East African coast. To the north of
Buganda, the outlook as he saw it was threatening.
Islamists in the Sudan were pressing south. Between them
and Buganda lay Kabalega's kingdom of Bunyoro, also
hostile to him. Kabalega had substantial forces and many
guns, and a willingness to use both. The bishop's murder
cast a long shadow. Lugard believed that Mwanga's association with the pro-French, Roman Catholic political faction, against the British, was because he feared and
expected revenge for the killing.

The British government felt no need to avenge the death
of a private citizen. The following year it was proposed that
Stanley would lead an expedition into Equatoria. Sir Percy
Anderson of the Foreign Office wrote to the Cabinet with
familiar bureaucratic sang-froid: "... if he (Stanley) lost his
life there would be no more obligation on the British
Government to avenge him than there is to avenge Bishop
Hannington."

Protestants in Buganda remained without a bishop for
five more years, until the arrival of Bishop Alfred Tucker
in the last days of 1890. This was not through want of trying by the authorities. Soon after Hannington's death, the
second bishop of Eastern Equatorial Africa was consecrated: Henry Parker. He arrived near Lake Victoria safely
and stayed for a while at Usambiro. This was a CMS "safe
haven" south of the lake. But he died of a fever there in
1888. Tucker, however, survived in Uganda for many
years and was a major force in developing the Anglican
Church.

Hannington's murder left the Protestant missionaries at
Mengo in peril. Mwanga demanded to know how Ashe and
Mackay knew about the death, as Ashe recorded in *Two
Kings of Uganda*:

We put off our cross-examiners as well as we could; finally we said, "We have not come here to 'ropa' (inform on) people." Whereupon they waxed angry, and the king called us hypocrites, and added that we were "bagwagwa" (the most stupid), the most insulting term in the language. Manoga, the king's tailor, now came back to the question of who had told us about the Bishop. The king said, "They refuse to tell because they think I shall kill the person." Then he tried a wheedling tone. "Tell me," he said, "and you will be 'baganze enyo' (great favourites)." Our continued silence made them very wroth, and then came angry words about killing. "What if I kill you?" said the king. "What could Queeni (Queen Victoria) do? Was she able to touch Lukonge or Mirambo (chiefs outside Buganda) when they killed white men? What could she do, or all Bulaya (Europe) together? How would they come – would they fly?" Père Lourdel now kindly attempted to create a diversion in our favour. He said, "If you killed these white men, then I should not care to stay in your country." "If I killed them," insolently replied the king, "should I spare you? Are you not a white man like them?" The Père reflected on this in silence during the remainder of the interview.

Mwanga then said he would not have the east road used. Was he not the king? Who was Queeni?

We replied, "We are not messengers of Queeni, but messengers of God".

Despite the defiant talk, Mwanga feared to kill the missionaries but, encouraged by the Muslims, he showed no inhibitions about persecuting the African converts. The master of the king's pages, a Catholic called Joseph Balikudembe, was killed for remonstrating with the kabaka over Bishop Hannington's murder.

In the great terror of the following year, 1886, about 200 Christians – Roman Catholics and Protestants – were killed for the faith. Anyone attending a Christian meeting or receiving religious instruction risked betrayal and death. Yet still the number of converts grew including some of the senior chiefs surrounding Mwanga. The martyrs' willingness to die for a faith so recently learnt made the profoundest impression in both Buganda and Europe. The kabaka could not understand why young men and women went to their deaths praying joyfully instead of voicing the customary mournful wails.

A young boy, Kiwobe, asked to be baptised at the height of the persecution. He became Samweli (Samuel) and a pillar of the Christian community. He was so conscientious to duty that he fled only after delivering a tribute of cowrie shells that he had been entrusted with.

The terror reached a ghastly climax when 32 were burnt on a single pyre at the Namugongo execution ground, triggered, according to Ashe, by a royal page, Sabagabo, refusing to be sodomised. The victims included Walukaga, a smith, who had warning but refused to flee. The Christians were accused of disloyalty and sedition. Walukaga wanted to plead his case, but his confidence in the justice system was tragically misplaced. Much uncertainty surrounds who died there, and even the precise number, but by one count the dead included 13 named Catholics and nine named Protestants. Ironically, some non-Christians may have found themselves on the pyre having been caught in the round-up.

A small incident is supposed to have triggered the mass burning. Mwanga had spent an unsuccessful day hippo hunting. On his return he found no pages to attend him. He flew into a rage when he realised they had been having religious instruction. Every Christian he could find he handed over to the executioners. The executions were a calculated act, however. Another week went by while the funeral pyre was made ready. Mwanga, backed by some of the chiefs, had decided to rid himself of the Christians.

Official lists of the Uganda martyrs show the various ways in which they died: dismembered and burnt, burnt to death, speared, speared and hacked to pieces, speared and beheaded, speared and savaged by dogs, castrated, clubbed and burnt, hacked to pieces, dismembered and left to die, beheaded, beheaded and hacked to pieces, beheaded and thrown into swamp.

For Mwanga the burning of the 32 was a serious mistake. Nothing better dramatises the cause you are trying to suppress, or enlists spectators' emotions on the other side, than a public burning. You hope for a very visible recantation but you are unlikely to get it. The victims are beyond that; they have in a sense already crossed to the other side.

So Mwanga's terror did not destroy Christianity in Buganda but entrenched it. The Roman Catholic Church later canonised 22 of its converts who died in the great persecution, including Charles Lwanga, the Catholic leader. Jocelyn Murray, in her history of the Church Missionary Society, *Proclaim the Good News*, writes: "In no other Anglican mission has there ever been such a testing and such a response." H.P. Gale, in *Uganda and the Mill Hill Fathers* (although this group of Roman Catholic missionaries did not arrive until 1895), remarks that the persecution had the opposite effect to that intended: it forged the two Christian groups into "parties", opposed to the Muslims and traditionalists. The Christian parties were known as the ba-Fransa and the ba-Ingleza from their association with the French Catholic and English Protestant missions respectively.

Frederick Lugard spoke of the admiration and sympathy in England for the martyred Christians, recalling as they did the zeal and fortitude of the early Church. "Men asked what kind of people were these [he wrote] who would thus brave death for their belief, and ceased to scoff at the reality of conversions which could stand so terrible a test." *(The Rise of Our East African Empire)*

An article in the (London) Times said:

> The existence of the Mission, lying altogether in Mwanga's power, yet staying against his declared will, is infinitely more conclusive evidence of the strength of Christianity in Africa than would be its predominance by the tyrant's dethronement. There would have been no shame had the Mission voluntarily broken itself up in the face of the young king's insolent enmity. Its persistency is not merely magnanimous; it is the one way of testing the ability of Christian truth and humanity to hold its ground, without the accessories of gunboats and rifles, against both Heathendom and Islam.

Mwanga's actions were driven by immaturity but he was not the crazed and blood-soaked tyrant sometimes depicted by European writers. He was also illiterate, unlike some of his chiefs. Ashe described how he tried but failed to teach Mwanga to read: "... wayward and flighty, he

seemed unable to concentrate his attention on the same
thing for any length of time." In his near-contemporary
account (1893) of the event, Lugard acknowledged that
from Mwanga's point of view both Christian and Muslim
religions were dangerous because they were "disintegrat-
ing his country". Mwanga's fears were rational enough,
but under the influence of bhang – a commonly smoked
narcotic in Buganda – he was capable, according to
Mackay, "of the wildest unpremeditated actions".

Ado K. Tiberondwa, in *Missionary Teachers as Agents of
Colonialism*, argues that Mwanga was not brutal for the
sake of it, but was aiming to defend his power and his people by cutting out elements that threatened to destroy
them. His persecution of the Christians was fuelled by
anger that their first loyalty was to God, not the king.

Mwanga knew – the three boy readers proved it – that,
unlike his predecessors, he could not through his deified
status as kabaka automatically command the allegiance of
the Christians. They listened also to their ministers, their
priests and their consciences.

For the moment the state, in the person of Mwanga, had
the upper hand, and some of the missionaries decided to
withdraw. Two of the Catholic priests left in the caravan of
Wilhelm Junker, a traveller who arrived from Equatoria in
June, and was allowed to continue to the coast. In August
Ashe left. Mackay and three of the French fathers
remained in Mengo.

Junker brought out with him letters from Emin and his
own apocalyptic assessment of the situation in Emin's
Equatoria and Buganda. Emin was under extreme pressure from Islamists from the north of the Sudan. By
August Junker was at Msalala, from where he wrote in
emotional terms to a friend, Dr Schweinfurth:

> Escaped at last from the clutches of Mwanga at Uganda ...
> Must we believe that nothing will ever be done for these
> unhappy Equatorial Provinces? Write, write on, dear friend!
> Send forth words of thunder that will open the eyes of all the
> world! ... It is absolutely necessary that Emin Bey should
> receive help without delay ... It is with this hope alone that I
> essay to return to Europe. (Quoted by Iain R. Smith: *The
> Emin Pasha Relief Expedition, 1886-1890*)

Junker's information reached Frederic Holmwood, the acting British consul-general in Zanzibar the following
month. He immediately cabled London in melodramatic
style: "News from Uganda, 12 July. Junker left for
Zanzibar. Terrible persecution broken out, all native
Christians being put to death. Missionaries in extreme
danger; urgently requests our demanding from King their
being allowed to withdraw. Emin at Wadelai holds
province, but urgently needs ammunition and stores.
Objects, if he can avoid it, deserting the 4,000 loyal
Egyptian subjects there. No time to be lost if assistance
decided on."

In Britain, momentum developed to send help to Emin.
The Buganda mission, which Holmwood had made clear
was also threatened, attracted less attention, although
many hoped that a relief expedition could help both situa-
tions. Eugene Stock, in his official *History of the Church
Missionary Society* (1899), complained that the British
newspapers were not interested in the plight of Mackay,
now on his own at Mengo: "For the English missionary
they cared nothing; for the Austrian Pasha (Emin) they
cared a great deal."

Charles Allen of the Anti-Slavery Society published a
letter from Emin; so did Robert Felkin, who had been in
Buganda as a missionary in the earliest days. Felkin, who
was campaigning for Emin in Scotland, wrote to Allen:

> In order to get the Scotch to stir I must have a good humani-
> tarian, utilitarian and several other "arian" objects in my
> paper. Can you help me? Do try – think of all poor Emin has
> tried to do and really has done, of his long weary holding out."
> (Quoted by Smith, see above)

All this effort had its effect. The British cabinet on
December 3, 1886, approved the idea of a relief expedition.
The details were uncertain but one thing was clear: there
would be no official British government involvement.

The missionaries and their supporters were not
Mwanga's only target. He accelerated Buganda's raids into
Bunyoro, and these turned into full-scale war in 1886. At
one point Kabalega found himself on the run. Gaetano
Casati, an Italian who was the Equatoria envoy in

Bunyoro, described how the mukama's fighting career might have been prematurely ended.

"If I had chosen to put an end to the tyrant's existence, a word or gesture would have been sufficient; but although my life had been continuously plotted against, I would not act otherwise than as a loyal guest," he wrote in *Ten Years in Equatoria and the Return with Emin Pasha.*

At the time of the Ganda invasion Kabalega had more than one thousand guns, Casati reported. Many were Remingtons; a few were Sniders. There were also percussion muskets, breech loaders and muzzle loaders. At the Battle of Rwengabi, Kabalega is said to have personally shot and killed the opposing general, the kangawo.

African wars were not usually aimed at conquest but at quick victories and the seizure of booty including goods and slaves – children as servants and women as wives.

A second Ganda invasion followed in 1887. Kabalega had Casati arrested, with his personal servant, an Egyptian soldier and a Zanzibari named Mohammed Biri.

At a signal from the royal vizier, Casati wrote, an "unbridled crowd" pounced on them. He continued:

> (W)e were seized and barbarously tied to the large trees close to the great magician (a reference to the high priest). I was stripped of my tarboosh (fez) and my pockets were rifled; my neck, arms, wrists, knees and ankles were bound to a tree with such atrocious force that I was unable to make the least movement. The rope round my neck was so tight that my respiration was hindered and one of my arms was twisted and tied in a painful position.

The vizier addressed the crowd about the captives:

> "This man," he said pointing me out, "together with that other, Biri, brought the Waganda to our country; he was the cause of your children and wives being ravished, your goods stolen and your crops destroyed. For these crimes the King has struck them with his justice and entrusted his vengeance to my arm".

It is easy to see why Casati was suspected of being a spy. Casati, as the Equatoria envoy, wanted to open a route to the coast through Buganda, to replace the northern route through the Sudan which was blocked by the Mahdist uprising. To further this aim, he dealt with Alexander Mackay in Buganda.

Improbably, Casati, his servant and the Egyptian soldier (Biri was left behind, and later died) managed to escape from their place of execution, only to be seized within sight of the lake and safety by the barusura, Kabalega's elite force. Yet they escaped again. One of Emin's steamers appeared on the lake. This threw their captors into a panic and they fled. Casati and his party were safe.

Buganda and Bunyoro were fighting almost continuously for three years, while in Buganda persecution and harassment of the Christians continued sporadically. Mackay stayed on for almost a year after Ashe left. He completed his translation of St Matthew's gospel into Luganda. He was careful that the translation was authentic — "every page criticized and revised by the most advanced pupils," as he put it.

Eventually Mwanga demanded that he leave, but he would not do so until a successor had been arranged. The brave person who agreed to take over was E.C. Gordon. There was to be a short gap until he arrived. Relations between the two Christian missions were at best mixed, but Mackay's last action before leaving Mengo in July 1887 was to hand over the key of the mission building to the French fathers.

Mackay had not been home throughout his 10 years in Buganda. Headquarters had often tried to persuade him to take leave. Again he turned down the entreaties. He went no farther than Usambiro, south of the lake, but it was far enough to be beyond Mwanga's reach.

Gordon was joined by Robert Walker. After all the bloodletting and with continued risks, between 150 and 200 attended morning service one Sunday, with nearly as many at two o'clock. This moved Walker to remark: "Really Ashe, Mackay, and the others have done, by the grace of God, a glorious work here."

During the persecution of the Christians Mackay and Ashe clandestinely distributed a message to their followers. It read:

People of Jesus who are in Buganda. Our Friends, – We, your friends and teachers, write to you to send you words of cheer and comfort, which we have taken from the Epistle of Peter the Apostle of Christ. In days of old, Christians were hated, were hunted, were driven out, and were persecuted for Jesus' sake; and thus it is to-day.

Our beloved brethren, do not deny our Lord Jesus, and He will not deny you on that great day when He shall come with glory. Remember the words of our Saviour, how He told his disciples not to fear men, who are only able to kill the body: but He bid them to fear God, Who is able to destroy the body together with the soul in the fire of Gehenna.

Do not cease to pray exceedingly, and to pray for our brethren who are in affliction, and for those who do not know God. May God give you His spirit and His blessing! May He deliver you out of all your afflictions! May He give you entrance to eternal life through Jesus Christ our Saviour!

Farewell. We are the white men: we are your brethren indeed who have written to you."

The passage printed on the back was from 1 Peter ch 4, v 12 to the end. The passage begins: "Beloved, think it not strange concerning the fiery trial which is to try you, as though some strange things happened unto you: But rejoice, inasmuch as ye are partakers of Christ's sufferings; that, when his glory shall be revealed, ye may be glad also with exceeding joy."

It was both a message of encouragement and a call to martyrdom. The missionaries could have said flee. They could have said stay quiet. Instead, they asked the converts to acknowledge their faith even though renouncing it would save their lives. It was a great responsibility Mackay and Ashe were taking on themselves.

After the mass burning at Namugongo, the persecution of the Christians continued although with less intensity. In London the Church Missionary Society was pleased to receive this letter from Buganda converts:

Buganda Mission, May 13th, 1887

Beloved of authority in the Church of Jesus Christ, our English fathers, and all Christians who love us; our brethren. We, your Buganda brethren, write to you to thank you for the letter which you sent us. We rejoice much to hear news which came from where you are to cheer our hearts through our Lord Jesus Christ.

We thank God that you have heard of our being persecuted. Thank God who brought our brother where you are, whom we love, Mr Ashe, and made you understand the evil which has befallen us Christians in Buganda, your children whom you have begotten in the Gospel.

Mr Ashe has told you how we are hunted, and burned in the fire, and beheaded, and called sorcerers, for the name of Jesus our Lord. And do you thank God who has granted us to suffer here at this time for the Gospel of Christ.

We hope indeed for this thing which you hoped for us in your letter, namely, that in a short time other teachers will come to teach. And you who have authority continue earnestly to beseech Almighty God, who turned the Emperor of Rome to become a Christian, who formerly persecuted the name of Jesus as to-day this our king in Buganda persecutes us. And do you our fathers hope that we do not in the least degree give up the Word of Christ Jesus. We are willing, indeed, to die for the Word of Jesus; but do you pray for us that the Lord may help us. Finally, our friends, let your ears and eyes and hearts be open to this place where we are at Buganda. Now we are in tribulation at being left alone. Mr Mackay, the Arabs have driven away out of Buganda. Oh, friends, pity us in our calamity. We, your brethren, who are in Buganda, send you greetings. May God Almighty give you His blessing. May He preserve you in Europe. We remain, your children who love you,

HENRY WRIGHT DUTA.
EDWARD.
ISAYA MAYANJA.

The date of the letter was a puzzle for the CMS because Mackay did not leave until July. The letter may have been started in May, when he was expected to leave, and finished in July after he went.

The following year, 1888, Mwanga overreached himself by plotting with traditionalists at court to destroy all the foreigners – that is, both sets of missionaries and the Arabs – and their followers. To unite the Christians and the Muslims was a mistake that his father, with his sensitivities to the balance of forces, could not have made.

After consulting sorcerers, Mwanga laid plans for a general massacre, but the news leaked out. His next attempt was more subtle. The Mukasa, the embodiment of the Lubale, the Ganda god, lived on an island in the lake. The kabaka announced that the island was to be attacked and Lubale worship extinguished. The real intention was to lure the Christian and the Muslim fighters onto a nearby island under the guise of assembling for the attack; then leave them there to starve. With the loss of most of the men in their prime, the heart would have been torn out of the two communities.

This plan, too, became known. Leaders of the three groups – Honorat Nyonyintono (Catholic), Apolo Kaggwa (Protestant) and Lubanga (Muslim) – agreed on united resistance. In September Mwanga ordered the fighters to board the war canoes for the fake attack, but few obeyed him. He fled into his palace and was later allowed to leave Mengo unharmed. He went south of the lake with a retinue of pages and a small following, finding refuge first with Arabs and later at Bukumbi, the Roman Catholic mission station.

Leaving Mwanga alive was a mistake of realpolitik. The kabaka, good or bad, *was* Buganda, so a living ex-kabaka was a standing challenge to the legitimacy of the replacement. The crucial need to have a kabaka in place was underlined by the forced installation of Mwanga's eldest brother, Kiwewa. Nyonyintono became the new katikiro, and a Protestant and a Muslim were appointed respectively for the key roles of mukwenda and kimbugwe.

During Kiwewa's brief reign all the religious groups were able to practise their faith openly. Posts were distributed among the factions – Catholic, Protestant, Muslim and traditionalist. It was too good to last, and it lasted less than two months. The Muslims were by far the weakest of the religious factions. They had an estimated 300 guns against 1,000 apiece for the Catholics and the Protestants.

Even so, the next month (October) they succeeded with a coup d'etat, forcing the two Christian groups out of the capital. Nyonyintono and Kaggwa led their followers westwards to Ankole, where they were welcomed by King Ntare.

Alexander Mackay, in exile at Usambiro, wrote a vivid account of the exodus:

> That sad 12th of October will never be forgotten by our people. Chiefs and commons, rich and poor, free and slave, they fled before their foes, who hotly pursued them. Everything was lost; wives and children, home and country. No man could return to take anything from his house. Clothes, books, their all, gone.

It was not a mass movement. The numbers affected by these manoeuvres at court were relatively small – about 200 Protestants, rather more Catholics. The missionaries decided to stay in the capital. The mission stations were attacked and pillaged. The missionaries were detained and then expelled. Kiwewa, who had refused the Muslim rite of circumcision, fled but was soon captured.

The new kabaka was another of Mwanga's brothers, Kalema. He was much more receptive to Islam. His order for universal circumcision was resisted with much violence and bloodshed.

The missionaries went into exile together: Gordon and Walker of the CMS, and four White Fathers, including Bishop Livinhac and Père Lourdel, with around 30 followers between them. They used the Anglican mission's sailing boat, the Eleanor, which Mackay's sister in Scotland described as "a poor, comfortless thing compared with a Scotch herring-boat, being perfectly open, and having neither cabin nor deck, nor any protection for the crew from the pitiless rains". On the road to the lake Walker was robbed of his hat, coat and even trousers. One of the Frenchmen gave him a pair of corduroy trousers and a blanket.

During the crossing, the Eleanor was attacked by a hippopotamus, causing it to capsize. An island was nearby. Some swam to land, others clung to the boat until rescued by an islander in a canoe; even the Eleanor herself was recovered. The occasion was suffused with sadness, however. Although all the missionaries were safe, five Ganda boys drowned.

Walker set to with an ingenuity that vied with Mackay's when he repaired the Daisy (the Eleanor's predecessor), finding ways to make the damaged boat lakeworthy again.

The party finally reached the Catholic mission station at Bukumbi. After being hospitably entertained by the priests, Gordon and Walker moved on to join Mackay at the CMS station of Usambiro, which was nearby.

We do not have to imagine Père Lourdel's sad feelings about being forced into exile because he expressed them in a letter:

> After shipwreck and the many miseries of the crossing, fever, and dysentery, caused by the emotions and fatigue of the voyage, have come in their turn to pay us a visit. I am beginning to recover a little and I have not lost hope of returning again to dear Uganda, which was producing such fine apostolic fruit and promising even more ... The trials and miseries do not discourage one's spirit but they make the flesh feel weak and aged, so that at 35 years I find myself old; my hair and my beard are becoming white.

Mwanga with an entourage arrived at Bukumbi in December 1888, having slipped away from his Arab hosts in exile, whom he found too demanding. The fathers could not condone polygamy so he was lodged with one wife in quarters for married converts and his other wives lived separately. In April 1889 he received envoys speaking for both Ganda Christian communities in Ankole, asking him to join them in their bid to overthrow the Muslims in Buganda. A steady flow of refugees had boosted the exile numbers to the point where Honorat Nyonyintono and Apolo Kaggwa believed they could beat Kalema. It is curious that the Christians should want to reinstate as kabaka the man who had persecuted their brethren, but Mwanga listed among his present virtues the fact that he was not Kalema: installing him as king would mean that the Muslims were beaten. No doubt also the Christian chiefs hoped to control a restored and chastened kabaka.

The missionaries were in a quandary. A revival of the

civil war to overthrow Islam could increase the persecution of the Christians. For the Protestants, a further issue was that Mwanga seemed more closely linked than ever to the Catholics. The movement went ahead anyway. Mackay refused the use of the Eleanor, but the king found the former missionary turned arms trader, Charles Stokes, ready to oblige. They crossed the lake and landed in Budu, where the king was well received. He was joined by the Christian army after a successful encounter with Kalema's forces, during which the Christian leader, Honorat Nyonyintono, had been killed – apparently needlessly as the Christian forces launched a helter-skelter pursuit of the fleeing Muslims.

Nine months of see-saw fortunes for the two sides followed. Mwanga was obliged to leave the mainland for Sese, a large and strategically sited cluster of islands, while his army dispersed towards Ankole. The Sese islanders, like the people of Budu, declared for Mwanga, which gave him control of the lake. Kalema, however, had a big advantage in firepower: some 2,000 guns, twice as many as Mwanga.

Kalema, faced with the invasion threat, responded by killing over 30 of his relatives including his brother, Kiwewa, the former kabaka. These gruesome acts further boosted support for Mwanga (who had an even greater number of ghastly murders to his name).

In June Mwanga moved to the small island of Bulingugwe, less than a mile (1.6 km) from the mainland and close to Mengo. Because Kalema did not have the war canoes to attack the island, the Christians were brilliantly sited close to the centre of Muslim power. From Bulingugwe Mwanga invited both sets of missionaries to join him. Père Lourdel and Père Denoit – another of the party that crossed in the Eleanor – came in Stokes's boat; Gordon and Walker from the CMS entrusted themselves to a canoe. Mwanga also wrote appealing for support to Frederick Jackson of the Imperial British East Africa Company, who was at that time believed to be in Kavirondo. This was like inviting a leopard up for a meat tea – of oneself.

In October 1889 the Christian forces under Apolo Kaggwa drove the Muslims out of the capital. Kalema fled and the Christians returned to Mengo a year almost to the day after they had been driven out. Kaggwa became katikiro, a post he was to hold for many years. Mackay, from Usambiro, wrote:

> The greatest, and, till recently, the most tyrannical power in all East Africa is now in the hands of men who rejoice in the name of CHRISTIAN. But is the power in the hand of *Christianity*? Shall a nation be born in a day? It is born, but being only just born it is at this moment in the most helpless and critical condition conceivable.

The October victory proved to be transient. Next month Kalema's forces, reinforced by Kabalega of Bunyoro, retook the capital. Mwanga went back to the fastness of Bulingugwe, where Père Lourdel lamented conditions on the overcrowded island:

> In our island, disease and famine, following the flow of war, rage more violently each day! How many poor folk have not even a rag with which to cover themselves! And how many sick people die of cold and misery! The bark-cloth with which the Baganda clothe themselves is nearly all used up, and no-one is able to make more because of the disturbed conditions ...

Instead of the Protestant Apolo Kaggwa, the Christian forces now agreed to serve under a young Roman Catholic, Gabriel Kintu. By February 1890 he had 3,370 guns under his command and was able to drive the Muslims out of Mengo, this time for good. True to a pact they had made before the decisive battles with the Muslims, the Catholics and the Protestants shared out the official posts and the shambas (landed estates) that went with them. Chiefdoms were allocated between the two groups, each office-holder having a member of the opposite faith under him, and so on down the line.

The distribution was admirably fair in theory, but became the source of many problems in practice. Given the hostility between the two Christian groups, which had been put aside for the fight with the Muslims but not ended, members of the opposing faiths found it hard to work together. Then there was the matter of what happened to the post – and the shambas – when someone wanted to change faiths. This was particularly a problem for the Protestants. With the kabaka supporting the Catholics, loyal Baganda were tugged that way.

At this point in Buganda's affairs, Walker of the CMS identified three separate interests among the Europeans. The CMS missionaries wanted to see a British occupation "to ensure peace, and to put an end to the ceaseless war and carnage". The White Fathers, who through Lourdel had exclusive influence over the king, believed that Buganda should be left alone and Africans able to buy arms for their defence. The third interest was the arms trader and former missionary, Charles Stokes, who wanted to be able to offer terms to any Europeans who came to Buganda. It is a measure of Stokes's extraordinary position that Walker picked him out for mention alongside the two religious groups.

John S. Galbraith, in *Mackinnon and East Africa 1878-1895*, makes clear that the "French" and "English" labels, while deriving from the presence of the two missions, referred essentially to politics, not religion:

> In the convulsions in Buganda after the death of Mutesa, the "Arab" party derived much of its strength from the fear of the extension of European influence and European values, and Mwanga when he had initially accepted Muslim support had been similarly motivated. Bunyoro's backing of the Muslims after Mwanga had shifted to the Christian party had nothing to do with doctrine, much with the ambitions of its ruler, Kabarega, to restore his kingdom to its earlier greatness by capitalizing on the internal weaknesses of rival Buganda. The Fransa and Ingleza chiefs, on the other hand, saw the future of Buganda as within the sphere of European influence but were divided as to which of the European powers should be their protector.

The defeated Kalema retreated northwards towards the Bunyoro border. He soon died of smallpox and the Muslim succession went back a generation, to Mbogo, a brother of Mutesa. As Elizabeth Mary Matheson points out in *An Enterprise So Perilous* (a history of the White Fathers), Mbogo was "one of the few (royal) survivors of the 1889 massacre". He was "much less aggressive a character than his predecessor, though his followers carried on raiding in

Singo and Kyagwe county for some time". Indeed, while the two Christian groups aimed to settle their differences after their joint victory, the Muslims remained an unintegrated part of the Buganda body politic. Walker's contemporaneous comment was: "The Mohammedans were for the moment overpowered, but neither was their strength nor their spirit broken."

The incoming Europeans held Kabalega's support for the Muslims against him. In their minds, it cemented Bunyoro in opposition to the main forces in the Ganda state.

8 Emin beleaguered

Egypt's provinces stretched deep into Africa, even gnawing from time to time at the Great Lakes kingdoms of Bunyoro and Buganda. For the most part it was not settled administration, but rather garrisons of troops more or less holding down recalcitrant tribes. Further, the country had ruined itself in the cause of modernisation. Over much of the 19th century Khedive Muhammad Ali and his successors set about modernising Egypt in everything from education to cotton growing.

Nominally part of the crumbling Turkish empire, the country had achieved considerable autonomy and wanted to find its place in the modern world. Meanwhile, costs mounted. Debt, particularly to British and French investors, eventually became unsustainable.

In 1875 Khedive Ismael, to raise money, sold his 44 per cent holding in the Suez Canal to Britain, giving that country control of its vital link with India. In 1876 he was obliged to accept an international commission to manage the Egyptian debt. In 1879 the British and French seized the arteries of Egyptian self-rule, taking over the treasury, customs, telegraphs and railways. In 1880, according to Lawrence James in *The Rise and Fall of the British Empire*, Egypt's debts were more than £100 million – or about eight times the average annual value of her exports, £13 million.

Anglo-French control of Egypt was challenged the following year (1881) when a high-ranking soldier, Urabi Pasha, staged a coup d'etat. Foreign control was only one of the issues. Urabi and his associates had grievances over pay and conditions; behind them stood the Egypt for the Egyptians movement of constitutional reformers.

What united them was a determination to break the power of the Turkish oligarchy [writes Thomas Pakenham in *The Scramble for Africa*]. They were not, at least at first, anti-Western. Indeed, they admired Western institutions and planned to set up a Western-style democracy with an elected

Parliament and with the Khedive playing the role of constitutional monarch.

Doubtless Urabi's admiration of things western did not extend to the ironclads that in July 1882 bombarded Alexandria. When this did not do any good, a substantial British expeditionary force of about 30,000 was landed at Ismaelia. It engaged Urabi's army in September at Tel-el-Kebir, 60 miles (97 km) from Cairo. The commander, Sir Garnet Wolseley, decided on a daring night attack. It took the enemy by surprise. The battle was over in just 35 minutes.

"Down the slopes, through the camps, over the railway and across the Canal, the white-clad fugitives were flying south and west in dots, in dozens, in hundreds." The words were written by a battle participant, Colonel William Butler. He praised the fighting spirit of Urabi's forces:

> Not a moment was given them to awake, form up, prepare, or move into position. The assault fell upon them like a thunderbolt might fall upon a man asleep ... they fought stoutly wherever ten or twenty or fifty of them could get together in the works ... the heaps of dead lying with and across their rifles facing the upcoming sun bore eloquent testimony to that final resolve of those poor fellows. (Quoted by James: *The Rise and Fall of the British Empire*)

Urabi gave himself up, Wolseley returned to Cairo in style and British control over Egypt was consolidated. The khedive, by now Ismael's son, Tewfik, nominally stayed in control, but the real power was with his British officials. Already, though, the government's tenuous control of the country was threatened from another direction – the south.

The uprising of Muhammad Ahmad, a boat-builder who was hailed as the Mahdi (the Expected One or the Redeemer) protested at the westernising agenda of the Egyption government. Soon the Mahdi had much of the Sudan in his grip. An army of 10,000 was sent against him under Colonel William Hicks (Hicks Pasha). On November 5, 1883, this large force was ambushed, overcome and massacred at El Obeid in the southern Sudanese province of Kordofan. El Obeid is one of the few African battles where

weight of numbers prevailed against better armed and better disciplined, European-led forces.

The zeal of the Dervishes, as the Mahdi's troops were
known to the Europeans, was shown again 14 months later
at the Battle of Abu Klea, where they nearly managed
another massacre by prising open the British defensive
square.

Rudyard Kipling produced a famous poem about the
battle. His brilliant metre and rhyming has worn better
than the language of this Cockney soldier's tribute to his
opponents. The final lines are:

So 'ere's to you, Fuzzy-Wuzzy, at your 'ome in the Soudan;
You're a poor benighted 'eathen but a first-class fightin'
man;
An 'ere's to you, Fuzzy-Wuzzy, with your 'ayrick 'ead of
'air –
You big black boundin' beggar – for you broke a British
square!

After El Obeid the British Cabinet decided to separate
Egypt from the Sudan. General Gordon was sent to
Khartoum to supervise the withdrawal of the Egyptian
garrisons. He allowed himself and the garrison to become
trapped by the Mahdists. Eventually, a relief expedition
under Sir Garnet Wolseley was sent. Wolseley was advancing slowly – too slowly, the critics charged afterwards –
through Abu Klea, where the battle was fought, and Al
Matamma. His forces arrived just too late to save Gordon.
Ironically, it was the news of the relieving force that drove
the Mahdi to risk storming the city on January 26, 1885.

Gordon's death echoed across Europe. In the Equatorial
Province, or Equatoria, his lieutenant, the German-born
Emin, remained cut off and under threat. Slatin Bey and
Lupton Bey, other European satraps ruling provinces of
the Sudan for the khedive, had surrendered to the
Mahdists. Only Emin remained. A correspondent wrote
the the Times: "Having betrayed the master (Gordon), we
might well exert ourselves a little to deliver his man."

Comes the moment comes the man ... Henry Morton
Stanley re-enters the story with a mission to bring relief to
the beleaguered governor. Stanley had spent several years

working for King Leopold of Belgium after he finished the expedition upon which he met Kabaka Mutesa. Travelling west, he traced a then-unidentified river, which turned out to be the infant Congo. He followed it to its mouth, completing an historic east-west crossing of Africa. For Leopold he knocked heads together and split rocks apart to make the roads that created the Congo state, earning himself his African name, the Breaker of Rocks. The Conference of Berlin in 1885 – the defining event in modern African history because in European terms it legitimated the scramble for Africa – recognised the Congo Free State as the king's private property.

As Emin's admirers saw it, the governor of Equatoria was keeping alight the flame of civilisation in the heart of Africa. Local tribes, as Iain Smith shows in *The Emin Pasha Relief Expedition, 1886-1890*, saw instead a string of garrison stations, administering little more than themselves but still exacting supplies, concubines and taxes from the surrounding countryside.

Emin as not yet trapped. He could have fled south through Bunyoro to the south, abandoning "Emin's people" – the soldiers, administrators and clerks who had come up from Cairo, Alexandria and Khartoum. Heroically, the governor stayed put. But his position was untenable both short-term and long-term. He lacked the military strength to stop the Mahdists. He had abandoned Lado (near the present-day Sudanese city of Juba) as his headquarters, and moved ever southwards along the Nile: to Muggi, Labore and finally Wadelai (the last in modern Uganda). Emin also lacked reliable supply routes. The Nile route was closed indefinitely while astride the other feasible routes were the powerful kingdoms of Bunyoro and Buganda. He had no assured ways of bringing in equipment, spare parts or the ammunition on which his rule ultimately depended.

The route that brought Emin to Wadelai was long in miles and even longer in terms of a life's journey. He was born Eduard Schnitzer in Germany in 1840, and qualified as a doctor. However, he failed to complete the formal requirements to practise medicine in his own country so that employment in his profession was impossible. In a wandering life he found himself employed in the medical

service of the Ottoman Empire, calling himself by a
Muslim name. Later, he assumed a different Muslim name
– Emin. By an oddity of history, Emin and Henry Stanley
met and greeted each other by names that were not their
own, Stanley having been born John Rowland.

Emin from his time in Turkey became enthused by
Islamic culture so it was natural to drift to North Africa.
He arrived in Equatoria when Gordon was the governor,
and their association for the better part of a decade fixed
him in the public mind as "Gordon's man". Emin by every
account was a most likeable character, unselfish and asce-
tic. Even as governor he treated medical patients. It is no
surprise that he won the loyalty of his ragbag of soldiers
and followers. As a keen naturalist, Emin was greatly
pained that in the eventual evacuation of Wadelai he had
to leave his collections behind. He was not, however, heroic in appearance. He was extremely short-sighted. He is
said to have several times passed by the famous
Ruwenzori Mountains (the Mountains of the Moon) and
never known they were there. He was also quite short,
around 5 ft 7 in (1.7 m). Stanley brought a pair of trousers
for Emin. They had been made in Cairo to measurements
based on a traveller's account of the pasha, and 6 in (15
cm) had to be cut off the legs for them to fit.

In 1884, the year before the fall of Khartoum, Equatoria
reached its fullest extent. According to Major C.H.
Stigand, a British officer who served in the area years
later, the province consisted of the following districts and
stations: 1. Rol. Capital Ayak plus five stations; 2. Lado.
Capital Lado plus five stations; 3. Makaraka. Capital
Wandi plus 11 stations; 4. Mangbettu. Capital Mbaga plus
five stations; 5. Kiri. Capital Labore plus three stations; 6.
Dufile. Capital Dufile plus two stations including Wadelai;
7. Fowera. Capital Foda plus one station; 8. Fadibek.
Capital Fajuli plus five stations; 9. Latuka. Capital
Tarangole plus three stations; 10. Bor. Capital Bor, no
other stations.

The forces in the province were two regular battalions,
about 1,300 men, and 3,000 irregular troops. The expatriate population also included Egyptian and Sudanese
administrators and clerks, many of them with criminal
records because Equatoria was seen as a virtual penal

colony, and their dependants. Emin had with him two
faithful associates, who stayed with him to the end: the
Italian Captain Gaetano Casati, and a Tunisian medical
dispenser, Vita Hassan. Emin's Abyssinian wife died
before the final evacuation, leaving him with a young
daughter.

Stigand's account suggests a degree of structure in the
province that it never actually had. For the tribes of the
area life went on more or less irrespective of the local station. In that sense Equatoria was more of a construct in
the European mind than a reality on the ground. Emin
never enjoyed the resource base, the infrastructure and
the involvement of the local population to move beyond
garrisoning to complete administration. However, the
regime did make successful efforts to reduce the slave
trade in its area.

Paradoxically, the humane government of Equatoria
was involved in heavy stockpiling of ivory, which was
obtained at terrible human cost. In pursuit of slaves and
ivory, Arab traders fought their way into Africa's deepest
recesses. Stanley wrote in *In Darkest Africa* (not specifically about Equatoria):

> Every tusk, piece and scrap in the possession of an Arab trad-
> er has been steeped and dyed in blood. Every pound weight
> (0.45 kg) has cost the life of a man, woman or child, for every
> five pounds (2.3 kg) a hut has been burned, for every two tusks
> a whole village has been destroyed, every twenty tusks have
> been obtained at the price of a district with all its people, vil-
> lages and plantations. It is simply incredible that, because
> ivory is required for ornaments or billiard games, the rich
> heart of Africa should be laid waste at this late year of the
> nineteenth century ...

Emin wrote a letter from Wadelai on the last day of 1885
which, when it was published in The (London) Times
months later, caused a sensation and started the movement to bring him "relief", in the classic term of the period. The letter was to Charles Allen of the Anti-Slavery
Society:

> Forgotten, and abandoned by the (Egyptian) Government, we
> have been compelled to make a virtue of necessity. Since the

occupation of the Bahr-Ghazal we have been vigorously attacked, and I do not know how to describe to you the admirable devotion of my black troops throughout a long war, which for them at least, has no advantage. Deprived of the most necessary things for a long time without any pay, my men fought valiantly, and when at last hunger weakened them, when, after nineteen days of incredible privation and sufferings, their strength was exhausted, and when the last torn leather of the last boot had been eaten, then they cut away through the midst of their enemies and succeeded in saving themselves.

In the same month Emin sent a "local letter" to Mackay in Buganda, which ominously foreshadowed the events to come. One of Mackay's many roles was to act as Emin's postmaster, establishing regular contact between Equatoria and Buganda and from there to the world beyond via the route to the coast. Emin told Mackay: "All my people, but especially the negro troops, entertain a strong objection against a march to the south and thence to Egypt, and mean to remain here until they can be taken north."

That route, using the Nile, was closed by the Mahdists. This sentiment was not realised in London when the Emin Pasha Relief Expedition was created. The task was taken up by William Mackinnon, whose Imperial British East Africa Company had an avowed philanthropic as well as trading purpose. The IBEA Company included among its sponsors one of Britain's most influential African specialists, Sir John Kirk. He had travelled with Livingstone and in the 1870s was the British consul-general in Zanzibar. Like the Doctor, he believed that commerce was the way to bring civilisation to Africa.

When Kirk was in post in Zanzibar, Frederick Jackson (*Early Days in East Africa*) found Kirk's knowledge of what was going on, both important and trivial, "little less than downright uncanny". It was founded on a great network of eyes and ears. At Jackson's first meeting with Kirk, the consul led him on about his trip and then threw in "Oh yes, that's where you gave the headman far too much baksheesh (gratuity)", or "I know, you shot a topi there", or "And then the gun-bearers you dismissed came along and frightened them away", and so on.

Mackinnon and his colleagues were inspired by the East India Company's success as a trading company that also exercised the powers of government, but the IBEA Company lacked some of the crucial advantages of the earlier company. The east African coastal hinterland was not favoured with great natural resources and was not very promising for cultivation; nor were the tribes advanced in social development. The company was in its earliest days when Stanley was appointed leader of the Emin expedition, but it soon became obvious that if the company was to have a future, that future lay in Buganda and the surrounding states. Here the soil was fertile and the population advanced.

On the British side the Emin Pasha Relief Expedition was entirely privately funded. The Egyptian government met almost half of the expedition's costs. Stanley was not the only possible leader, especially because he was still in the service of King Leopold of Belgium building the Congo State, but he was by far the most eminent and experienced explorer available. He was the natural choice, although another well known explorer, Joseph Thomson, was disappointed not to have been chosen.

Stanley's instructions, which were later the subject of bitter controversy, appear to have been to (a) invite Emin with his men to accept repatriation to Egypt, all to receive arrears of pay and allowances from the Egyptian government, or (b) to stay under another flag, in which case the Egyptian government accepted no further financial responsibility. Emin himself wanted nothing more than resupply of goods and ammunition, which begged the question of what would happen when they in turn ran out. In any case, there were bigger stakes in play.

Controversy soon broke out over the route to reach Emin at his base near Lake Albert. The more established course ran from Bagamoyo on the coast of present-day Tanzania north-westwards and around the southern tip of Lake Victoria. Thomson suggested leaving from Mombasa in what is now Kenya and passing the opposite (northern) end of Lake Victoria. This was the shorter route, although it was far more dangerous. It ran through Masai country and also Busoga, the "back door" to Buganda. This was the Buganda road that cost Bishop Hannington his life. The

Baganda were very sensitive about this strategic area, so there was a risk that an expedition taking this route would destabilise the situation for the Christians in Buganda still further. The same could and was said to a smaller extent against the route from Bagamoyo.

Stanley now proposed the seemingly extraordinary idea of starting from the other (west) side of the continent, using the River Congo and its tributaries to reach the deep interior. This route meant circumnavigating half the continent to reach the starting point and was more than double the distance across land. It also meant crossing the unexplored vastness of the Ituri Rainforest.

Stanley put the weight of his reputation behind the route. He stressed that desertion would be easier if the expedition started from the east coast, and the desertion of porters with valuable supplies had wrecked other expeditions. He made the Congo route sound easy: the river would take the expedition to barely more than 300 miles (480 km) as the crow flies from Lake Albert, its destination. He conjured up dangers of the other routes, like the Wanyankori with the unimaginable number of 200,000 spears.

Even so, Stanley could not prevail over the organising committee until providentially – too providentially, some historians have felt – a letter was received from King Leopold's aide, the Comte de Borchgrave. The king, Stanley learnt, "considers that he would be failing in his duty towards the (Congo) State were he to deprive it of your services" over the 18 months the expedition was expected to take via the east coast. Stanley's estimated time for the Congo route was the same – 18 months – but by passing through untraversed parts of Leopold's domains he would be combining exploring with the relief of Emin.

A letter from Mackinnon to Stanley showed that Leopold's intention had been understood:

> I had a pleasant short letter from the King [wrote Mackinnon] showing how anxious he is the Congo route should be taken, and how unwilling to allow a break in the continuity of your connection with the Congo State, as he considers you a pillar of the State.

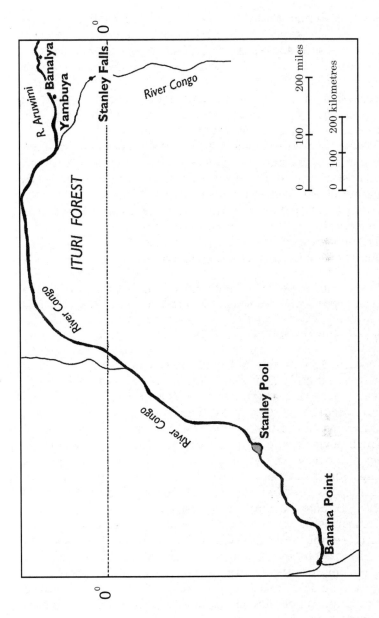

Map 4: The Emin Pasha Expedition – outbound to Yambuya

So, the Congo route it was. It is hard to believe that
Stanley, the servant of King Leopold, did not have a double agenda in suggesting the Congo route. It was not dis-
honourable to allow for Emin bringing Equatoria under
the the king's flag. This was one of the possible outcomes
of the expedition. It depended on adequate communication
across the Nile-Congo watershed. The traverse of the
unexplored Ituri Forest might establish that.

Mackinnon and Leopold were closely associated in business activities and as friends. Mackinnon had been an
early supporter of the International Association, Leopold's
means of establishing himself in the Congo. Mackinnon,
like Stanley, believed in the Congo as an important area
for British investment. But the pair failed in a bid to build
a Congo railway, which Leopold wanted built by Belgians.
Iain Smith sees this as a crucial event:

> September 1886 (when the railway contract was lost) marks
> an important watershed in the careers of both Mackinnon and
> Stanley. After this date, they both turn away from the Congo
> and their real interest is in East Africa.

Leopold, Mackinnon, Stanley, the Germans on the coastal
strip of what is now mainland Tanzania would all have
been aware that at the heart of Africa there was the political vacuum of two established but unstable states,
Equatoria and Buganda. It was becoming a question of
which power would fill that vacuum. Equatoria was unstable because of the Mahdist threat and lack of supplies;
Buganda because of chronic unrest under Mwanga.
Stanley was in what now would be called a conflict of interest, although he may have seen it as simply advancing
civilisation in whatever way was to hand. He was working
for one employer and seconded from another, both of whom
wanted to possess Equatoria. In Zanzibar before the expedition set out, Stanley underlined his dual allegiance with
what he called "a little commission" to the ailing Sultan
Barghash. He persuaded the sultan to grant Britain a concession over what is now the coast of Kenya. This was the
springboard from which Frederick Lugard half a decade
later penetrated the interior on behalf of Mackinnon's company.

An Anglo-German agreement in 1886 settled arrangements along the East African coast. Kirk described it
enthusiastically to Mackinnon as covering deep into the
interior:

> Thus we have Mombasa under the Sultan (of Zanzibar) and a
> free run inland to the Lake (Victoria) etc. but not Kilimanjaro.
> We have the best of any line for a rail if ever one is made. We
> also have the Equatorial Province now held by the brave Emin
> Bey, well-governed and quiet to this day. Germany will rent
> Dar Salaam from the Sultan, which arrangement we may
> make at Mombasa. This is the outline of the scheme and you
> will see we have an opening as good as any." (Quoted by
> Smith: *The Emin Pasha Relief Expedition, 1886-1890*)

The Emin Pasha Relief Expedition was organised on military lines, despite its leader's only army experience being
as a ranker in the American Civil War. Stanley answered
operationally to Mackinnon and the relief committee in
London, but the expedition flew the Egyptian flag and was
partly funded by the Egyptian government. From these
military arrangements Stanley could perhaps claim legitimacy for the harsh discipline he imposed on his men,
including execution, and his readiness to fight tribespeople
in his path – actions that otherwise would be common
assault and murder. Three army officers were among the
seven expedition officers chosen in England. Two more
expedition officers were added en route.

The soldiers were Major E.M. Barttelot, Captain R.H.
Nelson and Lieutenant W.G. Stairs. A Congo veteran,
John Rose Troup, and William Bonny, who was to be the
medical assistant, were selected. The two other civilians
were James S. Jameson, a naturalist, and A.J. Mounteney-
Jephson, whose merits included their willingness to pay
the then enormous sum of £1,000 each for a place on the
expedition. A medical doctor, Thomas H. Parke, joined the
party in Cairo. The final officer to join, when the expedition was already on the march, was Herbert Ward, a veteran of service with Stanley in his Congo state-building
days.

In Cairo, the khedive gave Stanley 61 Sudanese soldiers
and he later recruited about a dozen Somalis. In Zanzibar

620 men and boys were recruited, mainly as porters, most of them slaves.

Stanley now made the fateful decision to bring about the appointment of Tippu Tip as governor of Stanley Falls (near present-day Kisangani) on the River Congo, a few days' march from the expedition's staging point of Yambuya. Tippu Tip was a Arab trader of strongly negroid appearance, a slaver or reputedly ex-slaver, whom Stanley knew from years before. The Arabs had reached all over the eastern side of Africa, many of them seeking slaves and ivory. They were spreading ever westwards and had become a force in the Congo. When Stanley crossed the Ituri Forest on this expedition, it was unexplored by Europeans but already well known to Arabs, who had opened up trails across it and built villages. Tippu Tip was "an uncrowned king of the region between Stanley Falls and Tanganika Lake" who had the power to disrupt the expedition, and worse. The loads of ammunition being carried for Emin might be expected to attract attack; between Tippu Tip and Mwanga of Buganda Stanley felt "there was only the choice of the frying-pan and the fire". Once landed in the Congo, the expedition would need more carriers. Who better to supply them from the local tribes than Tippu Tip?

The trader was found to be "fully prepared for any eventuality – to fight me, or be employed by me". Stanley chose the second, and Tippu Tip was duly appointed as a salaried official under King Leopold. He was to defend the expedition's base against all Arabs and natives; defeat and capture slave raiders; and abstain from slave-raiding himself. He had also to accept a European officer as Resident to see that the duties were carried out. Otherwise he was free to carry on his trading activities.

Tippu Tip's main value to Stanley was as the provider of carriers: he was to supply 600 carriers to take ammunition to Emin Pasha and to return with ivory. Each man was to carry 70 lb (32 kg) of ivory. The matter-of-fact way in which Stanley described this arrangement in *In Darkest Africa* does not play well alongside his impassioned plea against the ivory trade, quoted above. Tippu Tip was named as governor of the Falls over the strong opposition of many of Stanley's Belgian colleagues, who doubted the depth of the trader's conversion to king and country. As the events of the Emin Pasha Relief Expedition unfolded, the 600 carriers were indeed to decide the outcome of the whole venture.

In February 1887, the SS Madura left Zanzibar on its improbable route to relieve Emin: down the east coast of Africa, around the Cape of Good Hope, then up the west coast to the mouth of the Congo at Banana Point. Included in the cargo was a Maxim automatic gun, which Lieutenant Stairs demonstrated at 330 shots per minute to general admiration.

Stanley left Zanzibar with 706 men plus Tippu Tip and his party, making about 100 more. The casualty rate was to be extraordinarily high, for only 246 returned to Zanzibar in December 1889 after the winding down of the expedition. Almost all the rest had either died or deserted, with little to choose between the two outcomes. No doubt some of the deserters did survive among alien tribes and impossibly far from home, but most were condemning themselves to death the fast way.

From the Congo mouth the expedition's route lay up the river to Stanley Pool, where the young settlement of Leopoldville (now Kinshasa) was located, then continuing upriver to Bangala and, after the main river forked away to Stanley Falls, along the Aruwimi to Yambuya. The navigation was interrupted in several places by cataracts, requiring long and tedious treks.

Herbert Ward, the last officer to join, engagingly tells how he ran after the expedition when it was in the lower Congo – stretched out in line of march with almost medieval magnificence and colour – and persuaded Stanley to sign him up:

> (I)n the distance coming over the brow of a hill I saw a tall Soudanese soldier bearing Gordon Bennett's yacht flag. (Bennett was the proprietor of the New York Herald, who sent Stanley on the expedition to find Livingstone.) Behind him and astride of a fine henna-stained mule, whose silver-plated strappings shone in the morning sun, was Mr Henry M. Stanley, attired in his famous African costume. Following immediately in his rear were his personal servants, Somalis with their curious braised waist-coats and white robes. Then

came Zanzibaris with their blankets, water-bottles, ammunition belts and guns. Stalwart Soudanese soldiers with dark-
hooded coats, their rifles on their backs, and innumerable
straps and leather belts around their bodies; and Zanzibari
porters bearing iron-bound boxes of ammunition, to which
were fastened axes and shovels as well as their little bundles
of clothing which were rolled up in coarse sandy-coloured
blankets.

... Passing along I became further acquainted with the consti-
tution of Stanley's great cavalcade. At one point a steel whale-
boat was being carried in sections, suspended from poles
which were each borne by four men; donkeys heavily laden
with sacks of rice were next met with, and a little further on
the women of Tippoo Tib's harem, their faces partly concealed,
and their bodies draped in gaudily-covered cloths; then at
intervals along the line of march an English officer with
whom, of course, I exchanged friendly salutations; then several large-horned East African goats, driven by saucy little
Zanzibari boys. A short distance further on, an abrupt turn of
the narrow footpath brought into view the dignified form of
the renowned Tippoo Tib, as he strode along majestically in
his flowing Arab robes of dazzling whiteness, and carrying
over his left shoulder a richly-decorated sabre, which was an
emblem of office conferred on him by H.H. the Sultan of
Zanzibar. Behind him at a respectful distance followed several Arab sheiks, whose bearing was quiet and dignified. In
response to my salutation they bowed most gracefully.

"Haijambo," said I. "Sijambo," they replied. "Khabari gani?"
(what news?), I inquired. "Khabai njema" (good news), was the
reply, and in that way I passed along the line of 700 men, in
whose ranks were represented various types from all parts of
eastern equatorial Africa, each wearing the distinguishing
garb of his own country. All the costumes and accoutrements
looked bright and gay, for the Expedition had disembarked
but a few days previously. As the procession filed along the
narrow, rugged path, it produced an effect no less brilliant
than striking. Its unbroken line extended over a distance of
probably four miles (6.4 km).

Stanley reached Leopoldville on April 1887 and two
months later (June 15), with two steamers, had reached
Yambuya. The inhabitants being unwilling to share their
village with the arrivals, it was occupied by force and the

villagers driven off. Yambuya was the starting point for
the crossing of the Ituri Forest and the Congo/Nile watershed. It was also the point where things started to go
wrong.

9 Horrors of the forest

Between Stanley and Emin Pasha lay many miles of fearsome jungle, uncrossed by Europeans. Stanley's column to find Emin left Yambuya on June 28, 1887. He had with him 388 men including four European officers. The rear column under Barttelot, which was to follow, had more than a third of the men and most of the supplies for Emin. Stanley expected he would take two months to reach Lake Albert. In the event, he took 5 1/2 months – a difference that proved crucial in several ways. When the rear column failed to come up as arranged, Stanley made two more traverses of what he called "this region of horrors", to find the missing column and then to rejoin the main party.

The difficulties and delays of crossing the great Congo forest, which Stanley described as measuring 321,057 square miles (831,538 sq km), were caused by the terrain and the pigmy inhabitants. The atmosphere of the trek is well caught by Frank Hird in an authorised biography of Stanley:

> For over five months he and his men had marched through a continuous, unbroken primeval forest under conditions which equalled some of the horrors in Dante's Inferno. At high noon only a dim green light filtered through the foliage from forty to a hundred feet (12-31 m) thick above them. When they started the day's march at six o'clock in the morning, the forest would be buried in a cheerless twilight, the morning mist making every tree shadowy and indistinct. A path had to be hacked with bill-hooks, cutlasses, and axes through thick and entangled undergrowth, along which the Column crept slowly, the carriers often sinking to their necks in quagmires of stagnant water and decaying vegetation. Moisture dripped from the archway of impenetrable green above them; they were stung by wasps and hornets, and during many nights sat shivering under ceaseless torrents of rain. Underfoot the ground was soft black mud; oozy creeks had to be forded or bridged, causing hours of delay.

Stanley himself wrote of the long months "without ever having seen a bit of greensward of the size of a cottage chamber floor. Nothing but miles and miles, endless miles of forest ..." Colin Turnbull, an anthropologist who two generations later befriended the ba-Mbuti pigmies who so beset Stanley, acknowledges (in *The Forest People*) how overpowering the forest can be:

> ... the heaviness of everything; the damp air, the gigantic, water-laden trees that are constantly dripping, never quite drying out between the violent storms that come with monotonous regularity ... the seeming silence and the age-old remoteness and loneliness of it all.

Turnbull might have added the threatening feeling of disorientation, when one can wander 10 yards (metres) off the trail and amid the dense vegetation not find it again.

For most of the route the advance column followed the river (the Aruwimi changes its name to the Ituri), so except where there were rapids a river party and a land party were formed. The expedition had a portable steel boat, the Advance, which Jephson soon assembled, and some canoes were acquired along the way. The Advance was in 44 sections, representing 44 loads, and could carry 50 loads and at least 10 sick. That meant relief for 100 or so porters.

The expedition ate what it could find in the rainforest. A staple was patties of vegetables, herbs and leaves of the manioc. Some tribes were happy to trade: sugar cane, Indian corn (maize) and tobacco were bartered for empty sardine boxes, jam and milk cans and cartridge cases. Dr Parke bagged weaver birds with his gun. On October 15 Stanley's faithful donkey from Zanzibar, which had been ill, became part of the food chain. The meat was fairly shared, but a free-for-all occurred over the skin. Bones and hoofs were used; "a pack of hyaenas could not have made a more thorough disposal of it".

In a very Victorian comment, Stanley said:

> That constituent of the human being which marks him as superior to all others of the animal creation was so deadened by hunger that our men had become merely carnivorous bipeds, inclined to be as ferocious as any beast of prey.

With the constant preoccupation of obtaining food, it was perhaps inevitable that someone of Stanley's temperament would clash with the forest inhabitants. As perceived by Stanley, the ba-Mbuti were vicious dwarves and cunning thieves. All this from a people described as ranging from 3 ft to 4 ft 6 in in height. (Turnbull in the 1950s found them averaging 4 ft 6 in although, curiously, he does not distinguish male and female heights.) An average male might weigh 90 lb. One man was measured very comprehensively by William Bonny, the expedition medical assistant, whose findings include: height 4 ft 0 in, length of leg 22 in, length of foot $6^{1/4}$ in, length of arm to tip of finger $19^{3/4}$ in.*

Stanley felt sorry for the settled tribes around the forest. They "have much to bear from these fierce little people who glue themselves to their clearings, flatter them when well fed, but oppress them in their extortions and robberies". The expedition was often attacked by the pigmies, armed with poison-tipped arrows. Stanley supposed one of the poisons was made from a species of arum. Another seemed to be made from dried red ants, which with even deadlier insects gave the pigmies a limitless supply of poison. The main antidote was a heavy solution of carbonate of ammonium injected into the wound, after it had been sucked out and syringed. There were deaths, however, which Stanley ascribed to the poison not having been fully removed.

For all Stanley's hatred of the pigmies as a people, he had with the expedition for a year and more two individuals, a young man and a girl, both of whom he described affectionately. The "damsel" was the servant of Dr Parke, carrying his satchel, collecting fuel for his fire and preparing the surgeon's "cheering cup of tea". She became ill and was eventually left with a chief far beyond her forest home, on the way to the coast. The young man, who worked for one of the other officers, was frequently robbed of his stock

---

* The metric equivalents are: 0.9 m to 1.4 m in height. (Turnbull in the 1950s found them averaging 1.4 m.) An average male might weigh 41 kg. One man was measured very comprehensively by William Bonny, the expedition medical assistant, whose findings include: height 1.2 m, length of leg 56 cm, length of foot 15.9 cm, length of arm to tip of finger 50.2 cm

of fuelwood. He "would show his distress by his looks, but presently gathering courage he would abandon it and collect another pile, as though time was too precious to waste in useless argument over the inevitable". Stanley commented sententiously: "And thus the Pigmies showed by their conduct that they were related to all that was best and noble in human nature."

When Colin Turnbull lived with the pigmies two generations later, he found that Stanley's expedition was only too well remembered. A chief of one of the settled tribes had a father who was a boy when the expedition came through. Old Effundi Somali "used to tell stories of the dreadful wars that were fought in those days, and of the trail of destruction that Stanley had left behind him". Yet Turnbull found the pigmy world essentially non-violent. The ba-Mbuti are hunter-gatherers who roam about the forest in hunting groups. They have no chiefs and no hierarchy. Punishment means ostracism rather than chastisement. Pigmy wars, which are about territory, consist of mutual threats until, after a respectable interval, the group that invaded runs away.

While Stanley commiserated with the villagers for the way the pigmies "glued themselves" to the clearings and stole the villagers' goods, Turnbull contended that this was the expression of an extraordinary symbiotic relationship. The two sides dislike each other but need each other. The villagers supply the pigmies with vegetables, plantains and metal arrowheads; the pigmies provide meat from the forest, where the villagers rarely care, or dare, to go. The pigmies steal from the villagers and have no sense of guilt about it. The villagers scarcely react. It is sanctioned thievery, as one might indulge a child.

The tribes of the villages claim to "own" the pigmies. Individuals have "their" pigmies, but the supposed rights are often unenforceable. For much of the time the pigmies are in the forest and out of reach; but when they are in the villages the pigmies go along with the system because it suits them. This even extends to the nkumbi initiation ceremony for boys, with its painful circumcision rites. The pigmies go through the nkumbi because it would be inconvenient for their young men not to be accepted as adults in the villages, but every mu-Mbuti knows that the only real initiation is in the forest hunt.

Turnbull lived with the boys at the nkumbi camp, a privilege normally allowed only to the "fathers" of the boys (brothers sometimes fill the role), and saw what the ceremony really meant to the pigmies. One played punchball with the sacred banana; another mockingly imitated the action of the bull-roarer, which the candidates were supposed to think was the voice of a forest demon. The boys washed themselves in a rain shower, although they ought to have kept the white clay on as a sign of their death as children. All of this was not mere play:

> The villagers hoped [wrote Turnbull] that the nkumbi would place the pigmies directly under the supernatural authority of the village tribal ancestors, the pigmies naturally took good care that nothing of the sort happened, proving it to themselves by this conscious flaunting of custom.

This must have been as an insurance policy because pigmies, Turnbull found, do not believe in the power of the dead. The villagers live in constant fear of spirits and those who summon them. The pigmies' god is the forest, but they revere it rather than worship it. Stanley's "region of horrors" is to them a cool, friendly and familiar place. Since the forest is god, why should one be afraid of it? Turnbull in his three years with the ba-Mbuti felt at home there too, but even towards the end of his time he acknowledged the forest's capacity to frighten. He wanted to make a final visit to a favourite spot, but he had to force himself to go alone:

> (T)here is something about the forest, not exactly threatening, but challenging, that dares you to travel alone ... I knew what that challenge was: for to be alone was as though you were daring to look on the face of the great God of the Forest himself, so overpowering was the goodness and beauty of the world all around.

The pigmies' own great ceremony is the molimo, which Turnbull witnessed daily for a month. The music was made by two "trumpets" (hollow tubes) found in the forest. Turnbull had been expecting elaborate and beautiful ritual objects. Instead, the pigmies picked up a couple of metal pipes left behind by construction gangs. "What does it matter what the molimo is made of?" he was asked. "This one makes a great sound and besides, it does not rot like wood. It is much trouble to make a wooden one, and then it rots away and you have to make another." The dancing, with dramatic spurts out of the forest and rampages through the camp, was strictly by the men. The women were bundled into the huts before it started. They were supposed to think the molimo was an animal of the forest and to see it meant death. Needless to say, they didn't think that, and later Turnbull was surprised to find the women singing the sacred songs, led by an old woman under a head-dress of vine and feathers and backed by the camp belle, with the men in supporting roles.

Finally, old Moke explained the meaning of the molimo. He said:

> Normally everything goes well in our world. But at night when we are sleeping sometimes things go wrong, because we are not awake to stop them from going wrong. Army ants invade the camp, leopards may come in and steal a hunting dog or even a child. If we were awake these things would not happen. So when something big goes wrong, like illness or bad hunting or death, it must be because the forest is sleeping and not looking after its children. So what do we do? We wake it up. We wake it up by singing to it, and we do this because we want it to awaken happy. Then everything will be well and good again. And when our world is going well then we also sing to the forest because we want it to share our happiness.

Turnbull found that the pigmies have a strange perception of death. Life and death are not either/or states. The daughter of a man called Cephu was announced to be dead, but the child was actually still alive although critically ill with dysentery. Degrees of illness are expressed as hot, with fever, ill, completely or absolutely dead and finally, dead for ever. Unhappily, the next day the girl was dead for ever. After Stanley's forays in the Ituri Forest so were many others.

For all the ordeals of the crossings, Stanley maintained his meticulous observations. Among the trees and bushes he noted were cottonwood, teak, camwood, mahogony, greenheart, lignum vitae, ironwood, yellowwood,

skinkwood, ebony, copalwood, wild mango, wild orange,
wild fig, butter tree, acacia and mpafu.

Even in the gloomy rainforest, there were better times,
although Stanley's way of describing them is curiously but-
toned-up. The master of the vivid journalistic phrase was
not at his best describing the lyricism of nature:

> But during the march, Providence was gracious; the sun
> shone, and streamed in a million beams of soft light through
> the woods, which brightened our feelings, and caused the
> aisles and corridors of the woods to be of Divine beauty, con-
> verted the graceful thin tree-shafts into marbly-grey pillars,
> and the dew and rain-drops into sparkling brilliants; cheered
> the invisible birds to pour out, with spirit, their varied reper-
> tory of songs; inspired parrot flocks to vent gleeful screams
> and whistlings; roused hosts of monkeys to exert their wildest
> antics; while now and then some deep, bass roar in far-away
> recesses indicated a family of soko or chimpanzees enjoying
> some savage sport.

Breaking out of the forest at last was dramatic and the
entire column was overjoyed:

> ... then, to our undisguised joy, [we] emerged upon a rolling
> plain, green as an English lawn, into broadest, sweetest day-
> light, and warm and glorious sunshine, to inhale the pure air
> with an uncontrollable rapture. Judging of the feelings of oth-
> ers by my own, we felt as if we had thrown all age and a score
> of years away, as we stepped with invigorated limbs upon the
> soft sward of young grass. We strode forward at a pace most
> unusual, and finally, unable to suppress our emotions, the
> whole caravan broke into a run ... Leagues upon leagues of
> bright green pasture land undulated in gentle waves ... far
> away to the east rose some frowning ranges of mountains
> beyond which we were certain slept in its deep gulf the blue
> Albert.

That was on December 5, 1887. A few days later (December
13) they had completed the easy route to the shores of Lake
Albert. Crossing the forest had taken a terrible toll. Of the
389 including Stanley who started from Yambuya, only 169
now stood beside him. The rest had died, deserted (which far
from home came to the same thing) or had been left sick at
several points along the route.

At the cost of fragmenting his expedition, Stanley had made finding Emin his overriding priority. It had all been for nothing, though. Beside Lake Albert, Stanley was astonished to find that the local people not only had no message from Emin but did not even know who he was. It was to be four more months before the two met. Meanwhile, there was nothing for it but to create a stockaded camp, which Stanley did inland from the lake at a site he called Fort Bodo.

The pressing need was to reunite the scattered expedition. Lieutenant Stairs led a party back into the forest making for Ipoto, a settlement founded by Arab slave traders, where a section of the advance column under Captain Nelson was stranded. Also there were another of the expedition's officers, the surgeon, Thomas Parke, the Maxim gun and the portable steel boat. Stairs brought them all back to Fort Bodo and before long – in February 1888 – he had dived into the forest again. This time he was sent even further, to a settlement called Ugarrowwa's, where more sick had been left. Stairs's mission was to find news of the rear column, which was overdue. Stanley had hoped that by a detailed system of marking trees and blocking forks in the trail the rear column would have made good time through the forest.

In April, Stanley led a party on a return to the lake, making camp close by at Kavalli's. This time there was a letter from Emin. It was dated from Tunguru, a station on the lake northwards. Jephson was sent in search of the elusive pasha, and before the end of the month (April 29) a steamer brought Emin to meet Stanley on the lakeshore. It was evening and dark. We can imagine that Stanley was conscious of his poor record in historic greetings, stating the obvious to Livingstone and getting the wrong man with Mutesa of Buganda. This time he played it straight. As *In Darkest Africa* told it:

> At eight o'clock, amid great rejoicing, and after repeated salutes from rifles, Emin Pasha himself walked into camp, accompanied by Captain Casati and Mr Jephson, and one of the Pasha's officers. I shook hands with all, and asked which was Emin Pasha? Then one rather small, slight figure, wearing glasses, arrested my attention by saying in excellent

English, "I owe you a thousand thanks, Mr Stanley; I really do
not know how to express my thanks to you".

"Ah, you are Emin Pasha. Do not mention thanks, but come in
and sit down. It is so dark out here we cannot see one another".

The object of the Emin Pasha Relief Expedition appeared
in clean suit of snowy cotton drill, "well-ironed and of perfect fit", as Stanley noted. He wore a well kept fez. As for
his face, there was "not a trace on it of ill-health or anxiety; it rather indicated good condition of body and peace of
mind". It was the rescuers who from their appearance were
more in need of relief. Stanley and Emin spent almost a
month together at Kavalli's. But there were few supplies to
hand over: before the "relief" of Emin could be completed,
Stanley had to rescue his own rear column, about which
there was still no news.

It was agreed that Emin, accompanied by Jephson,
would tour the stations of the Equatorial province to
explain arrangements to the garrisons and to sound out
their opinions, while Stanley would make a return journey
through the Ituri Forest to find the missing column. On
June 16 he started the return march accompanied by his
personal servant (if he was going to starve, he would do so
in style), 113 Zanzibaris and 95 carriers supplied by Emin.
It was an astonishingly determined crossing of the forest:
the party was back at Banalya, only 90 miles (145 km)
from the original starting point of Yambuya, in 62 days
(the outbound march had taken 2 1/2 times as long). At
Banalya Stanley saw from the river a camp flying the
Egyptian flag. Asked who they were, they answered, "We
are Stanley's men." This was the rear column, or what was
left of it.

It was a terrible tragedy. Of the officers, only Bonny, the
medical assistant, remained at the camp. An incredulous
Stanley heard that the commander, Major Barttelot, had
been assassinated by one of the carriers over a trivial dispute, Troup had been invalided home, Ward had been sent
1,500 miles (2,400 km) down the Congo to send a telegram
to the expedition committee in London, and Jameson had
also gone downriver in yet another hunt for carriers. On
the very day that Stanley reached Banalya, Jameson died
of fever at Bangala nursed by Ward.

Stanley caused Bonny to make a return of all personnel at Banalya on August 17, 1888. It showed 75 Zanzibaris present out of 223 accounted for when Stanley handed over command of the rear column to Barttelot. Ten more were with Jameson at Bangala, but there had been 78 deaths – more than one third of the total – and many desertions. Of 53 Sudanese, Somalis and Syrians, 22 were present and 23 were dead. The futility of these deaths was particularly shocking because for whatever reason – and that became a bitter national, indeed international, controversy – the rear column had not moved for almost a year and when it did, it got just a fraction of the way. Stanley's role was naturally at the centre of the storm that followed.

Stanley had left Barttelot with detailed written instructions that at least in theory covered every possibility. But Barttelot was in an unfavourable position from the start. The rear column was already split with Troup, Ward, Bonny and their parties downriver bringing up more loads. Nor had Tippu Tip, upon whom so much depended for the supply of carriers, arrived in Stanley Falls yet. The question arises why Stanley rushed on when the situation at Yambuya was unresolved. The memory of Gordon's death at Khartoum just 2 1/2 years earlier, when a British relieving force arrived hours too late, must have been fresh and haunting. Now the Mahdists were threatening Emin, one of Gordon's loyal lieutenants, and Stanley would not want to repeat that tragic delay. With his odd dual loyalty to King Leopold and to the British, he would know that the Germans might get to the interior territories first and annexe them. Nor did Stanley's temperament lend itself to waiting and watching.

And so Stanley marched away into the jungle. In his detailed instructions, he told Barttelot:

> The goods that will be brought up are the currency needed for transit through the regions beyond the Lakes; there will be a vast store of ammunition and provisions, which are of equal importance to us. The loss of these men and goods would be certain ruin to us, and the Advance Force itself would need to solicit relief in its turn.

If Tippu Tip did not supply enough carriers

... you must consider, after rope, sacking, tools, such as shovels (never discard an axe or bill-hook), how many sacks of provisions you can distribute among your men to enable you to
march ... If you still cannot march, then it would be better to
make two marches of six miles (10 km) twice over, if you prefer marching to staying for our arrival, than throw too many
things away.

Barttelot never attempted this plan of short double marches, which would have allowed the expedition to move with
half the complement of carriers and all the loads. Instead,
he awaited for many months the full strength of carriers,
seemingly always about to turn up. The waiting proved as
lethal as the forest. Food was inadequate: for much of the
time the men lived on nothing but the manioc root, while
the Europeans managed with boiled rice and fried plantains. Arab slave traders and ivory hunters camped nearby competed with the expedition for supplies from the surrounding countryside. One by one, day by day, men died of
fever or malnutrition.

The question at the crux of the tragedy was whether
Barttelot had been instructed to move in some form or
another. Stanley afterwards expressed amazement that
Barttelot did not carry out the double marches, but it
seems clear, even from a dispassionate reading of *In
Darkest Africa*, that Stanley left Barttelot with the option
of moving or staying. That was how the rear column commander understood matters. It appears Stanley expected
to return rather than necessarily wait for the rear column
to find him. He planned to be back in five months. As it
was, it took almost 14 months. Whatever the instructions,
the ultimate cause of the tragedy was Stanley's under-esti-
mate of the terrain.

The wasting away of the rear column was graphically
chronicled by Herbert Ward, who had joined the expedition
when it was already in the Congo in the hope of adventure
and found himself, like the rest at Yambuya, hungry,
fever-ridden and bored. He spent much of the time sketching and writing his diary.

Rheumatism, fever, and biliousness was the order of the day
amongst the white men [Ward wrote], while the poor fellows
under us were growing weaker and weaker, and dropping off

day by day. By December 5 there were thirty-one deaths amongst the blacks. Each morning a miserable sight met our eyes as, crowding round Bonny's hut, their number growing each day, a mass of suffering Zanzibaris and Soudanese sought relief and medicine, from the scanty store he had at his disposal. The wet weather, the wretched food, and the weary, miserable existence we were forced to lead was telling on us all, but with most deadly effect on the poor creatures, whose uncared-for flesh broke into festering sores of the most painful character.

On February 18, 1888 – with the rear column still at Yambuya almost eight months after Stanley left – Ward commented in his diary: "Death is written in plain letters on many faces in this camp. Almost as many lives will be lost over this philanthropic mission as there are lives to save of Emin's people."

The Manyemas, a tribe much used by the Arabs, had a reputation for cannibalism. Ward records: "Had a chat with Selim bin Mohammed this morning about cannibals. He told me he had frequently seen the natives he used to have with him in these parts ... kill a slave, cut it up, and eat the flesh in front of him." A few days later, matter-of-factly: "To-day was very hot, the sun registering 135° (Fahrenheit [57 C]) outside; no news of the captured Arabs; they have undoubtedly been eaten. Drew two Manyema warriors this morning, and sketched a number of heads &c."

If small episodes can tell all, Ward's description, from his diary entry of January 10, of how he and his fellow officers spent their time is revealing: "Jameson and I are generally sketching; Major B. walking up and down; Troup and Bonny smoking, chatting, reading, &c." The least productive of these activities was "walking up and down". For the commander to extricate the expedition, more was needed.

The jungle trail from Yambuya on the Aruwimi to Tippu Tip's base at Stanley Falls on the Congo was relatively short, around five days' marches. Barttelot and his fellow officers made the journey several times: Jameson and Ward in August 1887, Barttelot and Troup in October, Barttelot and Jameson in February 1888, and Barttelot again in April and May. They were kindly received by

Tippu Tip or, in his absence, by other leaders, but the necessary carriers did not appear. The reason has always been disputed. That Tippu Tip was hoping to bring about the final wreck of the rear column so he could plunder its guns and other stores is the most unfavourable construction. Another possibility is that as governor of Stanley Falls he felt he had been promised money and assistance by Stanley that had not been given. He may have been unwilling to help Stanley until the debt had been paid. He may simply have been unable to produce such a large number of carriers (600) at any one time. Whatever the reason, the Europeans would never have been told No and would have thought just a little bit longer ... With no word about Stanley for almost a year, and with a growing feeling that the advance column must have met with disaster, the rear column officers would have felt even less inclined to venture into the Ituri Forest. They had fewer men than Stanley – and he had the Maxim gun.

Finally, Barttelot managed to collect 430 Manyema carriers (still only two-thirds of the number specified by Stanley) and on June 11, 1888, the rear column left Yambuya, almost a year after the advance column. On the other side of the great Congo forest, Stanley had met Emin Pasha and was about to trek back in search of the missing rear column.

Barttelot was a well qualified army officer and an able commander of his Sudanese soldiers, but he now showed he was no Stanley in the control of a mob of irregulars. Amid much chaos and very slowly, the column reached Banalya, 90 miles (145 km) upriver. While it was halted there, Barttelot was shot dead in the most trivial circumstances. He complained to a woman about the noise of her singing during a Manyema festival and her husband, taking offence, killed him. This was on July 19, one month before Stanley's return.

Stanley found only 60 men "likely to survive" and scarcely one-third of the loads. The fear he had expressed to Barttelot the year before, that the loss of the men and the goods "would be certain ruin to us", had nearly come about. The lack of supplies that Stanley was able to offer Emin had a direct bearing on what the pasha did next, which in turn affected the course of events in Equatoria and Buganda. Stanley now led the bedraggled expedition through the Ituri Forest – some, like him, traversing the forest for the third time. Passing through Fort Bodo, he was back at Lake Albert in January 1889. There he found astonishing news. There had been a rebellion in Equatoria. Emin and Stanley's lieutenant, Jephson, were prisoners. The beloved pasha upholding civilisation in the wilderness became a captive of his own men.

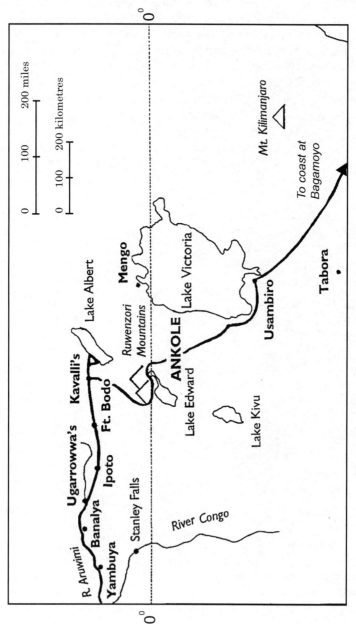

Map 5. The Emin Pasha Expedition – to the lake and coast

10 Adieu to Equatoria

After Stanley left to find the missing rear party, Emin made a tour of his stations to discover the views of the garrisons. He was accompanied by Jephson and just three soldiers from the relief expedition. This was a misjudgment by Stanley: Emin's troops could not believe that their master, the mighty khedive of Egypt, would send word to them with such a meagre force. Thus even before the message was delivered, the messengers had failed to convince. As the governor explained the khedive's options, the suspicion grew that Emin had "turned" and was about to betray them. Jephson was clearly an imposter, it was felt. Emin must be planning to march them away and sell them into slavery.

In their month together by the lake, Stanley and Emin had reviewed the choices offered by the khedive's message. The proposition was for Emin and his people to come out, and receive their arrears of pay and allowances, or to stay on without further Egyptian responsibility. Only after Emin had said he wished to stay did Stanley feel able to mention the offers from his two employers: King Leopold wanted Emin to attach Equatoria to the Congo state and to continue as governor; Mackinnon wanted Emin to work with his Imperial British East Africa Company, which involved relocating his people to Kavirondo (at the northeast end of Lake Victoria). Both Stanley and Emin seemed inclined towards the Kavirondo scheme, but to sell it to the garrisons might be another matter.

Most of the main stations of Equatoria could be reached by steamer, being on Lake Albert or along the Nile. In the south-north direction taken by Emin and Jephson, they were: Mswa and Tunguru (in present-day Congo); Wadelai, Bora and Dufile (now in Uganda); Labore, Muggi, Kirri, Bedan, Rejaf and Gondokoro (still in Sudan). These stations were strung out over more than 200 miles (320 km). Lado, the former capital of Equatoria, further north still and near modern Juba, had been abandoned the year before because of fire.

Emin and Jephson began their tour of the stations in
June 1888. The first stop was Tunguru. In his address to
the troops and other station residents, the governor did not
mention the Kavirondo scheme but presented the khedive's choice of evacuating the province or staying on
under another master. The message was not well received.
The idea of going to Cairo was deeply unattractive to many
Sudanese, who saw destitution staring at them in an alien
city. Moreover, since everyone knew that the seat of the
khedive lay downriver, the plan to evacuate by marching
in another direction was profoundly suspect.

It was the same reaction at other stations. At Wadelai,
Emin's capital, Jephson nevertheless was impressed by
the neatness and order with which the governor had
arranged the station. Emin's own comfortable quarters,
filled with his well arranged natural history collections,
described the man. After passing through Dufile, Emin
and Jephson reached Labore where, on August 13, the
unthinkable happened: one of the once loyal troops made a
rush at the governor. The incident was contained, but it
was a portent.

Stanley's expedition had brought next to no relief – just
34 cases of ammunition and two bales of calico – because
most of the loads were with the rear party. His presence,
however, combined with the Mahdist threat to bring about
the unravelling of Equatoria. The same effect was felt in
Bunyoro, where Captain Casati was Emin's emissary to
Kabalega. When the king heard about the expedition, he
had Casati arrested.

Above Labore, Emin learnt that the 1st Battalion in
Rejaf had mutinied and he was advised not to proceed farther north. The party returned to Dufile, but it was too
late. The disaffection had spread to the 2nd Battalion and
Emin, with Jephson, was put under house arrest. On
August 31 evacuees from Rejaf, which was under threat
from the Mahdists, reached Dufile. Three years after the
event, the garrisons finally began to accept the truth of
Khartoum's fall.

On September 3 Jephson was freed so he could tell the
southern stations how things stood. Using Emin's steamer
Khedive, he visited Wadelai, Tunguru and Mswa. Then,
showing a Roman sense of honour, he returned to Dufile.

Emin was deposed on September 27. The state of Equatoria, what remained of it, was in the hands of two of the officers, Fadl al-Mula and Hamad Agha. Selim Bey, the governor of Labore station, who was to play a continuing part in the Buganda story, was consistently loyal to Emin.

Late in October came the news that the Mahdists had captured Rejaf. Emin and Jephson were freed. On November 17 they left for Wadelai, but even that southerly station began to look insecure as the Mahdists swept on. On December 4 Emin heard that the Mahdists had taken more northern stations including Labore, and had attacked, but failed to take, Dufile, the scene of his recent captivity. It was later taken by one of the local tribes, the Danagla, who no doubt relished the chance to pay back the soldiers for their oppression.

Two days after he heard about the Mahdists' capture of the northern stations, Emin began to evacuate Wadelai. To his great regret, he had to leave behind his books, instruments and natural history collections. On February 17, 1889, he reached Stanley's camp at Kavalli's with just 65 followers. These included the loyalist Selim Bey. At this point the governor (or former governor, because he refused to take up his old title) looked more like a refugee than a ruler with a choice of action. Stanley, it seems, now dropped the plan for Emin to settle in Kavirondo and simply prepared to bring his charge out.

The day after Emin reached Kavalli's, Captain Nelson, Lieutenant Stairs and Dr Parke returned to the camp with more loads. Mostly these were too late to do any good: with the collapse of Emin's administration, the ammunition was superfluous and much of it was buried and left. Since Jephson and Bonny were already with Stanley, the surviving expedition officers were reunited for the first time in two years. Two others were dead (Barttelot and Jameson) and two more had been repatriated (Troup and Ward).

An example of the protracted time scale that was typical of those days and which we find so hard to relate to followed. It was almost two more months before the march to the coast began. Partly this delay was caused by Emin's temporising. He must have known that Equatoria held nothing for him any more, but he may also have felt the shame of making the journey, figuratively, in Stanley's baggage train. Or perhaps it was less rational than that; perhaps he just could not make up his mind. Meanwhile, Selim Bey returned to Wadelai with the invitation to the troops and their followers to join the evacuation.

Eventually, it all became too long even by the more relaxed pace of the times, and Stanley set a deadline for departure. He had become obsessed with the idea that some of the Sudanese were planning to seize the expedition's ammunition and stores. After an attempt was made to steal guns from the Zanzibaris, Stanley announced that he was assuming control of the entire party – a move that humiliated Emin. Stanley refused Selim's pleas for more time to gather the troops, or to wait en route, although he did promise to go slowly so the late-comers could catch them up.

The expedition set off from Kavalli's on April 10, a ragbag crowd of about 1,500. It was a far cry from the splendid force that Herbert Ward so vividly described after it first landed in the Congo. To Stanley's depleted original force he had added 130 Manyema carriers recruited from the Arabs, and more than 500 carriers press-ganged into service locally. Emin's people numbered 570 men, women and children, but the men were administrators and clerks, not troops. In other words, the Emin Pasha Relief Expedition was relieving Emin himself, but it was leaving behind far more of Equatoria's expatriate population than it was bringing out.

Nor did the soldiers join the expedition later, even though the expedition soon halted for a month because Stanley had fever. Selim Bey was driven out of Wadelai by Fadl al-Mula, and established himself at Kavalli's – helped by finding the buried ammunition – with about 90 soldiers plus women and children.

Relations between Emin and Stanley quickly became strained. Even without the gun incident, that was always likely between men of such different temperaments: the all-action and brutal Breaker of Rocks and the scholarly, caring, indecisive German. In Emin's reduced circumstances they did not march as equals, and it was clear to all whose expedition it was.

Stanley was drawn by Captain Casati in a vivid and balanced pen-picture:

> Stanley is a man remarkable for strength of character, resolution, promptness of thought and iron will. Jealous of his own authority, he does not tolerate exterior influences, nor ask advice. Difficulties do not deter him, disasters do not dismay him. With an extraordinary readiness of mind he improvises means, and draws himself out of a difficulty; absolute and severe in the execution of his duty, he is not always prudent, or free from hasty and erroneous judgments. Irresolution and hesitation irritate him, disturbing his accustomed gravity; his countenance is usually serious. Reserved, laconic and not very sociable, he does not awaken sympathy; but on closer acquaintance he is found very agreeable, from the frankness of his manner, his brilliant conversation and his gentlemanly courtesy. (Quoted by Stanhope White: *Lost Empire on the Nile*)

Emin now found himself doing what he had always insisted he did not want to do – leave. His wish to hand over his province to Britain had come to nothing. His withdrawal left behind a dangerously unstable situation with remnant military groups and Stanley's buried arms.

The expedition had hardly even fulfilled its first duty, to survive. Two of the European officers were dead, and the overall loss rate by death or desertion was awful. It was to be almost two-thirds at the end of the journey. Consul Holmwood's hope that the expedition could also help with the troubled situation in Buganda had long been off the agenda. The subject was about to return, however. This was the time when the Ganda Christians were in exile in the kingdom of Ankole, looking for ways to go home.

The expedition came out by the south-western route, passing through Ankole. Here Stanley went through a blood-brotherhood ceremony with one of King Ntare's sons. Two emissaries from the Ganda Christians – one of them Samweli, the boy who insisted on delivering the king's cowrie shells before fleeing from the king's persecution – to ask for his help to overthrow the Muslims in Buganda. The expedition was soon to meet both sets of missionaries, now established south of the lake. Stanley's officers were fed by the Protestants (British) and re-clothed by the Catholics (French), although, doctrinal considerations apart, they might have done better by reversing the sequence.

Stanley refused the Christian refugees' request to intervene in Buganda. With his motley party, far more followers than fighters, he was hardly in a position to. However,
he had a Maxim gun, that single-handed conqueror of
thousands, and for those who see an imperialistic master-
plan behind the expedition the decision is hard to read. By
now it was not a question of whether a European power
would take over Buganda, but which and when. In 1889
tensions between Germany and Britain over the interior
were at their peak. The governments in both countries,
headed by Bismarck and Salisbury respectively, were
deeply involved with chartered companies that ostensibly
ruled over East Africa. In Britain's case this was the
Imperial British East Africa Company, led by William
Mackinnon, the chief sponsor of the Emin Pasha expedition. Stanley had been in the African interior for more
than two years, and may not have fully realised how far
the scramble had moved into its end-game.

From Ankole, Stanley's expedition continued through
Karagwe, where according to the leader the numbers were
down to 800, or scarcely more than half the total starting
from Kavalli's. Losses came from deaths and illness, desertions or simply being unable to keep up. It was a fearsome
loss rate, however, over relatively known and straightfor-
ward terrain.

On August 28 the expedition reached Usambiro and
Stanley came face to face for the first time with Alexander
Mackay. This was the man who more than any other was
the embodiment of Stanley's famous appeal for missionaries to serve in Buganda. Emin, too, was able to meet the
man with whom he had corresponded for so long. Mackay
had come out with the first Church Missionary Society
party in 1876 and, amazingly, had never been home since.
Sometimes alone, sometimes with one or two colleagues,
Mackay survived against the odds in Buganda until at last
he was compelled to continue his work and witness south
of the lake in what is now Tanzania.

Stanley left readers of *In Darkest Africa* in no doubt
about Mackay's fortitude:

A clever writer lately wrote a book about a man who spent much time in Africa, which from beginning to end is a long-drawn wail. It would have cured both writer and hero of all moping to have seen the manner of Mackay's life. He has no time to fret and groan and weep, and God knows if ever man had reason to think of "graves and worms and oblivion," and to be doleful and lonely and sad, Mackay had, when, after murdering his Bishop (James Hannington, killed on Mwanga's orders when approaching Buganda), and burning his pupils, and strangling his converts, and clubbing to death his dark friends, Mwanga turned his eye of death on him. And yet the little man met it with calm blue eyes that never winked. To see one man of this kind, working day and night for twelve years bravely, and without a syllable of complaint or a moan amid the "wildernesses," and to hear him lead his little flock to show forth God's loving kindness in the morning, and His faithfulness every night, is worth going a long journey, for the moral courage and contentment that one derives from it.

Mackay himself, dressed in white linen and grey Tyrolese hat, came out to greet the visitors. The mission station was in a rather barren location but was within sight of an inlet of Lake Victoria. Stanley found the station full of activity, with an extensive workshop, the boiler from a launch being prepared, a canoe under repair, sawpits, a cattle fold, a goat pen and scores of fowls pecking around. Boys of all ages looked "uncommonly sleek and happy" and quiet labourers wished the visitors a polite good morning.

Stanley was shown into a room with substantial, 2 ft (0.6 m) thick clay walls, which were evenly plastered and covered with missionary pictures and placards. The room was filled with books. The headman confided: "Mackay has thousands of books, in the dining-room, bedroom, the church, everywhere."

The expedition stayed at Usambiro for three weeks, enjoying the company of Mackay and another missionary, David Deekes. Everyone was able to catch up on good food and rest. Stanley enjoyed real coffee and home-made bread and butter for the first time in 30 months. On the party's final night, September 16, Mackay and Deekes produced a sumptuous dinner of roast beef, roast fowls, stews, rice and curry, plum pudding and wine. The last item was described by Stanley as "a bottle of medical wine", presumably to avoid giving the impression of a mission awash with alcohol. The healths of Emin and Stanley were drunk.

Stanley's high opinion of Mackay was reciprocated. Mackay's comment after meeting the explorer adds to the paradox of Stanley because its portrayal of the kind uncle differs from the more familiar view:

> He is a man of an iron will and sound judgment, and besides is most patient with the natives. He never allows any one of his followers to oppress or even insult a native. If he has had occasionally to use force in order to effect a passage, I am certain that he only resorted to arms when all other means failed.

On another occasion Mackay wrote:

> Wherever I find myself in Stanley's track, in Uganda, Ugogo or even Ukerewe itself, I find his treatment of the natives has invariably been such as to win from them the highest respect for the face of a white man.

The expedition left Usambiro and continued better equipped towards the coast. Fourteen pack donkeys were distributed to Emin's followers, and three riding asses – for the pasha, Stanley and Captain Casati – were bought from the Roman Catholic missionaries at their nearby Bukumbi station. From the French, Stanley's officers were able to buy much-needed items of clothing.

Stanley received a letter from Mackay dated January 5, 1890, in which he noted "what a strange loneliness hung about this place – physically and mentally – after you left". He was active as always: the steam engine, including the "serious job" of the boiler, had been fitted up; the canoe that Stanley saw was about to be transformed into a steam launch. This work was behind because of other jobs, including printing for Buganda. Mackay was both a printer and a translator of Christian texts. All this work ended a month later when, on February 8, 1890, Mackay died of fever, still only on the edge of middle age.

Mackay always took the broadest view of the Church's mission, raising his eyes beyond the day-to-day work of evangelising. In an earlier letter to his fellow missionary,

Robert Ashe, he wrote:

> To relieve men from the wrongs under which they perish, to
> secure freedom for the oppressed, yet not by Blut und Eisen
> (blood and iron), is a crux indeed for statesmanship. We want
> not so much an "arm of flesh," but heads of wisdom, human
> hearts, and helping hands. There is no need for gunpowder.
> That remedy is even worse than the disease.
>
> The rotten, mortifying state of this continent cannot be healed
> by more lacerations and wounds. A transfusion of fresh blood,
> and new life into it, not in miserable driblets as hitherto, but
> in a full stream, will alone save it from utter corruption.
>
> This African problem must be solved, and in God's name it
> shall be solved, for God means it to be solved. It is not for the
> sake of the few scattered and despised missionaries that we
> are determined that this end shall be attained, but for the
> sake of Africa itself.

Soon after he arrived at Usambiro, Mackay showed himself ever the realist, writing:

> Hereabouts we are so far from the reaping stage, that we can
> scarcely to be said even to be sowing. We are merely clearing
> the ground, and cutting down the natural growth of suspicion
> and jealousy, and clearing out the hard stones of ignorance
> and superstition. Only after the ground is thus in some meas-
> ure prepared and broken up, can we cast in the seed with hope
> of a harvest in God's good time.

Mackay's last public appeal was written just a month
before his death, and received by the CMS afterwards. It
was a call for more missionaries, which had strong echoes
of Stanley's letter that had won him for Africa:

> You sons of England, here is a field for your energies. Bring
> with you your highest education and your greatest talents,
> you will find scope for the exercise of them all. You men of God
> who have resolved to devote your lives to the cure of the souls
> of men, here is the proper field for you. It is not to win num-
> bers to a Church, but to win men to the Saviour, and who oth-
> erwise will be lost, that I entreat you to leave your work at
> home to the many that are ready to undertake it and to come

forth yourselves to reap this field now white to the harvest.
Rome is rushing in with her salvation by sacraments, and a
religion of carnal ordinances. We want men who will preach
Jesus and the Resurrection.

With this article, which was published in the CMS
Gleaner, was a personal message to the society's headquarters: "But what is this you write – 'Come home'?
Surely now, in our terrible dearth of workers, it is not the
time for any one to desert his post. Send us only our first
twenty men, and I may be tempted to come to help you to
find the second twenty."

Deekes, himself ill, was the only other missionary at
Usambiro when Mackay died. He arranged the burial, at
which the small band of Ganda Christians at the mission
sang the stirring hymn, All Hail the Power of Jesus' Name.
Later on, Mackay was moved to Kampala to lie alongside
Bishop Hannington.

From Usambiro, it took Stanley 79 days to reach the
coast at Bagamoyo, where the expedition arrived on
December 4, 1889. The German commandant gave a cele-
bratory banquet, during which there was a near-tragedy.
Emin fell from a first-floor window and sustained head
injuries. Being extremely short-sighted, he apparently
mistook the window for a balcony. He was unconscious for
several days.

Stanley had brought the expedition in at fearful human
cost. The people whom he had come to rescue – Emin's people – had been few enough to begin with. A total of 570
men, women and children had started for the coast, and
only 290 arrived. Stanley had left Zanzibar in February
1887 with 706 men and boys. This had become almost
exactly half, 350, at the start for the coast in April 1889
and a hundred or so more were to be lost before the expedition was wound down with 246 survivors. To this must
be added untold numbers from the tribes who died in
fights in the Ituri Forest and elsewhere. Nine European
officers were enrolled with the expedition, but only five finished it with Stanley.

While Stanley was on his march back to the coast
through most of 1889, the German Carl Peters was marching the other way, and his moves created near-panic

among the British government. Peters, a resourceful free-
wheeler not to mention loose cannon, headed another
Emin Pasha relief expedition, in the German interest,
which he himself called "no pleasure trip, but a large-scale,
colonial-political undertaking". Forbidden to proceed by
the German colonial authorities, who were co-operating
with the British, Peters made a secret landing on the
African east coast in June 1889. With very few men, he
managed to traverse Masai country and was quickly in the
region of Lake Victoria. He heard that Emin was coming
out with Stanley, but he made a discovery that offered better prospects. It was to raise the Buganda stakes dramatically. Peters did not act the gentlemen, however; he
opened and read letters sent by Mwanga and Lourdel to
Frederick Jackson of the IBEA Company. Mwanga in his
extremity against the Muslims asked for help in regaining
his throne. In return, the kabaka offered to accept the flag
of his rescuer, a trade monopoly and other inducements.
Peters saw his opportunity. He rushed to Buganda, where
he found Mwanga newly restored to his capital and in
February 1890 he signed a treaty with the king.

Jackson had been sent out with orders to make for
Wadelai. It greatly vexed Stanley when he learnt about it
that the company had seen fit to send a second expedition
in search of Emin. Jackson, who had a force of 500 men,
also had specific orders not to enter Buganda. This was the
reason for his lukewarm response to Mwanga's letter sent
in June 1889. Jackson offered a flag – which horrified the
kabaka – and not much else. The letters that Peters read
included one from Lourdel on behalf of the king, dated
December 1 and repeating Mwanga's appeal for help.

When Jackson returned to Kavirondo in March 1890
from an ivory hunt near Mount Elgon, he heard about
Peters's seizure of the letters, and knew he must put aside
his orginal orders and follow the German to Mengo, which
he reached in April after Peters had left.

By now Mwanga had little use for Jackson. The Muslims
had been driven out of Mengo, so Mwanga no longer felt
the need of military help. In any case, he had the treaty
with Peters. Frederick Lugard said the appearance of
Jackson's men was seen to compare badly with the scarlet
and gold lace of Peter's escort. The kabaka was strongly

under the influence of Lourdel, who was acting as his private secretary. British political control was the last thing
the French missionaries wanted. They associated it, quite
reasonably, with Protestant supremacy. Nor did they want
French rule (although this was never a practical possibility): France in the 19th century had a long history of anti-
clericalism. The fathers' choice was for the status quo ante
in which the Baganda would continue to rule themselves,
buying goods and arms (for self-defence) where they
would. Apart from Britain, the only European country in a
position to take over Buganda was Germany. Of the two
powers, the fathers preferred Germany.

With Mwanga and Lourdel both uninterested in his
treaty, Jackson was getting nowhere. It looked as if
Buganda, the "Pearl of Africa", was slipping away from the
IBEA Company and Great Britain. Jackson's presence further destabilised the fragile political situation. It was
decided to send two envoys, one Catholic and one
Protestant, to the coast to find out which country had the
stronger claim on Buganda. It was unclear because the
Anglo-German boundary agreement of 1886 had left the
hinterland undefined.

Jackson left empty-handed for the coast on May 14,
1890, leaving behind his colleague, Ernest Gedge, with
about 35 men and some 180 rifles. The day before Jackson
left, Lourdel died of fever. It was just three months after
Mackay's death. Lourdel, too, was a young man even
though he felt himself prematurely old. Like Mackay, he
had never been home. Mackay and Lourdel spent 14 years
and 11 years in Africa respectively.

Meanwhile, at Bagamoyo Emin Pasha had recovered
from his fall. In March 1890 he surprised the world, and
angered a chunk of it, by entering German government
service with a brief to open stations south of Lake Victoria
in the German sphere. The man whom Britain had rescued
at enormous financial and human cost was to return close
to Equatoria and even closer to Buganda, which was still
the unpicked plum. The ultimate destination, it is clear,
was Buganda itself. It was too much for the Times correspondent, who wrote from Zanzibar:

The news of Emin's decision is received very unfavourably here. His rescue, effected at so great an expenditure of time and money is absolutely resultless regarding himself. Within four months of reaching the coast he returns, as a paid subordinate of the German Company, to the very latitude where he so recently lived as heroic governor of immense provinces amid world-wide admiration.

Worldwide admiration was at first Stanley's lot, too. Soon, however, he was caught up in a vicious controversy as the relatives of the dead officers, and the surviving officers of the expedition, had their say.

Major Barttelot's brother issued a rejoinder to Stanley. Jameson's widow published her late husband's letters and diaries. The nation and beyond were caught up in a heated debate about Stanley's decision to split the expedition at Yambuya. Stanley himself was forced into a series of public pronouncements in his own defence. He had already produced an eloquent account of the expedition with *In Darkest Africa* (1890). His raw energy – in a man approaching 50 – is shown as clearly in this production as it was in marching three times through the Ituri Forest.

For speed of writing, it is one of the most astonishing feats of authorship of all time. Stanley immured himself in a Cairo hotel and generated the text of about 400,000 words in 50 days. This is an astonishing 8,000 words on average, or around 20 printed pages per day, where many modern writers consider they have done a day's work in producing 1,000 words.

Stanley made – and gave away – a fortune from newspaper articles about the Emin Pasha expedition. He donated his fees to the expedition funds: at £2,200 they were 6.9 per cent of overall income.

Stanley's book was candid about what the author saw as Barttelot's inexplicable failures at Yambuya, although if he had been able to foresee the controversy to come it would no doubt have been even stronger. He was answered with equal eloquence, but with brevity in place of length, by H.R. Fox Bourne in *The Other Side of the Emin Pasha Relief Expedition* (1891). This is high-quality journalistic commentary, which still reads well today.

Without claiming to any first-hand knowledge of the

events, Fox Bourne put the "case for the prosecution". Stanley, he argued, promised Emin ample ammunition and stores to be delivered to Wadelai. In fact, he came late and never got to Wadelai; by sending Jephson there with Emin, but accompanied by just three soldiers, he "quickened and strengthened the disaffection" among the pasha's people.

Fox Bourne was among many to claim that Emin was brought out of Equatoria as a captive. He pointed out that barely more than half of the pasha's followers who left with the expedition survived to reach the coast. Interestingly for the period, he complained about the colonialism behind the expedition: it was a pretence for an "empire-making errand" for Mackinnon's company.

Fox Bourne quoted from *In Darkest Africa* and ended his book with a venomous comment:

> How to adhere to a promise seems to me to be the most difficult of all tasks to 999,999 men out of every million whom I meet.

> For Mr Stanley himself the task was too difficult. He has shown that he, at any rate, is not the one man among a million who can be trusted to keep a promise.

While Fox Bourne was concerned about Stanley's failure to relieve Emin in the way originally announced, the dead officers' supporters wanted to drive home the point that the decision to split the expedition at Yambuya effectively condemned Barttelot and Jameson to their deaths. Splitting an expedition in difficult terrain is always hazardous. This expedition was not so much split as scattered, with Troup, Ward and Bonny still at various points downriver when Stanley left Yambuya. Barttelot was an accomplished officer, but he was unproved in Africa. Much depended on Tippu Tip, but Barttelot was also unversed in dealing with Arabs. Yet again, it remains hard to explain why Barttelot and the other rear party officers were seized with inaction while the force wasted away over many weeks.

Stanley, amid all the controversy, had been portrayed in newspapers and elsewhere as "a nineteenth-century conquistador resolutely cutting his way across Africa at the head of a slave army and leaving a wake of destruction behind him", says Iain R. Smith (*The Emin Pasha Relief Expedition 1886-1890*). In typical British fashion, the questions over his conduct did not prevent Stanley going on to continued successes. Until now a lifelong bachelor, he married. He became an MP and a knight of the realm. He was able to build a fine house in Surrey. But he remained the former work-house boy and not everyone was won over. His fellow explorer, Colonel James Grant, had been unable to get Stanley into membership of the Athenaeum Club in London before the Emin Pasha expedition; afterwards (Smith records) he quite despaired of doing so.

In the wreckage of the expedition, one fact was clear. The huge loss of life was the consequence of Stanley's choosing the west coast route. The east coast routes were by then relatively established. They were shorter, and lacked the forests and mountains that bedevilled the western approach. As we have seen, however, Stanley had mixed motives in his choice of route. The Emin Pasha expedition was never simply about reaching Emin.

11 Lugard walks in

As 1890 progressed, three of the main elements in the Uganda story were arranged as follows:

- An uneasy peace prevailed in Buganda after years of war both among the internal factions and with Kabalega of Bunyoro. The country was eyed by Britain and Germany.

- Kabalega continued with his bid to regain Bunyoro's greatness, and supported the defeated Muslims of Buganda as part of the strategy.

- Equatoria had ceased to exist, but organised groups of Sudanese troops and their followers remained in the territory.

By mid-year, the affairs of the region were about to took a decisive turn with Captain Frederick Lugard's departure from Mombasa, bound for Buganda. He was in his early thirties, and possessed those ideal accompaniments of the Victorian expeditioner: a war wound and a broken heart. He had followed his lady from India to England, to suffer the traumatic shock of finding her in a hopelessly compromising position with a lover. In the circumstances the isolation and danger promised in Buganda can have been no hardship for Lugard, who was the first choice of the Imperial British East Africa Company for the job.

The Company needed Buganda as much as it considered Buganda needed the Company. Half a decade earlier, Stanley had won it land cessions from the sultan of Zanzibar, but its rule had been lethargic. Little development had taken place. The interior remained largely untouched, with few stations established. Part of the problem was that much of East Africa lacked exportable natural resources. The IBEA Company's chief, William Mackinnon, had declared that its shareholders would "take their dividends in philanthropy". So far, however, there was little economic or humanitarian activity to pay dividends on. Buganda was the Company's inevitable destination. It had become well known in Britain through the explorers and missionaries. There were massive supplies of ivory and an established system of agriculture. On the back of commercial success, the war against Arab-led slave-raiding would be successfully prosecuted.

Stanley's advice to Mackinnon caused a delay with Lugard's expedition. The advice was that a major force would be needed to assure control of Buganda. In the Mackinnon Papers, John S. Galbraith (in *Mackinnon and East Africa 1878-1895*) found that Stanley advised 500 white men, 2,000 porters and an expenditure of at least £100,000. He also suggested that the undertaking was not worthwhile until a railway was built.

An expedition on that scale was far beyond the resources of the Company. It was obvious that successful trade with Buganda depended on a rail link to the coast, but to delay until the line was built – it was actually completed in 1901 – would be to hand the country to other powers. Buganda, from the point of view of Europe, was a political vacuum. Stanley's advice was so wayward that we must wonder at the motive behind it.

Lugard proved Stanley completely wrong about the size of the force needed. He was eventually cleared to proceed to Buganda with three other Europeans, a Somali interpreter called Dualla and about 300 porters. The fighting force, such as it was, consisted of 50 Sudanese and Somali soldiers, but backed by a Maxim gun – the weapon that wrote the history of Africa in the closing years of the century:

Whatever happens we have got
The Maxim gun, and they have not.

As Hilaire Belloc put it.

The expedition left Mombasa on August 6, 1890. With the porters carrying standard loads of 65-70 lb (30-32 kg) each, it covered up to 20 miles (32 km) a day but usually much less. On September 20 the Company post of Machakos (later to be the seat of Britain's Kenya adminis-

tration before yielding place to Nairobi with the coming of
the railway) was reached. Lugard passed uneventfully
through Masailand and Busoga, the "back door to
Buganda" where Bishop Hannington had been killed, to
cross the Nile on December 13 and enter Buganda proper.
Five days later he was flying his flag on Kampala hill near
the kabaka's palace on Mengo hill (Mwanga had moved the
palace here from the nearby Rubaga hill site used by
Mutesa). Lugard coolly helped himself to the campsite as a
show of strength, as his book *The Rise of Our East African
Empire* makes clear.

Lugard was fortified by the knowledge that earlier in
the year Germany, as Britain's main European rival for
Buganda, had given up its claim. The Peters treaty with
Mwanga was washed away by the Anglo-German agreement of May 1890. Germany accepted Britain's protectorate authority over Buganda and Equatoria, as well as
Zanzibar. Britain ceded Heligoland to Germany. This barren rock in the North Sea was of vital strategic importance
to Germany because it was the key to the Kiel Canal and
the country's main naval base. But Britain also had to give
up a five-mile (8 km) wide strip of land in Central Africa,
which marked the end of the Cape-to-Cairo dream of a railway taking the "red route" – running in British territory
throughout.

If Lugard was afraid that his tiny armed band could
simply be swept away by Mwanga's thousands of warriors,
there is no suggestion of it in this passage from his book:

> As a result of international negotiation, Uganda and the coun-
> tries round about had been ceded to the influence of Great
> Britain. I, myself an officer of the army, had been deputed, as
> the representative of a great chartered Company, to make a
> treaty with a semi-savage king noted for his cruelty and inca-
> pacity. I sought no unfair advantage, no acquisition of territo-
> ry, no monopoly of trade, no annexation of revenues. My task
> was to save the country from itself; and for such a treaty as I
> proposed to make, I saw no need to stoop to bargaining by
> presents (of arms, a Maxim gun, &c., as had at first been sug-
> gested), and no cause for obeisance or deference. It was for
> this reason, as well as to hasten my arrival before any crisis
> between the factions took place, or the expected munitions
> reached Uganda, that I crossed the Nile without waiting for

permission, and, marching rapidly on the capital, selected my own camping-ground. Mackay and Ashe relate how they knelt before the king, when praying for permission to leave the country. Such an attitude seemed to me to lower the prestige of Europeans, and I determined to make my own methods the more marked by contrast.

Robert Ashe in his *Two Kings of Uganda,* published in 1889, told how he and Mackay always followed local custom by kneeling or sitting in the presence of the ruler, never standing. The missionaries lacked both Lugard's sense of status and his 50 armed men.

Lugard rubbed the point in by declining Mwanga's invitation to call at the palace on the day he arrived, saying he was tired and had much work to do. The first meeting took place the next day (December 19). He took a dozen Sudanese whose bugle flourishes vied with the fervour of the king's drummers. The durbar hut was packed with a mass of humanity. Lugard, who had been warned on the point, was careful not to tread on the king's carpet. He then shook hands with Mwanga "cordially and frankly". (He discovered only later that it was Mwanga who ordered the death of Bishop Hannington.) The kabaka's face, he felt, "betokens irresolution, a weak character, and a good deal of sensuality".

Lugard explained that he had come in the hope of bringing peace to the country and he had full powers to make treaties. For the present he was there to pay salaams; he would talk of other matters "by-and-by". The court was very relieved that there had been no mention of a flag, "understanding that it means that they give away their country". Carl Peters, Frederick Jackson and other visitors had "talked of nothing but a flag", Lugard found, but he was much more delicate in the matter: "If I can get a treaty, the flag will come of its own accord, and at their own request later on."

Lugard must have felt he had taken the initiative firmly into his hands as he left the first meeting. Meanwhile, on Kampala hill the tiny force was making sure of its security. A neat, stockaded camp was created. The fort was close to the Protestant (Church Missionary Society) settlement at Namirembe. The major buildings and compounds of the capital were scattered among banana groves and dense high grass on several hills. Across the valley from the CMS mission, on Rubaga hill about one mile (1.6 km) away, was the Roman Catholic mission of the White Fathers. The royal palace was at the apex of a triangle with Namirembe-Rubaga as the base and was about two miles (3.2 km) from each. The layout of the place afforded plenty of space for politicking while the location of the church missions, facing each other across a valley, symbolised the bad feelings between the supposed brothers and sisters in Christ.

Lugard wanted to regularise his position and pressed for a quick treaty. On December 24 a preliminary meeting was interrupted by armed rowdies, and he narrowly escaped being shot. On Christmas Day he missed the magnificent dinner, with champagne, that had been put up by the tiny European community in Mengo in order to confer with the kimbugwe, the senior chief of the Roman Catholics. On December 26, the chiefs of the Catholic and Protestant factions came to the Company's camp to sign the treaty, then they all went to the king and obtained his signature. The scene gives us a glimpse of literacy in Buganda at that time: Mwanga made a mark and a ba-Fransa chief who could write put the king's name against his cross. Several of the other head chiefs were able to sign although "they took very long struggling with the letters of their names".

From a first impression of Mwanga's irresolution and sensuality, Lugard came to see the king as a monster of depravity. With the persecution of the Christians men had been "slowly hacked to pieces, each member being thrown into the fire, and lastly their mutilated but living limbless trunks", while the court was mired in immorality:

> Mwanga's court was the public scene of all the vices of Sodom and Gomorrah [Lugard wrote] – vices not indigenous, I believe, amongst African tribes, and the result of contact with coast people ... His dominant motive was a thirst for arbitrary despotic power, and his antagonism to European influence arose, not from high patriotism, but from a fear lest this exercise of despotism should be curtailed.

Lugard added that Mwanga was particularly afraid of the
British because he expected vengeance for the murder of
Bishop Hannington.

This character sketch of the king may or may not be
accurate, but it is no more than an artist's impression. It
cannot claim the first-hand authority of much of Lugard's
writing, nor does Lugard claim that he witnessed the vices
of Sodom and Gomorrah at court. His success (and the
style of the book matches the confidence he showed on the
ground) was founded on an unshakeable belief in the rightness of his mission – and strong genes. The empire builder
who created a British territory before Queen Victoria's dia-
mond jubilee lived to see the last stages of Hitler's war.
When Margery Perham was publishing her biography of
Lugard in the 1950s, a brother and a sister were still alive.

Although he was not a large man, his robustness apparently allowed Lugard to withstand the ailments big, small
or fatal that were everyday occurrences for Europeans in
Buganda. (Years later it was said that the anti-malarial
drug Paludrine created a new, less friendly society among
whites in the tropics because now everybody expected to
see tomorrow.) In his book Lugard compared his good
health with the problems of his associates in a way that
sounds hubristic:

> Williams came back (from a mission south of the lake) full of
> health, but broke down the day after his arrival, and was in a
> serious state of collapse. The others were ill from time to time.
> As for myself, I remained, as usual, impervious to all sickness,
> but neuralgia, toothache, and dizziness, &c., warned me that
> the strain was almost too great even for me.

Later he remarked:

> Grant and Wilson were both so unwell at this time that I
> advised their making a trip for a few days to our little island
> on the lake, which they did in the company of Mr Smith
> (Church Missionary Society). I was myself considerably pulled
> down, for I had hardly been outside my office for four months.
> The breaking out of the wound in my arm, accompanied by
> toothache and neuralgia, were the signs which always warned
> me that the pressure was a little too high.

The Rise of Our East African Empire is an important but
self-justifying account of Lugard's activities in Buganda
(and of a previous assignment around what is now Lake
Malawi). It was written when he was being challenged
over some of his actions. The style suggests the high self-
confidence of a man convinced about the morality of his
position. He had come to Buganda to take possession of it
as the property of the company he represented. It had been
awarded to Britain by the forces of international diploma-
cy, and the IBEA Company was the chartered representative of the British people. That the king or people of
Buganda had not asked to be taken over, or even consulted about it, would have seemed to Lugard beside the point:
in their state of under-development, although Buganda
was advanced compared with its neighbours, there was no
occasion to. The debt was the other way: the advanced
nations were bringing the blessings of commerce and
Christianity.

Lugard did not see himself as a conqueror but as a
treaty-maker and administrator. He was always careful to
follow the forms, as when he made blood-brotherhood with
the son of the king of Ankole:

> I made a very formal ceremony, drawing up all the Sudanese
> (troops) in a hollow square, which I had cleared of grass and
> bushes. I greatly pleased them by consenting to go through
> the full ceremony according to their own rites, and I founded
> upon our mutual pledges the treaty which I submitted to
> England. I had this treaty read and most carefully translated
> to them. Its main provisions were, that the British were to be
> free to pass through Ankoli, or to build and settle in it, and
> that the king would do all in his power to suppress the import
> of arms and powder, by the Waziba traders in German terri-
> tory to Kabarega and the Mohammedan Waganda, and would
> seize and confiscate all he could.

> In return, I gave him a flag and a copy of the treaty, and prom-
> ised him the protection and the alliance of the Company. We
> exchanged presents, and the ceremony was complete, and this
> large country of Ankoli was added to the Company's territory.

It is tempting to see in the last sentence a wry comment on
the unequalness of the bargain (particularly since the

Company lacked the means to guarantee protection), but that would be to use the hindsight of a later century.

Whatever the missionaries might say, Lugard had no illusions about the equality of the races in Buganda. The job of the whites was to hang together. Complaining about two of the leading Church Missionary Society members, he wrote:

> ... it became patent to me that both Mr Ashe and Mr Pilkington allowed the Waganda to imagine that they could turn to them with complaints against myself. "The pity of it!" I exclaim in my diary, "that natives should find that they can set off one Englishman against another. This means death to British prestige with black men; and once let our prestige go – by which alone we hold our own in Africa – and we must follow fast. Langheld, a German officer, was more loyal than my own countrymen. He told Williams that when they came to him "he very quickly let them understand that they could not play off one European against another," and that we all stand by each other.

Lugard was no Colonel Blimp but he was a paternalist, as we understand the word today. Throughout his book he made clear his respect for the Baganda, both in comparison with surrounding tribes and for their innate capacities. Even so, they were at a lower level of social evolution than Europeans, whose service to Africa lay in the models they represented of superior technology and development. This needed to be underpinned by social distance; appearance and form were vital. Even the katikiro, the king's chief minister, had to request an audience to see Lugard, and no followers were allowed to hang around the meeting place as was customary in Africa.

> Trivial as these things may appear [Lugard wrote], I think that in dealing with natives they are of the utmost importance ... the European should assert his superiority – not merely in intellect, in appliances, and in knowledge, but in his dwellings, his manners, his every surrounding; and the superiority, which he thus unostentatiously asserts, will be instinctively accorded to him. Above all this is important in Uganda, where a scale of deference is insisted upon, varying in its degree from the king down to the very pettiest chieflet,

and every slightest detail of etiquette is punctiliously followed
and understood by the smallest pageboy or most ignorant
peasant.

With the treaty obtained, Lugard was soon joined by two
other key players in the Buganda drama. Just after
Christmas 1890 Bishop Tucker reached Mengo. He was
the third CMS missionary bishop to be sent to the kingdom
and the first to reach it. He was to stay in post and build
up the Anglican Church for almost two decades. The country he found on arrival he described as "like a volcano on
the verge of an eruption". Early in the new year of 1891 a
second Maxim gun arrived, brought by Captain W.H.
Williams with 75 Sudanese soldiers and 100 porters. There
was the potentially ticklish problem of Williams being
slightly senior to Lugard in length of army service
although assigned to serve under him in Buganda, but the
two men hit it off. *The Rise of Our East African Empire* is
full of cordial references to Lugard's deputy.

If the first task had been to ensure the survival of the
tiny Company force amid rival factions awash with guns,
the second was to pacify the capital. With Kampala Fort
made safe from attack, Lugard set about securing the dispersed settlement beyond the stockade. He gave some of
the porters basic military training, creating a useful auxil-
iary force which he called the Zanzibari Levy. He used
these men to mount police patrols around Mengo.

At least twice, Lugard's soldiers prevented war between
the factions and he was able to bring about a shaky accord
between the Catholics (ba-Fransa) and the Protestants
(ba-Ingleza). The situation was made doubly unstable
because the kabaka was with the ba-Fransa. This was the
obvious political choice for Mwanga. The ba-Fransa were
the larger faction, and with the IBEA Company poised to
eat the country they were his best bet to thwart the
British. Lugard, officially neutral, inevitably found himself
in bed with the ba-Ingleza, the faction that took Britain's
side in Buganda.

The interchangeability of the terms ba-Fransa/Catholic
and ba-Ingleza/Protestant was a contemporary recognition
of how politics and religion had become mixed up. The factions were not essentially about religion, but religious

belief affected the political equation because the triumph of one or other European power would entrench one or other religion. This duly happened under British rule, when the Protestants grew in support and political influence at the expense of the Roman Catholics.

It was sensible for the Ganda supporter of French or British political hegemony to attach himself to the appropriate religious faction. However, not everyone was motivated by such cynical calculation. Buganda had purchased its admission to the Christian world with the blood of martyrs. Many of the leaders were sincere Christian converts; others just adopted religion as a useful label for a political cause. Meanwhile, followers for the most part accepted the religious denomination of their feudal lord.

> The two factions called Wa Ingleza (English) and Wa Fransa (French) were led by chiefs of the Protestant and Roman Catholic creeds respectively [Lugard explained]. These chiefs were the rulers of the country, and the lesser chiefs and peasantry, who followed them in war as their retainers or serfs, declared themselves, of course, of the same faction as their lords. The two parties were thus composed largely of men of no religion, nor were they religious in their designation. But religious differences had embittered the leaders and a large portion of the rank and file against each other, and their animosity was taken up and intensified by their respective followers.

The Catholics and the Protestants were in temporary alliance, but the third main faction, the Arab party (the Muslims), remained to be dealt with. They had fled towards and into Bunyoro, where they were helped by Kabalega. Whatever his feelings towards Islam, the Muslims were a good weapon for the king against the traditional enemy, Buganda, now that Mwanga had gone over to the Christians.

A large army set out from Mengo in April led by the katikiro, Apolo Kaggwa. Lugard and Williams followed a week later with about 600 men. Half of these were former porters, now proud members of the Zanzibari Levy. Lugard estimated the Baganda fighters at about 25,000. Spears outnumbered rifles by five to one, and there was a vast following to carry the guns, bedding and other equip-

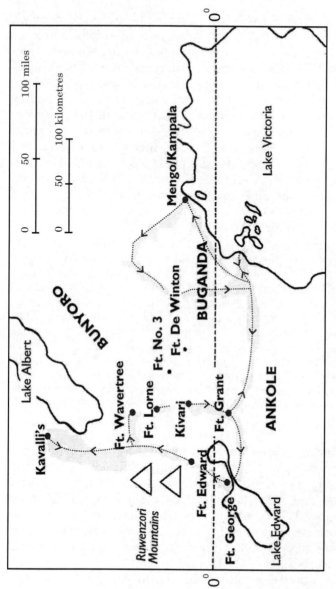

Map 6: Lugard's marches

ment. He was mystified over where the food was found for
such a host.

Just inside the Bunyoro border, on May 7, the army
overcame the Muslims, who had a sizeable stiffening of
Kabalega's rifles, despite the disadvantages of attacking
uphill. Lugard's force was scarcely involved, and the
Maxim guns could not be used because of the dense grass.
The victory was achieved by turning the enemy so they
fled rather than wearing them down with heavy casual-
ties: deaths on the Christian side were about 30 while the
Muslims lost 300-400 killed, many of them butchered after
capture.

Lugard could not persuade the Baganda to march with
him on Kabalega's capital so the army broke up with the
warriors dispersing to their home areas. Williams
returned to Kampala, taking one of the Maxim guns and
fewer than a dozen soldiers. Including the troops already
there, the fort would find itself with barely more than 200
soldiers while Lugard went marching away to the west
with 110 of his own troops, some Baganda (whose numbers
he does not give) and the more effective Maxim gun. He
also had with him 138 of the Zanzibari Levy and 185
porters, as well as two European associates. At home later,
he was to be criticised for leaving the capital exposed, but
his luck held in that regard.

The Muslims and the forces of Bunyoro that lay behind
them had been checked but not mated. Lugard had
secured neither a total military victory over them nor a
political settlement with them. His object now, however,
was to make contact with the remants of Emin Pasha's
Equatoria garrisons known to be established at Kavalli's
under Selim Bey.

The expedition marched into Ankole, where the treaty
was signed with King Ntare, and on to Lake Edward,
where Lugard built a stockaded camp to control the salt
supplies at the adjacent Salt Lake. This camp – Fort
George, which he immediately garrisoned – was sited on a
neck of land only 40 yards (37 m) wide separating Lake
Edward from the Salt Lake.

On August 6, the expedition had the second of three
encounters with Kabalega's troops. It was a dramatic illustration of the power, actual and psychological, of the

repeating gun. Lugard, with only about 40 soldiers, had got ahead of the main party and at that moment ran into a large force of Banyoro by the River Mokia. The enemy delayed too long for their own good allowing some 60 more soldiers to join Lugard's small band. With night approaching, he ordered an advance and at the same time sprayed Maxim fire on a knoll 950 yards (870 m) off. This caused panic. Disciplined charges on the two flanks by Somali and Baganda completed the rout. Later they heard that the score or so of rounds from the Maxim had killed 20-30 Banyoro.

Three weeks later (August 26) the expedition, now numbering about 300, offered a remarkable example of the effect of disciplined movement by overturning an army of many thousands without firing a shot. The enemy was thought to contain a large portion of Kabalega's main army, with considerable firepower. Lugard described what happened next:

> We steadily came on, while the enemy kept up a tremendous firing. The bullets, however, came nowhere near us. We advanced without replying, and the Wanyoro fell back as we came on. The result was that, scared by the reports of our terrible shooting at incredible ranges, and at our stolid and orderly advance, they did not dare to await us at close quarters, and we actually defeated this great army without firing one single cartridge, and without the loss of one single life!

Heading generally north-east on a line between Lake Edward and Lake Albert, the expedition marched through a country near to paradise in the spectacular variety of its scenery. Constantly climbing, they crossed endless streams bringing snow-waters from the Ruwenzori Mountains. The terrain alternated between bush and elephant grass and great areas of cultivation. Vegetation was luxuriant. At 5,300 ft (1,615 m) they found a trio of pretty lakes. They dropped down into the Kiaya valley and down again onto the great plain of the River Semliki. Far away Lugard could see the edge of the Kavalli plateau – their destination.

The Semliki was at least 100 yards (90 m) wide. Some of the Zanzibaris, braving the crocodiles, swam across to obtain canoes on the other side, and in this way the party was able to get over. They were still shadowed by Kabalega's troops. They ran into heavy firing along the Semliki, although again without casualities. They entered swamp, sometimes up to the waist, troubled by grass with a fret-saw edge that caused deep gashes and with stalks shedding white thorns that produced intense irritation. A forest composed mainly of scarlet and yellow flowering trees, criss-crossed by paths of elephant and hippo, was followed by a park-like country studded with acacia bushes.

Hidden away in another stretch of forest the expedition came upon villagers of the Banyabuga people, whom Lugard described as "the most affable savages I had ever met, and ... the first friendly people we had seen since we left Fort George". The chief explained that they washed the saline hills and sold the salt; they dared not cultivate because they knew Kabalega's men would seize the produce. In fact, the Banyoro had recently visited them, carrying off everything. The chief also gave the welcome news that the Sudanese settlements were nearby.

Guides led the expedition into the hills. At 3,000 ft (914 m) they saw Lake Albert spread before them. Some of the Sudanese were veterans of the Emin Pasha Relief Expedition, including the leader, Shukri Aga. They could point out to Lugard the harbour from where the goods of Emin's people were humped up the edge of the plateau to Stanley's camp 10 miles (16 km) inland. Lugard wondered why the camp had not been made nearer, "that the tired men might be saved a part at least of their toil".

The expedition camped on the top of the plateau and were visited by several Sudanese officers from Kavalli's. Lugard, quoting from his diary, described the scene, although as he acknowledged himself without the "practised pen" of a Stanley:

> There was great joy and kissing of my hand (which they touch with their foreheads), and hand-shaking with Shukri and my Sudanese. Every one talked at the same time, and congratulated each other, and every one temporarily became a fool, and smiled extremely, and talked incessantly, as is right and proper on such an occasion.

Selim Bey, the commander of Kavalli's, was the master of substantial settlements with a population of around 8,000. Only about a 10th of these were soldiers; the rest were wives, children, slaves and the households of soldiers who had died in Equatoria. Buried among the tribal villages and completely cut off from the world, the Sudanese made do with cotton clothes of their own weaving if they were fortunate, with ox-hides if they were not. The women wore a thick fringe of black strings suspended from the waist, "which served fairly adequately the purposes of modesty and decency". Yet coinage circulated and clerks wrote out Selim's orders to his officers and the out-stations.

> In short [Lugard wrote], among all the outward savagery of soldiers dressed in hides, of naked women and grass huts, there was a noticeable, – almost pathetic, – attempt to maintain the status they claimed as soldiers of a civilised Government.

Despite Stanley's distrust of Selim Bey, Lugard found the commander to be "a man of very considerable character". He was a giant of a man and a devout Muslim who did not smoke or drink, even though many of his co-religionists at the settlements had wandered so far off the path as to distil their own liquor.

Lugard learnt what had happened to Selim since he had been unable to link up with Stanley's expedition to the coast two years before. Driven out of Wadelai by Fadl al-Mula supported by most of the troops, Selim had set up at Kavalli's with just 90 men. Finding the ammunition left behind by Stanley was a great bonus. He soon lost 50 men in an attack by tribespeople in retaliation for an attack by Stanley. Meanwhile, Fadl al-Mula began to treat with the Mahdists against the wishes of most of his soldiers. Eight hundred of these, with an astonishing 10,000 dependants and camp followers, deserted Fadl and joined Selim at Kavalli's.

Earlier that year (1891), Emin Pasha had turned up at Kavalli's on what was to be his last expedition. He was murdered in the interior soon afterwards. The subject of Stanley's relief expedition was himself mistaken for the reliever of the station, but he explained he was in German service and he failed to persuade Selim to abandon his loyalty to the khedive of Egypt.

Lugard faced the same problem of negotiation. However, he was able to say that Britain and the khedive were close allies. In this he was backed by Shukri Aga, who had even been to Cairo with Stanley. A complex agreement was struck whereby Selim and his men would serve under the British pending word from the khedive. If the khedive approved the association it would continue; if he did not and summoned them back to Egypt, Lugard would facilitate their journey to the coast in return for their service.

Both Lugard and Selim wanted to go to Wadelai but both recognised that this was not the time. Instead, the course was set for the Semliki plain and the Company's territory. On October 5, 1891, the evacuation of the 8,000 population of the Sudanese settlements began. Much of the time this host had to march single file along the narrow trails. The half of the expedition that Lugard was leading (i.e. 4,000 people) made a column seven miles (11 km) long – "Thus the head of the caravan would be nearly arriving in camp, by the time that the last of the people were leaving the old one ..."

Most of the Sudanese were settled in a chain of forts running north to south from western Bunyoro to the borders of Ankole, including Fort Wavertree, Fort Lorne and Fort Grant. Some of Lugard's own troops were sent to link up with the garrison at Fort George and secure the Salt Lake, which was being attacked by Manyema tribesman. When Lugard left for Kampala in early December the nearly 9,000 souls making up the expedition at its largest had become 1,200, among them Selim Bey and his retinue. There were "100 good fighting men" in the total of 600 Sudanese, also 350 widows and children to be repatriated to Egypt via the coast and 250 of Lugard's original soldiers.

In D.A. Low's phrase Lugard had established a "new model warband", consisting of Sudanese troops, Protestant allies among the Baganda and two Maxim guns. It established an hegemony that lasted 60 years.*

---

* *Fabrication of Empire*

December 13, 1891, was the anniversary of Lugard's crossing the Nile to enter Buganda proper. He could look back on a year of substantial soldierly achievement, which he set out unembarrassedly in *The Rise of Our East African Empire*. He could point to the preliminary settlement of Buganda, successful restraining battles with the Muslims, treaty relations with all the country west of Buganda to the the Congo State borders, the routes for the trade of arms and ammunition more or less closed, seven forts built, the Salt Lake annexed, the Sudanese relocated under their officers, the king of Toro (Kasagama) restored with a European to assist (one of Lugard's expedition associates, De Winton) and a feasible transport route opened between Lake Victoria and Lake Albert.

Excluded from this roll-call of activities was one principal party – Kabalega and Bunyoro. Lugard was frank about not wishing to come to terms with Kabalega, whom he did not trust to keep any engagement:

> (H)e outraged and insulted Major (sic) Casati when a guest at his court, and bound him naked to a tree. He fought against Stanley without cause. He gratuitously assisted the Mahommedan party when we had fought against them the previous year. He continuously fought against me in my expedition to Kavalli's. Recently he had sent an army against my Sudanese forts ... His cruelties to his people were the theme of all tongues.

Lugard proved himself to be the inheritor of Sir Samuel Baker's legacy. He never met Kabalega and never made any attempt to meet him. He wrote about the mukama:

> With him alone I felt little inclination to come to terms. For years he had exhibited a continued hostility to all Europeans, from the days of Baker and Gordon ... I knew his overtures to be insincere, and that, should opportunity offer, he would break all engagements, as he always had done.

Hence when Bunyoro envoys came treating for peace Lugard called their approaches insincere and said they were probably spies. Here was an unprovable negative: Kabalega could never prove that he would *NOT* break all engagements so the opportunity was never offered.

When Lugard's expedition returned to Kampala on New Year's Eve he well knew that the capital was bristling with arms and that tensions remained high between the ba-Fransa and the ba-Ingleza.

12 John Bull's baby

Among the mail waiting for Lugard at Kampala was a totally unexpected and wholly unwelcome instruction from the Imperial British East Africa Company, his employers: he was to evacuate Buganda immediately. The directors had decided that the occupation simply could not be afforded. There were some fig leaves. The Company might be back later. In the meantime, it was suggested, a British Resident might be found to work there without military support, which Lugard commented was like asking someone to volunteer to be hanged. He was flabbergasted at the directors' decision.

He shared the knowledge only with Williams. Both men were concerned about the breach of faith involved in withdrawal. Treaties had been made in which kings and chiefs had been induced to accept British suzerainty in exchange for military protection. They had been told that Britain had come to stay. Now the order was to scuttle out almost before the ink on the treaties was dry.

Lugard and Williams believed that the move would deal a fatal blow to British prestige. They also feared that Buganda would collapse into anarchy as the ba-Fransa took their revenge on the ba-Ingleza, who were the main supporters of the British administration. The Muslims, backed by Kabalega of Bunyoro, would then move in and massacre the Catholics. The position of the Protestant missionaries was inevitably threatened.

Feelings were running high with both men. Lugard did not even understand the instruction. From his point of view, the administration was virtually self-sustaining, particularly with the expected revenues from the Salt Lake. Williams declared that he could not hold up his head in society if he were party to such a betrayal of promises to the local people. He offered £4,000 (then a substantial sum) from his own funds to keep the administration going, and said he would use up all his resources if necessary. Lugard, who did not have much money, was deeply moved by the gesture. They were spared the need to disobey the

Company by the arrival of new instructions, which partly countermanded the first ones: the evacuation was to be postponed for 12 months, until the end of 1892. Later, there was to be another extension, to the end of March 1893.

The British prime minister, Lord Salisbury, accepted Mackinnon's plan for the Company to evacuate the country, but was essentially uninterested in the government saddling itself with the responsibility and the costs of a Uganda protectorate. The extensions were the result of intense lobbying in Britain, where the martyrdom of the Ganda Christian converts was well remembered. So too were the lonely deaths of Bishop Hannington and Alexander Mackay, the one murdered and the other a fever victim after 14 uninterrupted years in Africa. The Church Missionary Society – whose work in Buganda was at risk of being undone – raised funds by public donations to help the IBEA Company carry on. Lugard realised that he had to get to Britain to argue the case, but before he could leave he was caught up in another battle nearer to hand – in Mengo itself.

The showdown between the ba-Fransa and the ba-Ingleza was triggered when an Ingleza was killed by a sub-chief of the French faction in an argument over a gun. Mwanga acquitted the killer on the basis that the other man had entered his compound. To Lugard, this was not justice because the Ingleza was the owner of the gun, which had been seized by the Fransa. As Lugard's trusted Somali aide Dualla put it, if a leopard seized a goat would you not pursue it into its cave?

Since the kabaka belonged to the French faction, the political crisis that developed was a trial of strength between Mwanga and Lugard. According to the latter's acccount, he appealed in vain for the French bishop, Monsignor Hirth, and his priests to defuse the crisis. Their refusal, and their decision to stay put on Rubaga hill, was, he argued, evidence that they expected to win the coming battle.

The ba-Fransa were much more numerous in the capital, and on January 22 Lugard issued arms to the ba-Ingleza: 40 muzzle-loading guns and a 5 lb (2.3 kg) keg of powder. Lugard, then and now, has been criticised for fuelling the crisis in this way. D.A Low, for example, calls the action "very partisan".* Lugard, however, denied that "my own overwhelming force freed me from all apprehension of danger to ourselves". It was "very far from being the case". He knew that if the ba-Ingleza went down, the threat to his expedition would be immediate.

The Catholic Union of Great Britain saw matters in a totally opposite light when it issued its polemical *Notes on Uganda* the following year (1893). According to this analysis, the Protestants, otherwise outnumbered, had provoked the showdown at their time of maximum strength – when Lugard had returned to the capital with a reinforcement of crack Sudanese troops. The Company's force was not in any way vulnerable (the writer gave the example of two hundred Spaniards being enough to conquer Peru), and Lugard's issue of arms to the ba-Ingleza was with aggressive intent. The Catholics, the argument continued, would not have stayed quiet while the Company was at its weakest in Kampala and then pick a fight just when reinforcements had arrived.

Notes on Uganda blamed the Company – that is, Lugard – for the bloody results that followed:

> The armed natives, accustomed to a savage system of warfare, carrried their ferocity into the fight; and if the agents of the Company deplored the brutality which ensued and endeavoured to mitigate it, – as we may be quite certain they did, – yet, having armed and unloosened forces they could not control, the evil was done, and the responsibility for all that happened, can only fall on them.

For a time it seemed that the crisis would be contained without a fight, but on the morning on January 24, 1892, the ba-Fransa began to beat the war drums. Lugard issued more arms to the ba-Ingleza: 300 muzzle-loaders and 150 Sniders. The Catholic and Protestant forces were facing each other on opposing hills. The Catholic line extended from the king's compound to the White Fathers' Rubaga mission; the Protestant line was from Kampala fort to the CMS mission at Namirembe. Curiously, both sets of mis-

---

* *Fabrication of Empire*

sionaries refused to move, risking being caught up in the battle – which for the French is what happened. Although the forces were facing each other, their main strengths were not. The ba-Fransa's biggest strength was on Mengo hill facing Kampala, whereas the ba-Ingleza's biggest strength was at Namirembe opposite Rubaga, which was defended more lightly.

The Fransa planned to draw the Ingleza on and then create a wedge between them and the Company's troops at Kampala, allowing each to be dealt with separately and consecutively – a plan Lugard described as "extremely well devised". But, as a consequence of the unequal battle formation, the Protestants succeded in rushing Rubaga. Soon the great Roman Catholic church was in flames. Meanwhile, the Fransa charge from Mengo hill had been broken up by Lugard's Maxim, the second Maxim operated by Williams having failed with a smashed rivet-pin almost at the first shot. Terrified Baganda took shelter in a banana grove. Lugard claimed that the effect was mainly psychological, with only about half a dozen killed. He wrote in *The Rise of Our East African Empire*, with anxious italics: "On the West Coast, in the 'Jebu' war, undertaken by Government, I have been told that 'several thousands' were mowed down by the Maxim. *There was absolutely nothing of the kind in Uganda or previously in Unyoro* (original emphasis)."

Williams now led the Company's Sudanese and Zanzibaris into the battle, taking the king's compound to light opposition. With the defeated ba-Fransa streaming away to the lake, Williams turned his troops towards Rubaga to see what had happened to the fathers.

> As soon as the enemy turned [wrote Lugard], the spearmen and peasantry of the victorious side had rushed in (as is the custom of the Waganda) to complete the victory, and to loot and fire the houses. Flames rose in every direction, in spite of my indignant orders, for the Katikiro and chiefs were powerless to stay the excited rabble, who were scouring the country in every direction – mad to burn the houses of their detested rivals.

Mwanga and the ba-Fransa took refuge on Bulingugwe island in Lake Victoria. It was close to the shore and about seven miles (11 km) from Mengo. The Catholic bishop and his 10 priests accepted shelter at Kampala fort, where Lugard complained that their swarm of followers "swaggered about as though the place belonged to them". Williams gave the bishop his room and bed in the Europeans' house. Lugard, as he was doubtless happy to tell his readers, was living in a tent. Soon Bishop Hirth and all but two of the priests had left to join the ba-Fransa at Bulingugwe.

They were there when Williams, on Lugard's orders, attacked the island in support of the ba-Ingleza. Lugard acknowledged that he took offence at what he saw as an insulting message from the ba-Fransa, including the offer to return to the capital (which Lugard wanted for the general settlement of the country) if the ba-Ingleza – the winning faction – paid a fine for the fighting. There was also the trigger of the Catholics attacking Protestant estates on the mainland.

The island was only 400-500 yards (370-460 m) offshore, and most of the most of the damage was done by the Maxim firing from the mainland. The ba-Ingleza, according to Lugard's account, were ineffective in their canoes, hardly daring to land on the island even under covering fire. The ba-Fransa were driven back to the far end of the island. Mwanga and the bishop fled. The priests were brought to Williams and then returned to Kampala, where they stayed under a genteel form of house arrest. After the battle, Bulingugwe became "like a fair", with guns firing for fun and men dancing and fooling.

Williams's official report about the fighting put the killed and wounded on the island at 25 with 60 more killed in the Fransa canoes: he said he could have killed "several hundreds" if he had wanted to. More died in a panic to get away when they were not under fire or under pursuit.

Malumba Kiwanuka, in *A History of Buganda* (1971), argues that the battle was provoked by the Protestants at a time when they expected to win it – soon after Lugard had returned to the capital with his crack Sudanese troops. While for Lugard the fathers' refusal to leave Rubaga on the eve of the battle was a sign of their confidence in victory, for Kiwanuka they stayed because Lugard did not offer them the same facilities for safe evac-

uation as he had for the Protestant missionaries. The
Protestant whose death had started the chain of events
was in Kiwanuka's reading not the victim but the aggres-
sor. Mwanga was right under Ganda law to give judgement for the Catholic sub-chief.

It is crucial to Kiwanuka's position that Lugard's
actions have not been searchingly examined, largely
because of the influence of his principal biographer,
Margery Perham. She, it is argued, was too ready to rely
on Lugard's own explanations. Certainly Perham, in
Lugard: The Years of Adventure 1858-1898, does not hide
her closeness to her subject. They were on "Fred" and
"Margery" terms. This volume of a two-volume work was
published in 1956 – 11 years after Lugard's death – with
the active encouragement and help of his surviving brother and sister. Kiwanuka might have added that later writers were swayed also by the case so elegantly put by
Lugard himself in his book.

In this book Lugard described the claims that Williams
deliberately fired on fugitives including women as "hardly
worthy of serious refutation". He added: "Under any circumstances it is too monstrous to suppose that a British
officer would have purposefully fired on women." In
defence of his own role, he said simply that he took no part
in any alleged atrocities; he wasn't there.

After the events at Bulingugwe the Catholics, although
the larger faction, were roundly beaten with the kabaka a
fugitive in German East Africa. The Catholics held the
trump card, however: Mwanga himself. It was vital to get
him back to Mengo. A kabaka must always be on the
throne of Buganda. *Notes on Uganda* saw Lugard's moves
to get Mwanga back as a bid to give the Protestants legitimacy; Lugard presents them as the way to the settlement
of the country. Any kabaka was better than no kabaka. If
he could not get Mwanga back, he would even contemplate
installing Mbogo, the head of the Ganda Muslims and
Mwanga's uncle. Installing Mbogo, Lugard recognised
reluctantly, would mean Buganda was no longer a
Christian country.

However, following extensive negotiations Mwanga and
senior ba-Fransa chiefs returned to Mengo after a couple
of months (March 30). A treaty soon followed in which the

large and fertile – also formerly Protestant – province of
Budu was assigned to the French faction. Here Roman
Catholics could keep their arms; they were free to live else-
where provided they were unarmed. Lugard, who con-
stantly tried to separate religious differences
(Catholic:Protestant) from political differences (ba-
Fransa:ba-Ingleza), stressed that the Roman Catholic reli-
gion could be practised anywhere. Both the Fransa and the
Ingleza assailed the settlement as unfair, leading Lugard
to remark that this was proof of its fairness! The ba-
Ingleza were not given a special province, but as the vic-
tors in the war they had most of the country by default.

Notes on Uganda sought to rebut a key part of Lugard's
account – the alleged disloyalty of Monsignor Hirth.
Quoting several times the bishop's comment, "a very little
more, and it (Uganda) would have become a Catholic kingdom", it asked what would anyone expect a Catholic bishop to do but propagate his faith. The disloyalty of
Monsignor Hirth and his companions had "distinctly not
been proved". The writer continued, with the elaborate
syntax favoured at the time:

> Nay more, it is inconceivable to suppose that these Catholic
> missionaries could have been disloyal; for even were they
> French Nationalists before they were Catholics, the French
> were altogether outside of Uganda, and the interests of the
> White Fathers made them earnestly desire, that some civi-
> lized power should assume the direction of affairs in the
> Equatorial Provinces, to protect them from the
> Mohammedans, and to establish justice, liberty, and an
> enlightened government.

With his supporters coming to terms with Lugard,
Mwanga's power base had vanished. From now on, his
power would be what the British gave him. This was set
out in the general treaty of April 11, 1892. The kabaka
recognised the Company's suzerainty and would fly its
flag. Final authority no longer rested with the king or the
chiefs, but with the British Resident. The consent of the
Resident was needed "in all grave and serious affairs and
matters of the state", like raising taxes and appointments
of the higher chiefs.

Lugard in later years was to be known as the architect of "indirect rule", particularly in Nigeria. Here was an early demonstration of it. For a soldier who had turned up in the country, uninvited, with just 50 fighting men, the treaty was the culmination of an astonishing process of persistence, self-belief and legal correctness – all underpinned by the Maxim gun.

He was able, in time-honoured fashion, to turn to his advantage the divisions in the society. Doubtless, too, the Baganda, although famed for their warrior spirit, were growing tired of the fighting, which had lasted on and off for more than three years. Lugard was fortunate also in his deputy. Captain Williams had very much the back-up role, which must have been galling given his army seniority to his commanding officer. Williams played his part very loyally. He showed great commitment in offering money from his own pocket to keep the administration going, he literally held the fort at Kampala while Lugard was enjoying the more glamorous part of exploring the west and he continued the government in the spirit in which Lugard had left it for a few months until relieved.

Lugard's treaty, however, would be just paper unless the matter of the Ganda Muslims was settled. They possessed formidable military power – an estimated 10,000 soldiers – and occupied Singo province to the north of Mengo, towards Bunyoro. Lugard was clear that as long as the Muslims were unabsorbed, faction fighting could always break out again in Buganda. He wanted the Muslims to leave Singo and take over three small provinces in the centre of the country – Kitunzi, Butambala and Busujju. These were near Mengo and between lands occupied by the two Christian factions. Mbogo was to stand down as king and he would live in Mengo. He would not be allowed to reside in any of those provinces, where he might become a focus for disaffection.

Margery Perham in her definitive *Lugard: The Years of Adventure 1858-1898* cannot hide her puzzlement over why the Muslims, with a large undefeated army, accepted these severe terms without getting anything much in return. Certainly, the settlement and the earlier one between the Christian factions were hailed on all sides as "taking war out of the country", according to Lugard. In

the short time they were together, Mbogo and Lugard certainly seem to have hit it off. Thousands marched with the
two men to Kampala, where on May 28 they were greeted
by thousands more. After a rest, they went over to
Mwanga's compound on Mengo hill. With great courage,
Mbogo entered the compound unarmed and caused his
chiefs to do the same. He was trusting for his safety entirely to Lugard and his troops. In the event, help was not
needed.

Lugard vividly described the meeting between the rival
kings, uncle and nephew:

> Mwanga stood at his gate surrounded by his chiefs. He
> received Mbogo as though overpowered with delight. They
> held each other's hands, and gave vent to a long-drawn gut-
> tural Oh!-oh! then Ah!-ah! in a higher note, then long low
> whistles as they gazed into each other's faces. This went on for
> a long time, and became extremely ludicrous to a European
> conception; for at times, while thus indicating intense delight
> and surprise, their eyes would be roaming round in a very
> inconsequent manner. Then they fell on each other's necks
> and embraced, and then again began the former ceremony.
> Then Bambeja (princesses) who had followed Mbogo fell on
> Mwanga's neck, and those of Mwanga's suite fell on Mbogo's
> neck, and meanwhile the same performances were going on
> between chiefs and chieflets and common people on every side,
> till the crush became so great that it was hard to preserve
> one's balance among the gesticulating crowd.

The tale of the royal drum casts a pleasant light on the
characters of both Mbogo and Lugard. The sultan had in
his possession one of two large drums that were emblems
of Buganda kingship. (Mwanga had the other one.) Since
he was no longer a king, Mbogo gave the drum to Lugard.
It stayed for many years at Lugard's house in Abinger,
Surrey. In the 1930s, Lugard heard from Uganda that its
return would be appreciated. He sent it back at once, and
a copy was made for him.

At last, Lugard was able to leave for England, where he
knew he was urgently needed to fight for retention of the
British presence in Buganda. He had been north of the
lake for 18 months almost to the day, and within this neat
period he saw his activities falling into three broadly equal

phases: first half-year, preliminary settlement of Buganda, including containing the Muslims; second half-year, outside in tributary states (in the "march to the west" he brought the Sudanese remnant force out of Equatoria and resettled it, and also established treaty relations with the kings of Ankole and Toro); third-half year, the "closing of the story", with the Catholic, Protestant and Muslim factions united in acceptance of the British flag. It was a feat of will and energy, but the story was not quite as closed as Lugard liked to suggest. On Buganda's northern border, Kabalega of Bunyoro remained untamed and as well disposed to the British as a hungry leopard to an antelope.

At Kampala, Williams took charge. In haste, and to avoid depleting his successor's stock of arms, Lugard decided not to form his own caravan and joined the one being taken down to the coast by Captain James Macdonald, who had been conducting a railway survey. The party left on June 16. Lugard soon found himself in the same difficult position as Emin marching with Stanley: both were used to command but had to submit to someone else's decisions. Between Lugard and Macdonald there was much friction as the caravan marched for the coast. It was unfortunate for Lugard that Macdonald was the one chosen to inquire into his conduct of affairs in Buganda, the government's terms of reference requiring Macdonald to "explain the causes of the outbreak (of fighting) and the action of British officials". The surveyor's chief qualification for the work, it seems, was being on the spot and therefore cheap.

The following year, when he was in London, Lugard heard of the sad fate that had befallen Selim Bey at Macdonald's hands. The Sudanese commander was accused of treachery by conspiring with Muslim Baganda for the overthrow of the British. Already ill, he died on the way to the coast to answer the charge. Insisting that Selim's loyalty was beyond question and had been repeatedly proved, Lugard commented: "There must have been a strange want of tact to convert a loyalty so sincere into hostility, when Selim was even then a dying man!" Lugard defended the way that he and Williams had treated Selim as a dignitary by pointing out that he held the title of Bey, the highest rank but one in the Egyptian army (the high-

est being pasha) and for years had been in command of
large districts.

One of the most deeply felt passages in *The Rise of Our
East African Empire* is a tribute to Selim, the officer trusted by General Gordon, mistrusted by Stanley, whose remnant force Lugard had brought out of the wilderness that
was once Equatoria and resettled in and around Buganda:

> To me it is a sad contemplation, that this veteran, selected by
> Gordon for the command of Mruli; whose valour saved
> Dufileh; against whom no charge of disloyalty had ever yet
> been proved amidst all the faithlessness of the Sudan troops;
> and who had proved at the risk of his life his loyalty to me, –
> that this man should have been hurried off in a dying state,
> discredited and disgraced, to succumb on the march, a prison-
> er and an outcast.

Lugard reached London at a propitious time. Lord
Salisbury's Conservative government had been replaced in
the summer of 1892 by the Liberals under William
Gladstone. They were expected to be even less inclined to
take on Uganda. In fact, the new government was dead-
locked over what to do. The aged premier – 83 that year –
was the country's leading opponent of colonial involve-
ments. It was Gladstone who had delayed sending relief to
General Gordon in Khartoum until it was too late, so he
had redoubled reasons for not tying the country up in
another remote and unsuppliable place like Uganda. His
foreign secretary, Lord Rosebery, sought the opposite.
Under advice from Sir Percy Anderson at the Foreign
Office, Rosebery wanted Britain to declare a protectorate
over Uganda. It could then move into Equatoria to parry a
French threat to the upper Nile, mounted from their vast
north African territories. Gladstone needed to keep
Rosebery in the government, which meant that the far
younger man was playing his cards from a position of
strength.

Lugard, the Church Missionary Society and the
Imperial British East Africa Company all campaigned
strongly that autumn for a Uganda protectorate. Henry
Stanley gave his support. Lugard had to combine his campaigning with writing *The Rise of Our East African Empire*

to defend himself against the French fathers' claims being investigated by Macdonald. He addressed audiences all over the country. (How unimaginable now for the public to turn out for a talk on a foreign policy topic!) Rosebery may have been moved by the political imperative of blocking the French, others saw the economic potential of Buganda and the surrounding territories, but what interested Lugard's audience most were the plight of the missionaries and the Christian Baganda and the continued scourge of slavery in the region. As the leaves started to drop in Hyde Park and Kensington Gardens, not to mention in the Buckingham Palace and the 10 Downing Street gardens, it remained unclear who would win this battle for Uganda.

The IBEA Company's stay in Buganda had been extended by a year, to the end of 1892, thanks to the Church Missionary Society's hugely successful public appeal for funds. The CMS now played a leading part in the campaign for Britain to stay permanently. This was a cliff-hanger. It took three months to reach Buganda from the East African coast, so any instruction for the Kampala administration to stay put would have to be sent from the coast by October 1 at the latest.

A CMS deputation visited the foreign secretary, Lord Rosebery, a week before the cut-off date. With Rosebery it was pushing at an open door, but he had to get retention through the divided cabinet. A cable from Sir Gerald Portal, the British consul-general in Zanzibar, did the trick. It warned of anarchy and bloodshed in Buganda if the Company left. On September 30, 1892, with barely a day to spare, the cabinet agreed to pay for a three-month extension.

This was presented as allowing the Company time to wind up its affairs tidily, although every deferral made it more likely that the stay would be permanent. The retention campaign began in earnest, involving not only Lugard and Stanley but also Lord Salisbury, who only months earlier had shown little interest in Buganda as prime minister. Resolutions in favour of Britain staying in Buganda poured into the Foreign Office. Somehow, in November and December, the Uganda Question caught fire.

The big issue for the public was slavery. Professor D.A. Low, in *Buganda in Modern History*, comments:

The British public knew very little about Africa, but the preachings of Wilberforce, Buxton and Livingstone had sunk deep into the national mind, and any reverse in Africa instantly recalled the horror of slavery which was the one thing that most of them knew about Africa.

William Wilberforce's parliamentary act of 1807 outlawed the slave trade in the British Empire and wherever the Royal Navy reached. Thomas Buxton, Wilberforce's successor as leader of the anti-slavery movement in the British House of Commons, headed the campaign that in 1833 finally saw slaves throughout the British Empire given their freedom.

In an analysis of the resolutions, held in the Foreign Office archives, Low found that 104 out of 174 submissions mentioned slavery. Religious and commercial arguments were intermingled: 75 resolutions mentioned trade or commerce. The Victorian era did not see any conflict between the two. The Good Doctor himself (Livingstone) had proclaimed that commerce and Christianity went together as the way to develop civilisation. The leading politician Joseph Chamberlain, in a remark that now sounds ironical but presumably did not at the time, commented: "What is wanted for Uganda, is what Birmingham has got – an improvement scheme."

The Bishop of Chichester stressed that the argument was a big fuss about very little when he pointed out the cost of administering Uganda was "about the cost of a single picture in the National Gallery". More than half of the resolutions came from church sources, including 18 from CMS branches and seven from branches of another Anglican body, the Society for the Propagation of the Gospel. There was a noteworthy joint submission from the three heads of Scotland's disunited presbyterian churches. Few resolutions emerged from Ireland, underlining the inevitable connection between politics and religion. British colonial policy was officially secular, but Roman Catholic Ireland – at the height of her own home-rule struggle – was unlikely to summon much enthusiasm for Protestant Britain staying in Buganda.

Church people, with the fate of the missionaries and Ganda converts in mind, had the strongest motivation for demanding retention. Chambers of commerce were well aware of the trade possibilities of Buganda and the surrounding kingdoms. Much of the publicly voiced support came from Conservatives, not Liberals. But Lugard also addressed many crowded public meetings and the signatures on the resolutions came from all over the political spectrum. Low makes clear that the Uganda Question was not one just for the religious and right-wingers; it was a mass reaction that the government had to attend to.

The campaign was at its height after the cabinet had announced – on November 11 – a commission of inquiry into the retention issue. Sir Gerald Portal, who was to conduct the inquiry, could under his terms of reference recommend evacuation, but as a known enthusiast for retention he was hardly likely to. The campaigners might also have saved their energies if they had known about Rosebery's private directions to the consul (quoted by Low):

> ... I consider it as settled that your main duty will be to arrange the best means of administering Uganda ... There may, of course, be indicated to you the possibility that should the difficulty of retention be found insuperable, or at any rate too vast, you should so report. But as a rather one horse company has been able to administer I suppose the empire will be equal to it, and therefore that saving clause is mainly one of form.

A week later he told Portal:

> ... I may say this as my confident though not my official opinion, that public sentiment here (in Britain) will expect and support the maintenance of the British sphere of influence.

During Portal's short visit to Buganda, he made a new allocation of land between the Catholics and the Protestants. The Catholics had never come to terms with receiving only the province of Budu. Even Williams, his deputy and successor, thought Lugard's allocation was too restrictive for the Catholics. The Bishops' Agreement was so called because it was signed by Bishop Hirth for the Catholics and Bishop Tucker for the Protestants plus leading chiefs from both groups. As well as keeping Budu, the Catholics received two more mainland provinces (out of

the total of 10) and also the Sese Islands. They were given
shambas (estates) on the route to the capital so that
Catholic travellers did not have to camp on hostile territory.

The agreement, ingeniously but as it turned out tran-
siently, doubled up between the faith groups three of the
key posts in the kingdom. There was a Protestant katikiro
and a Catholic katikiro; likewise for the mujasi (chief of
soldiers) and the gabunga (chief of canoes). It did not last,
being abolished seven years later.

In the months that Portal was making his trip north of
the Great Lake, the Uganda Question stayed before the
British public. The retention campaign died away, but in
the following year (1893) came the sensational reports of
alleged British atrocities during the Battle of Mengo and
its aftermath on Bulingugwe Island. Both sides sent
accounts of the fighting to Europe, but the French ones
arrived first by several weeks. In May, while there was no
word from the British, a letter from the Roman Catholic
bishop, Monsignor Hirth, was published in France (and
republished in the Tablet in the UK). Bishop Hirth allowed
his emotions to get the better of him, and his language
throughout the crisis showed a hatred of Protestantism.
His letter concluded:

> It is not to the English officers that blame principally attach-
> es: they have only the blame of allowing themselves to be
> blinded by the Baganda, themselves persuaded by the
> "Reverends". We regret one thing – not to have been held wor-
> thy of the crown of martyrdom.

The Mengo/Bulingugwe episode became a major Anglo-
French international incident. Captain Macdonald's report
was highly critical of Lugard, but the latter won support
from his former deputy and successor, Captain Williams,
Bishop Tucker – and the British public. Eventually the
affair fizzled out, although the issue of compensation for
the White Fathers' buildings at Rubaga dragged on for several years.

The uproar had kept Uganda before the British public,
which paved the way for the eventual success of the retention campaign. Sir Gerald Portal, his own views and his

superior's expectations happily coinciding, duly reported in favour of keeping Uganda. On April 12, 1894, Britain announced a protectorate over Buganda and surrounding territories. The country became known as Uganda – the Swahili form of Buganda.

Punch magazine published a famous cartoon showing a black foundling labelled Uganda on John Bull's doorstep. Doughty old John Bull had no choice but to take the baby in.

Thus the Baganda, who less than four years earlier had co-operated with, even welcomed, Captain Lugard, signed away their independence. The Buganda government enjoyed substantial autonomy formalised by treaty relations, and as it turned out proved willing to take on the colonial authorities when it needed to. In Low's view, Buganda was in this favourable position because the country "made a quite unusually positive response to the western impact when it came, which earned it a quite unusual reward". Apolo Kaggwa, for instance, was the katikiro of Buganda from 1889, before the coming of the British, until 1926.

Part of that reward was a role as Britain's partner throughout the Uganda protectorate. Ganda armies fought under British leadership against Bunyoro and against rebel Sudanese; they served throughout the protectorate as tax collectors, clerks and administrators (offending local populations by demanding the use of their language, Luganda). If everywhere in the British Empire it was never as simple as coloniser and colonised, here was a notable example of a sub-imperialism.

For Malumba S.M.S. Kiwanuka it was specifically the Ganda Protestant elite that co-operated with the British, for the purpose of entrenching the victory of their faction. (*A History of Buganda*) He sees the ba-Ingleza chiefs as collaborators, no-one more so than Apolo Kaggwa.

Roland Oliver and Gervase Mathew, in Oxford University Press's *History of East Africa* (vol 1), underline how different was Bunyoro's response:

> While the most powerful elements in Ganda society identified their interests with those of the European administration, the most powerful elements in Nyoro society did the opposite.

Kabalega's hostility to Britain was the product of his long-standing fear of conquest, by the Egyptians, by the Ganda and, finally, by Buganda's British allies.

But for the moment Bunyoro remained free.

13 Decline and fall

With Buganda under control, the British were not to leave the defiant Kabalega unmolested. In the process, much of Bunyoro was laid waste by war, with crops destroyed and cattle driven away.

In late 1893 the Uganda commissioner, Colonel Henry Colvile, and his British officers invaded Bunyoro with upwards of 15,000 Ganda and Sudanese troops. The Ganda army was led by a Protestant leader, Semei Kakungulu.

The British found a country much like Buganda but flatter and with a smaller population. There were large forests and many swamps. The army marched first to the River Kafu. Kabalega's capital, Mparo, lay 20 miles (32 km) beyond. When the British reached Mparo they found it "all black and smouldering", as related earlier. Kabalega had torched the place and departed.

The mukama fought a series of rearguard actions, retreating to the Budongo forest and later to the far bank of the Nile. He was supported by the leading chiefs Rwabadongo, Ireyta and Byabacwezi. Colvile had his own problems. He was handicapped by the unwillingness of his Ganda allies to follow him further into Bunyoro (the same problem that Lugard encountered). He complained that they wanted only to return home "the richer by a few goats or head of cattle".

The hard-pressed Banyoro had reason to be grateful for the storage properties of their staple food, millet. During the British invasion, millet was hidden underground for long periods without spoiling. It was the same tactic they had used in the disturbed times of the 1860s and 1870s, when much of the country was plundered by the Baganda and Arab traders.

Kabalega had several brushes with death or capture. Kakungulu's Ganda troops caught him in the open. He ran from clump to clump, dropping his favourite rifle as he went. He would have been killed if anyone in the Ganda army could have shot straight, Colvile commented in his

account of the campaign, *The Land of the Nile Springs,
being chiefly an account of how we fought Kabarega.*

On one occasion the British came within 2,000 yards
(1,830 m) of Kabalega, although separated by a belt of forest. Major A.B. Thruston, one of Colvile's officers, was
amazed that the king's camp consisted of "an elaborate
and miniature town of grass huts". These, he learnt, could
be put up in half an hour by a thousand workers; the pro-
cedure was repeated at each camp.

Kabalega tried what today would be called "psy-ops". He
laid the British under an interdict. A human skull was
found with a live cormorant tied to it. A goat was killed
and half-buried, and "quaint miniature bridges of grass"
were put across the path as an ill omen for those who
crossed them.

In May 1894, the British took the mountain fortress of
Musaijamukuru. This rises 1,000 ft (305 m) above the surrounding plain, and was considered impregnable by the
Banyoro. The defenders fired high, however, and the
assailants successfully stormed the mountain.

Thruston, in his book *African Incidents,* described the
final stages of the assault in a passage that does not reflect
well on either side:

> The Wunyoro, who had apparently never imagined that the
> heights could be carried, were completely disorganised; they
> offered no resistance, but stood staring stupidly round them,
> and were shot down as quickly as the soldiers could reload
> their rifles.

> This slaughter lasted for about two minutes, when the
> remainder, suddenly awakening, turned, and with marvellous
> activity bounded down the sides of the hill. At its foot they
> afterwards suffered some further loss at the hands of the two
> sections and the irregulars, who were waiting for them.
> Among the killed was one of Kabarega's sons, who was second
> in command to Yabaswezi, the chief of the district. Yabaswezi
> himself was the first to run away, and he escaped.

In August, Kabalega's forces under the command of his son
Jasi and Ireyta mounted what Colvile described as "by far
the most important fight we had had since we crossed the
Unyoro frontier in January". The British-led forces includ-

ed 150 Sudanese, and Banyoro led by a dissident chief, Amara.

Kabalega's army gathered at his old capital, Mparo, to attack the new British fort at Hoima. The enemy, in Colvile's words, made "a good stand for some time". Thruston combined a flanking movement with a frontal attack: even then the Banyoro "would not own themselves beaten".

Eventually they scattered. The price of defiance had been high. Colvile said 200 riflemen and an unknown number of others had been killed, compared with eight wounded on the British side.

After this battle Kabalega sent a chief to a White Fathers' mission in Bugangaizi to help him finds ways of negotiating with the British. But this approach, like others before it, came to nothing.

Thruston nearly captured the mukama in November 1894, making a forced march in which he covered 35 miles (56 km) in a day. He moved so fast that he overtook the scouts who were on their way to warn Kabalega in his capital, Mashudi. They were killed in their sleeping hut, Thruston acknowledging that the incident was "very near to mere assassination". He said the needs of speed and avoiding noise meant no prisoners could be taken. The sleeping inhabitants in another village were left unmolested.

The king, surprised by Thruston's troops, was in such a hurry that he left behind valuable ivory, and the royal regalia: two brass spears and a brass tripod. The weather was on his side. "Had it been a bright night, there can be little doubt but that we should have taken him alive," Thruston commented.

Standing in the abandoned capital, Thruston – on Colvile's instruction – left a message in Arabic on a stick inviting Kabalega to submit to Britain. Whether or not it reached him, the mukama sought terms. Thruston granted a four-month truce, but was recalled from Bunyoro before anything more came of it. His successor, Captain Cunningham, continued the war.

In March 1895 Kabalega's forces had a success when British and Ganda forces attacked his position on the far (Lango) bank of the Victoria Nile near Masindi Port. The attack failed. Cunningham was shot in both hips, and another officer, Captain Dunning, died of his wounds.

A second British operation on the far bank next month led to the Banyoro withdrawing northwards. Kabalega's mother, his son Yosiya Kitahimbwa and a princess were captured, but the king, Scarlet Pimpernel-fashion, escaped again.

These events were playing out in northern Bunyoro and beyond because soon after the invasion Colvile had partitioned the country. In *The Land of the Nile Springs* he explained that he was unlikely finally to defeat Kabalega in an open fight (because a non-mechanised army would simply disperse and re-form) or, lacking cavalry or mounted infantry, run him down. His priority was to capture the king, but this he failed to do.

He decided instead to contain Kabalega in the northern part of his kingdom by building a line of forts from Kibiro on Lake Albert to Hoima. In the south of Bunyoro he formed a confederacy of friendly chiefs while the southernmost counties were allocated to Ganda chiefs, partly as a reward for help with the invasion. It was also, for Colvile, a cost-free way of paying for the chiefs' services. The land annexed to the Baganda became known as the Lost Counties – an issue that was to haunt Bunyoro for decades.

Another beneficiary was Kasagama, the ruler of Toro. He was restored to the throne from which Kabalega had driven him, and he was awarded chunks of Bunyoro territory.

A.D. Roberts, however, suggests* that rewarding the chiefs for containing Kabalega was a subsidiary reason for the annexation. The land in the hands of allies had strategic value for the British as they took control of more of Bunyoro. With the county of Buyaga in Ganda hands, Colvile had secure access to Lake Albert and the upper Nile. This was a British strategic objective.

For the near-contemporary commentator and African sympathiser, Professor J.W. Gregory, the justice of the war against Bunyoro was "open to doubt". In his book, *The Foundation of British East Africa* (1901), he suggested a

---

* "The 'Lost Counties' of Bunyoro", Uganda Journal, vol 26 pt 2 (1962)

less worthy motive for military activism than those publicly declared. This was the search for glory, even if it was
obtained with machine guns against spears.

> An adventurous policy has naturally been more popular in
> Uganda, for it has been better rewarded at home than
> attempts at the quiet development of the country [wrote
> Gregory]. The man, who made successfully one of those "nig-
> ger hunts", which in Equatorial Africa are misnamed wars,
> has gained distinction and decoration, in preference to the
> man who kept his province in peace by sympathetic and
> patient administration. The Chinese system of paying a doc-
> tor most when he attends his patient least might well be
> adopted for rewarding soldiers who have civilian duties.

Colvile while supervising the invasion found time to
observe the country about him. The terrain around the
River Kafu, he wrote in *The Land of the Nile Springs*, was
like Singo, a province of Buganda:

> Unyoro, however, is far more thickly populated and highly cul-
> tivated than its sister in Uganda, and its inhabitants, instead
> of courting starvation by relying on that favourite food of
> locusts, the banana, plant large quantities of beans and sweet
> potatoes, and seem generally to have some idea of laying by
> for a rainy day.

He found that wood from the bark cloth tree had the
unusual property of growing when stuck into the ground.
This meant that stockades built from this wood did not rot
as they aged but grew stronger.

Colvile had some praise for Kabalega. "He seems to be
an energetic old man" (he was about 40), who always
walked instead of being carried on shoulders – a soldierly
gesture for his followers. Kabaka Mwanga of Buganda was
praised in part:

> His face is a weak one, with half-covered, fishlike eyes, a rather
> squat nose, and a drooping mouth, but it shows no very marked
> signs of cruelty or debauchery ... He is a wretchedly weak crea-
> ture, utterly self-indulgent, a prey to timidity, and swayed by
> the opinion of the last comer; but after many opportunities of
> studying him carefully in all his many moods, I am inclined to
> think that he is not quite as black as he has been painted.

Thruston's book, *African Incidents*, gives a vivid and read-able account of the Bunyoro campaign. He found that Nyoro gunfire was not very effective. Muzzle loaders, he wrote, "are, in the hands of the natives, far often less dan-gerous weapons than the poisoned arrows and spears which they have in large measure superseded".

The point was interestingly echoed by Sir Winston Churchill in another setting. Churchill said of the American Indian tribes resisting the white advance in the later 19th century: "Their bows and arrows were much more effective than the muzzle-loading rifles with which the Federal troops were at first equipped."* The Indians' defeat came with the Winchester repeating rifle and the Colt revolver.

Published in 1900 three years after Thruston was killed, *African Incidents* has an engaging and honest feel – part-ly because the author set out to write an avowedly "light" book and perhaps because as a young and relatively junior man he carried little baggage. Its candour is such that a century later it was seized on as evidence by Banyoro seek-ing reparations from Britain. Episodes like the slaughter at Musaijamukuru, together with Colvile's acknowledged seizure of civilian food supplies, provided plenty for 21st century lawyers to get their teeth into.

Thruston lamented that "fate had set me down at the very furthest point from all civilisation, as a captain of Bashi-bazouks, a raider and an ivory thief". To contempo-rary readers this must have seemed deliciously to the point: the Bashi-bazouks were Turkish irregular soldiers famous for their lack of discipline, and the British at the time were trying to seize Kabalega's hoard of ivory.

African Incidents left Thruston's readers in no doubt about the nature of treaty-making upon which British pol-icy set such store. He carried a bundle of printed treaties, which he was supposed to make as many people sign as possible. The signing ceremony was "an amiable farce". He went on:

> The *modus operandi* is somewhat as follows: A ragged untidy European, who in any civilised country would be in danger of

---

* *The Great Republic* (Cassell, 2002, p232)

being taken up by the police as a vagrant, lands at a native village, the people run away; he shouts out after them to come back, holding out before them a shilling's worth of beads. Some one, braver than the rest, at last comes up; he is given a string of beads, and is told that if the chief comes he will get a great many more. Cupidity is, in the end, stronger than fear; the chief comes and receives his presents, the so-called interpreter pretends to explain the treaty to the chief. The chief does not understand a word of it, but he looks pleased, as he receives another present of beads; a mark is made on a printed treaty by the chief, and another by the interpreter, the vagrant, who professes to be the representative of a great empire, signs his name. The chief takes the paper, but with some hesitation, as he regards the whole performance as a new and therefore dangerous piece of witchcraft. The boat sails away, and the new ally and protege of England or France immediately throws the treaty into the fire.

This passage, damning in today's terms, did not have the same resonances at the time. Thruston's original readers would have seen the business as a farce but a farce to a good end. The author might even have argued that the passage was an exaggeration for comic effect, and that really the chiefs know what they were doing.

Thruston was no flaming radical. He held the conventional view of Kabalega as a treacherous rogue, but he respected his enemy and he was aware of what the war was doing to the country. He acknowledged that Kabalega was wise not to give battle but to keep up frequent guerrilla attacks. Some fellow officers obtusely blamed the mukama for not fighting pitched battles "like a man". Thruston, however, understood the rightness of these "Fabian tactics". He knew like Fabius, the Roman general who avoided open battles with the Carthaginian Hannibal and secured victory in the Second Punic War, that there is no military virtue in fighting battles to lose them. The officers sneering at Kabalega might also have learnt from Napoleon's conqueror, the Duke of Wellington, who was not afraid to refuse battle.

Thruston became "sick of the raids and bloodshed". He was amazed at the casualness with which his Ganda allies went about the business of killing the defeated enemy: "They were cheerful without being excited, and had the air of satisfaction which one would attribute to an honest Chicago workman when he had slaughtered the last ox of his daily task."

The soldiers often could not be prevented from executing captured enemy. A chief was shot behind him against Thruston's expressed order, and he saw a man killed on the ground while he had his hands up. Thruston himself was no softie, however. He ordered the execution of a Nyoro guide on the forced march to Mashudi. The man had broken down and started raving. He could not be set free and to leave him tied to a tree would expose him to a painful death from predator animals rather than the quick death of a bullet.

Thruston was unwell as well as weary. He asked to be relieved and to return to England. There, however, proved no better: "The climate was vile, the natives were yahoos, dirty in their persons, and rude in their manners; their restrictions I found tedious, their conventionalities artificial and insufferable." It was a feeling familiar to generations of returning expatriates to the present day. Before long he was back in Bunyoro, taking civil and military charge of the country.

The formal war between Britain and Bunyoro was over in 1895. Thereafter, as Edward I. Steinhart explains:

> Kabarega's resistance began to dwindle from a national war to a minor rebellion and finally to the personal struggle of a deposed monarch and his entourage in exile. (*Conflict and Collaboration: The Kingdoms of Western Uganda 1890-1907*)

Several of Kabalega's leading chiefs now surrendered to the British: Rwabadongo, Byabacwezi and Kikukule. The last was a Muganda by birth who was originally appointed to guard Bunyoro's approaches in what became the Lost Counties. After his release, he became a fighter for Kabalega again.

During a late stage in Kabalega's resistance, his call for a general rising among the chiefs received little response. Nor did the population at large show signs of rallying to the king. A mass insurrection or people's war might have been unsuccessful against Britain's military and organisational strength, says Steinhart, "but such tactics were never really attempted".

> Instead [Steinhart writes] Kabarega chose to rely on tried and
> proven instruments of royal power: his chiefly hierarchy, his
> barusura military units, and his traditional allies and diplo-
> matic supports. This reflects the habits of rule of a well-estab-
> lished monarch of a well-organized state. Although Kabarega
> has been portrayed and is remembered as a man of the people,
> he remained a monarch, remote from his people and reluctant
> to call upon them to mobilize and participate in a new kind of
> war, which was necessary (if not sufficient) to save his king-
> dom.

Yet Kabalega could hardly be a Mao Zedong or a Che
Guevara: as Steinhart acknowledges, the world did not see
this kind of guerrilla war until the 20th century.

In July 1896 the Uganda protectorate was extended to
Bunyoro, to the other historic kingdoms of Toro and
Ankole, and to the territory of Busoga. Kabalega, meanwhile, continued to offer guerrilla resistance from the far
side of the Nile, first in Acholi and then in Lango.

In Buganda, Kabaka Mwanga could not reconcile himself to the new state of affairs. His client status was underlined when he was fined for exporting ivory without
British permission. In 1897 he slipped away from Mengo
and went to the Catholic province of Budu. There he
declared a rebellion.

He was defeated in two battles – Kabuwoko and Nyendo
– before linking up with Kabalega – his old enemy – in
Lango.

For the Uganda authorities a more serious security
issue arose that year when three of the Sudanese companies which Lugard had brought out of Equatoria mutinied.

They had been ordered to join the Juba Expedition com-
manded by Major James Macdonald, which was to explore
the headwaters of the Nile. The secret objective was to
forestall France's advance from West Africa to the river.*
The mutiny delayed the plan. It fell to General Kitchener,
after his victory at Omdurman (see below, this chapter), to

---

* A.T. Matson's introduction to Macdonald's *Soldiering and Surveying in
  British East Africa 1891-1894*, edition published in 1973

face down the French at Fashoda, and so prevent them
from achieving their strategic aim of a band of territory
from west to east right across the continent.

The Sudanese mutineers were weary of constant soldiering away from their home bases, and unhappy over
pay and conditions. They marched to join a sympathetic
garrison at Luba's fort in Busoga, with Macdonald in pursuit.

With his Indian and Ganda forces, he laid siege to the
fort where the rebels were holding captive the fort commander, Major Thruston, and others. The siege of Luba's
saw the death of Thruston and three other Britons – one,
Lieutenant Feilding, in a fire fight outside the fort and two
executed by the mutineers.

An unsigned sequel section of Thruston's *African
Incidents* depicts the executions as wholly avoidable, a
combination of lethargy and intransigence by Macdonald
as commander of the relieving force.

After the battle where Feilding died, groups of mutineers allegedly offered to release the prisoners if the
rebels' lives were spared and an inquiry made into their
grievances. Macdonald was said to have precipitated the
tragedy by twice rejecting these unonerous terms,
demanding unconditional surrender. His refusal was not
mentioned in the official report of the events, the anony-
mous author pointed out.

Macdonald's answer to his critics remains unknown. So
sensitive was this challenge to Britain's burgeoning East
African empire that the Foreign Office refused him permission to publish a book covering this time in Uganda.

When Luba's was besieged, the rebels broke out and
went north to Lake Kyoga. They hoped to raise other
Sudanese in Bunyoro. The day was saved from the British
point of view when the Mruli garrison stayed loyal.
Kabalega joined in the attack on Mruli. His general,
Ireyta, was active in the fighting elsewhere.

In another part of the protectorate, Mwanga at the head
of Muslim Baganda, tried to link up with the rebel
Sudanese, but was repeatedly thwarted by loyal troops.
The mutiny was eventually put down after more than a
year.

Overall, the Sudanese Mutiny cost 280 lives on the British side: 185 Baganda, 39 Basoga, 25 Swahili, 24 loyal Sudanese and seven Europeans.

Yet the authorities' greatest fear had not been realised – that the mutineers would form a united front with the Muslim Baganda and the nationalists following Kabalega and Mwanga. A link-up like that would have imperilled the British hold on Uganda even more than the Battle of Mengo had in 1892.

Major H.H. Austin, who marched with Macdonald, put it succinctly. He said: "We all well understood that should such a junction be effected nothing could save Uganda from destruction." (*With Macdonald in Uganda*)

The mutiny was the first time that Indian troops – 220 Sikhs and 200 Muslims – had been brought to Uganda in significant numbers. The British authorities questioned what they had taken for granted – the dependability of the Sudanese troops as a whole. The Indians stayed and were absorbed into the Uganda army, adding another element to Uganda's complicated ethnic mix. (Amii Omara-Otunnu, *Politics and the Military in Uganda, 1890-1985*)

The mutiny was suppressed with the help of Ganda leaders. George Pilkington, the CMS missionary and translator of the bible into Luganda, was killed while observing an action against the rebel-held fort. He was there at the request of the Protestant Baganda, but a newspaper letter from an army officer underlined how ambiguous a missionary's situation could become. Captain C.H. Villiers told readers of The Times:

> It is owing to the attachment of the Protestant Waganda to men like Mr Pilkington that we have been able to hold Uganda so easily up to the present time. In Mr Pilkington's death the cause of civilization in Africa has received a severe blow and England has lost a devoted servant.

Pilkington was one of the most creative of the early CMS missionaries. His death was a great loss. He gave the Baganda the complete bible in their language, building on Mackay's work. With another CMS missionary, A.B. Fisher, he channelled a revival of religious interest among the Baganda into evangelical achievement. He called for evangelists to operate from "reading houses" (country churches). The result, says William Anderson in *The Church in East Africa, 1840-1974*, was "like magic". In January 1894 there were 20 reading houses outside the Mengo centre; by December there were at least 200.

In 1898, a faraway battle finally rendered Uganda's northern borders secure. The followers of the Khalifa, successor to the Mahdi, were routed at the Battle of Omdurman, outside Khartoum, leading to the end of the Mahdist state.

It was a dramatic demonstration of how rifles and spears are no match for artillery and machine guns. General Herbert Kitchener's force of British, Egyptian and Sudanese troops decisively defeated an army twice its size, with 48 dead in the British-led army to 10,000 among the Mahdists.

Kabalega's long campaign of resistance came to an end on April 9, 1899, in Lango. He and Mwanga were taken by surprise and driven into a swamp. Kabalega had refused Mwanga's suggestion to surrender and is supposed to have said (in the language of heroic embellishment):

> Everything has its time appointed; a woman travailing with child reaches the time of her deliverance; so also does a cow; the banana is planted and takes root; but when it arrives at fruition it must fall; and now we have reached the hour of our fate; and, if so be that our appointed time to die has come, let us not be faint-hearted.*

By now the mukama's active following may have dwindled to just 100. (A.R. Dunbar: *A History of Bunyoro-Kitara*) Kabalega fought bravely until he was shot and had to drop his gun. Kakungulu, the Ganda general who made the capture, with great difficulty prevented his men from killing the mukama on the spot.

He was defiant to the last. He asked one of his sons to remove the bandages: he preferred to bleed to death rather than live as a captive. Guards frustrated his wishes. His right arm was amputated and he survived.

---

* The account is given in Mrs A. Fisher's *Twilight Tales of the Black Baganda*

Until his capture no European is supposed to have seen Kabalega close up since Gaetano Casati in the mid-1880s. Few had tried.

A surgeon who attended the king related an anecdote about Kabalega in hospital. The king was displeased that the patient in an opposite bed was being attended to rather than himself. While the surgeon, Haig, bent over his patient, Kabalega wriggled himself into a position to kick the surgeon on the backside. "I didn't mind," said Haig. "It is not everyone who can claim to have had his bottom kicked by a king."

Kabalega's general, Ireyta, surrendered two months after his leader was taken. Kikukule, another staunch supporter, also surrendered after the capture of Kabalega had ended all effective Nyoro resistance.

The Nyoro historian, John Nyakatura, in his book, *Aspects of Bunyoro Customs and Tradition*, cited three heroes from this period apart from Kabalega himself. They were Rwabudongo, Ireyta and Kabalega's son, Prince Jasi Nyakimoso, who was said to be an exception to the Nyoro saying that a brave man does not have brave children.

Kabalega's spirit was admired by the colonial masters even as they subscribed to the narrative of his treachery and cruelties. Sir Frederick Jackson, who served in Uganda from 1894 and was governor of the protectorate 1911-17, said of the hospital incident:

> It certainly showed a truculence and a spirit of reckless defiance, even after the 'game was up', that excited some feeling of respect, and compared more than favourably with the cringing, abject condition of Mwanga, at the moment of his downfall. (*Early Days in East Africa*)

Jackson met Kabalega's mother. Fat was admired at the Nyoro court: the lady was so fat that she got stuck in a chair and had to be pulled out. The skin of her upper arms hung down like a dewlap. Jackson noted the "horribly cruel and revengeful expression of her hazel-red eyes", commenting: "No wonder her son was what he was."

Like many other Europeans, Jackson admired Kabalega's keeping up the fight.

From the first moment of succeeding his father, Kamrasi, he acquired for himself [Jackson wrote] a reputation for horrible cruelties, and cold-blooded butchery of his subjects, that almost rivalled that of his near neighbour Mutesa, and, later on, Mwanga. From the former he may be distinguished as possessing all the bad qualities, with the addition of the basest treachery, but none of the better ones; and from the latter, by possessing courage, and hatred of us that was so irreconcilable that he never once sued for peace, even when hard pressed; and never grovelled when captured. *In fact he always kept his end up, and in some ways was at least a man.* (Italics added)

This mixed verdict, from a man who was sympathetic to Africans, is far removed from modern. Nyoro perceptions of Kabalega. The Bunyoro-Kitara Cultural Trust, for instance, sees a sustained conspiracy against Bunyoro:

One may ask [says the trust] how a mighty empire, like Kitara, became whittled away to the present underpopulated and underdeveloped kingdom of Bunyoro-Kitara. This is the result of many years of orchestrated, intentional and malicious marginalization, dating back to the early colonial days.

The people of Bunyoro, under the reign of the mighty king Cwa II Kabalega, resisted colonial domination. Kabalega, and his well trained army of "Abarusuura", put his own life on the line by mounting a fierce, bloody resistance against the powers of colonialization. On April 9th, 1899, Kabalega was captured by the invading colonial forces and was sent into exile on the Seychelles Islands.

With the capture of Kabalega, the Banyoro were left in a weakened military, social and economic state, from which they have never fully recovered.

The paradox of Kabalega's resistance is that it worsened Bunyoro's situation by laying waste to the country and by creating in generations of colonial administrators the mindset that Bunyoro was the bad guy among the nations of Uganda.

John Roscoe, the CMS missionary, in a near-contemporaneous account (*The Bakitara*, 1923) estimated that the guerrilla war reduced the Nyoro population to just one fourth. It caused pasturage to be neglected. Cattle were driven away with Kabalega's party, never to return.

One who did not share the typical colonial mindset was J.R.P. Postlethwaite, a former district commissioner for Mubende, part of area annexed to Buganda by Colvile. "I like the Banyoro, and I do feel that their action in opposing foreign control hardly merited the consequences which have followed it," he wrote in *I Look Back*.

Kabalega in his long campaign of resistance had luck on his side. At least three times he escaped death or imminent capture – in 1886 when Gaetano Casati could have betrayed him to the Baganda, in 1894 when Ganda forces caught him in the open and missed a sitting duck, and later in 1894 when Thruston reached the Nyoro capital with a forced march, and the king left so quickly that he had to abandon the royal regalia.

He expected to be executed by the British, and he asked Kakungulu to look after his children. As it was, he began his exile to the Seychelles with the humiliation of being paraded through Kampala. Mwanga was with him. Mwanga soon died there, but Kabalega, the older man, lived on.

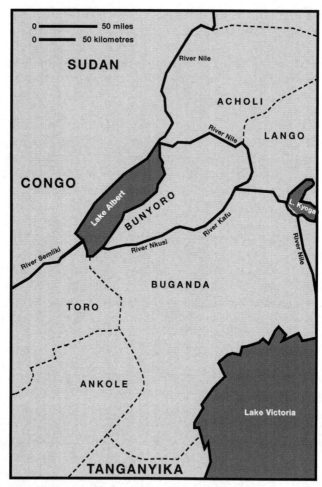

Map 7: The kingdom of Bunyoro and its neighbours after the British Conquest

14 Kings in exile

Kabalega was replaced as mukama by his son Kitahimbwa and later by another son, Andereya Duhaga. Mwanga was succeeded as kabaka by a child, his son Daudi Chwa.

In exile Kabalega was converted to Christianity, and learnt to read and write. (A.R. Dunbar, *Omukama Chwa II Kabarega*) One of his old associates, Abimileka, visited the ex-king at the behest of Duhaga, who was a keen Christian.

According to the missionary Ruth Fisher, Kabalega at first showed "the same obstinacy that had characterised him in the old days". (*Twilight Tales of the Black Baganda*) Abimileka persisted, however, and after two years the ex-king "surrendered himself to Christ". He took the Christian name of John, according to one account because John the Baptist had also been wrongly imprisoned.

Also exiled in the Seychelles was another African hero. This was Nana Prempeh I, the asantehene (king) of the Asante confederacy in what is now Ghana. The events that brought him there started many years earlier.

Unlike Buganda, where the presence of European missionaries was soon followed by takeover – in Barotseland the process was also quick – the Asante were in contact with the British for almost a century before colonisation was imposed. Nor did missionaries play a significant role.

The Asante confederacy occupied a great swathe of territory between the desert lands of the interior and the west African coast, where forts were built by the British, Dutch and Danes. Between Asante and the coastal settlements of the Gold Coast was Asante's rival, another confederacy, Fante.

The Asante supplied slaves from conquered territories and the Fante were middlemen for the European traders. (F.M. Bourret: *Ghana: The Road to Independence, 1919-1957*) In 1807, the British parliament outlawed the transatlantic slave trade, damaging the commercial interests of Asante.

Britain and her local allies fought Asante in a series of wars between 1803 and 1830. The Asante, a proud warrior nation, had a major success at the battle of Nsamankow (January 22, 1824): a British expeditionary force ran out of ammunition and was overwhelmed. The governor, Sir Charles MacCarthy, was among those killed.

A survivor, adjutant-general William Williams, was imprisoned for two months in a hut with the heads of MacCarthy and British officers. "These heads," W. Walton Claridge reported in his *History of the Gold Coast and Ashanti*, "had been so well preserved that the features of the Governor especially presented almost the same appearance as they had done in life." MacCarthy's liver was said to have been eaten as a tribute to his bravery.

The Asante continued their success by defeating the British and local allies at Efutu. The colonial authorities responded by putting together a formidable military force with the Fante, Ga, Akim and Denkyira peoples. This alliance overcame the Asante at the Battle of Dodowa (August 7, 1826). But Britain still felt itself unable to crush the warrior confederacy. It chose the opposite course for securing peace: it withdrew back to Sierra Leone and returned control of the forts to the merchants' committee that had owned them originally.

George Maclean, the merchants' president, reached an agreement in 1831 with the asantehene, Osei Yaw Akoto, successor to the revered Osei Bonsu. The Asante paid an indemnity in gold and provided hostages from the royal family.

Maclean was an effective operator, who without much real power or access to military force secured years of peace for the settlements and the coastal peoples (to 1844). Negotiations with the Asante were an art. An example of the required allusive speech was recorded at the time at a meeting between a later governor and an Asante embassy (Governor Sir Samuel Rowe in 1881):

Asante says: "If I cannot do this (stop leaks in a roof), we must have a new roof." Meaning: I have come for peace.

Governor replies: "I am not a mudfish." Meaning variously: I am not a fool (the mudfish buries itself and is not caught) or

the government is transparent (unlike the mudfish, which
stirs up mud) or I wish no harm (unlike the mudfish, which is
venomous) or the government is important (while the mudfish
is worthless). (Recorded by a contemporary, A.E. Ellis, and
cited by M.D. McLeod: The Asante)

After an inconclusive war from 1860 to 1864, yet another
struggle – which was to have devastating consequences for
the Asante – started a decade later. This was triggered by
the Dutch, who were allies of the Asante, selling their fort
at Elmina to the British. (The Danes had sold their forts to
the British earlier.) The Asante swept to the sea at Cape
Coast, the main British settlement, triggering panic
among the traders and the coastal nations.

Eventually Sir Garnet Wolseley – Britain's military
man for all seasons – turned the tables. He fought his way
to Kumase (1874) with a well armed force of 2,000, over-
coming the Asante army of 10 times that number. The
British occupied and then laid waste to the town.

The Asante were beaten but the British, as they had
done repeatedly over the years, praised the courage, discipline and warlike spirit of their adversaries.

By the Treaty of Fomena the Asante were to pay an
indemnity of 50,000 oz of gold. More than 1,000 oz were
paid on the spot; the rest was awaited. The asantehene
had to open Kumase for trade, including the building of a
road to the state boundary at the River Pra, and abolish
human sacrifice.

Wolseley had created a power vacuum in Asante by
destroying the authority of the government and leaving
nothing in its place. Years of confusion and civil war followed. The asantehene, Mensa Bonsu, fled Kumase in
1883. Agyeman Prempeh was not enstooled until 1888 in a
disputed succession. He formally became asantehene in
1894.

Nana Prempeh turned down a treaty with Britain that
would have removed Asante's independence in 1891. He
was willing to ask Britain for help in restoring order. None
appeared, and the situation continued to drift.

The Treaty of Fomena had called for the end of human
sacrifice, as described above. Thomas J. Lewin, in *Asante
Before the British*, argues that Prempeh kept the death

penalty only for a range of criminal offences (including adultery between a wife of the asantehene and her lover).

> The British either misunderstood or purposely disregarded the legitimate nature of the executions carried out at Prempe's court [writes Lewin], and continued to manipulate the issue of "human sacrifice" to justify their forward policy in Asante.

The defining year for Asante was 1896. By now Britain had become aware that the French or the Germans, both established in adjacent territories, might beat them to Kumase.

Realising the gathering threat to his kingdom, Prempeh sent an embassy to London to put the case direct to the government there. This was headed by the two Ansah brothers, who found official doors closed to them. Britain preferred to leave it to its officials on the ground.

Matters were not helped when it was found that a letter of authority presented by the Ansahs was a counterfeit. Prempeh's mark had been forged and the seal made in London.

As the embassy returned in failure, the governor, Sir William Maxwell, was on the march. British troops under the command of Colonel Sir Francis Scott entered Kumase on January 17, 1896, with the governor following the next day. There was no resistance, on Prempeh's orders. The Asante took the precaution of taking into hiding the Golden Stool, supreme emblem of the asantehene as the king of kings, and the bodies of kings in the mausoleum.

Maxwell now proceeded in an arrogant manner, acting the role of conqueror. Fortifications were dug without permission, and he summoned Prempeh in his own capital to attend on him.

> The net results of this expedition [wrote W. Walton Claridge as early as 1915], therefore, were the overthrow of the Ashanti dynasty and the loss of the country's independence, its acquisition as a valuable hinterland to the Gold Coast Colony under British protection, and the birth of deep and lasting feelings of anger and resentment in the hearts of the Ashantis at the way in which these ends had been attained." (Emphasis added.) (A History of the Gold Coast and Ashanti, vols I and II)

Prempeh ordered his warriors not to fight because he believed Britain had promised to leave him in place if he agreed to terms. These were principally to accept a British resident (that is, British suzerainty) and to pay the indemnity of gold due required by the Treaty of Fomena two decades earlier. Under the guns of the occupying troops, he would also have been aware of the futility of resistance.

What followed was high drama and "an act of deliberate treachery", according to Claridge.

The meeting between the king and the governor took place at the palaver ground before a huge crowd. Prempeh – who was a young man in his mid-twenties – and his mother, Yaa Akyaa, were required to make submission. This they did by prostrating themselves before the governor. It horrified the watching nobles and people.

Maxwell now demanded 50,000 oz of gold*, to defray the costs of the expedition – the Asante were asked to finance their own conquest! – and to meet the outstanding indemnity from the Treaty of Fomena. Only 680 oz were produced, the Asante saying that no more was immediately available. Crucially, Maxwell had authority from the government in London to reduce the indemnity "proportionate to the resources of the king". He chose not to do so.

The prickly governor chose instead to view the 680 oz as a studied insult. For Claridge, however, the amount of gold demanded was impossible. The country had been impoverished by years of civil war. Prempeh even had to borrow money to pay for his enstoolment, and raised a special tax to send the Ansahs to London.

Maxwell gave himself no time to inquire into the matter. To the amazement of all at the ceremony, he ordered Prempeh to be arrested on the spot. Arrested with him were the queen mother (Yaa Akyaa) and four other family members, two chiefs and three kings of nations within the confederacy.

With foreign troops in control of the capital, the Asante

---

* Accounts vary about how much gold Maxwell demanded, from 50,000 oz – the full amount required by the Treaty of Fomena – to 48,000 oz, which would allow for more than was paid originally. Those nearest the event, Casely Hayford (1903) and Claridge (1915), both say 50,000 oz

confederacy had fallen to a coup d'etat.

> The absence of all resistance to the advance of the troops
> [wrote Claridge] ... was really due to the repeated promises
> that the Government (the British) had no intention to depose
> the King provided that he acceded to the terms that would be
> imposed. This, so far as the Ashantis knew, he could and was
> willing to do; but had they known that impossible terms would
> be demanded, or had the least suspicion that their King would
> be carried away into captivity, there is not a shadow of doubt
> that they would have fought most determinedly.

Nor did the disputed money exist, in Claridge's view. He
saw as "proof, almost positive" the fact that the money was
never produced; if it had existed it "would assuredly have
been forthcoming".

Nana Prempeh and a party of more than 40 – family
members, royal counsellors and three kings of confederate
states – were exiled to Sierra Leone. Maxwell did not survive long to contemplate his actions in Kumase. He died
the following year (1897) on a boat back to England.

David Kimble, in *A Political History of Ghana, 1850-
1928*, echoes Claridge's conclusion of two generations earlier:

> (T)he manner in which British supremacy was asserted in
> Ashanti, by the unexpected arrest and deportation of
> Prempeh, ensured the persistence of a strong, and often
> embittered, national sentiment.

He concludes, however, that the fall of Asante was almost
inevitable. The power of the confederacy had waned from
1883 after the flight of Mensa Bonsu, and internal dissen-
sion flourished. A previous British governor had preferred
to wait and "gather the fruit when it is ripe". The time had
come.

An Asante who talked to Prempeh before he went into
exile gave this version of events:

> (W)hen the British came, the Asantes did not fight because
> Nana Prempe told them not to ... Okomfo Anokye, the shrine
> priest who lived at the time of Osei Tutu (founder of the
> Asante confederacy, early 18th century), made a prediction

that the whites would come to Kumase, would arrest Prempe, and would eventually rule all of Asante. He made this prediction through the tail of a cow. This shrine priest was believed by the Asantes because he enabled the Asantes to conquer the Akyems (Akims), Denkyiras, Gyamans, Fantes, and Assins. Okomfo Anokye's prophecies all came true. The Asantes were very successful. Prempe believed that the whites would come to arrest him. Prempe believed the predictions. He told Yaa Akyaa, his mother, that he would go quietly. He was proud of his country. He was proud of his people. Prempe asked the Asantes not to react when he was taken away. Asantes were very sad. We all cried. (Quoted by Thomas J. Lewin: *Asante Before the British*)

As Asante began life under colonialism, the way was open for Christian missionaries. The Basel Society, a prominent Protestant missionary group, was invited in by the governor. It had been first into the coastal settlements in 1828.* It went on to pioneer the introduction of the Gold Coast's major export crop, cocoa. (Stephen Neill: *A History of Christian Missions*)

With its roots in Swiss Reformed Christianity and German Lutheranism, the Basel Society or Basel Mission put ecumenism into practice long before that approach became standard currency. It trained recruits for the (Anglican) Church Missionary Society – Alexander Mackay, as described earlier, lamented that the CMS could not find enough home-grown missionaries – as well as running its own centres. It also supplied Dutch mission societies.

The Basel Mission became the Presbyterian Church of the Gold Coast in 1926, then the Presbyterian Church of Ghana.

Unlike in Uganda and Barotseland (where Francois Coillard facilitated the presence of Cecil Rhodes's Chartered Company), missionaries were not prominent in bringing colonialism to Asante. However, the Wesleyans

---

* The Anglicans can claim the solitary case of Philip Quaque in the later 18th century. Thanks to devoted missionary work by the Rev Thomas Thompson, Quaque was baptised in 1759. Six years later he became the first African to take holy orders in the Church of England. He died at Cape Coast in 1816 after more than 50 years' service to Christianity. (Stephen Neill, see above)

(Methodists) built a church in Kumase in 1841, only six years after they established themselves in the coastal settlements and long before the British takeover in Asante. But conditions were not favourable. The mission had to be re-established in Kumase in 1884.

The Roman Catholics were not established in Asante until 1910 – long after the advent of colonialism. This was in striking contrast to Uganda, where they vied with the Protestants from the start.

The Christian missionaries were not to everyone's taste. J.E. Casely Hayford, a highly educated man of colour and a member of the Gold Coast legislative council, bitterly questioned their concern for their charges:

> The very missionary who preaches the gospel of universal brotherhood seems to scout the idea of the black man, cultured or uncultured, being on the same plane of life as himself. He beholds the Aborigines afar off, and believes in the Native being kept in his place. He merely intends to raise him a wee bit higher in order that he may be useful to his white brother by more intelligently hewing his wood and drawing his water, which the latter is too good to do for himself. This is the black man's burden. (*Gold Coast Native Institutions*, 1903)

This was still the era where notions of God's ordained order of society died hard; where one of the world's best loved hymns, All Things Bright and Beautiful, included lines now expunged from modern hymn books:

The rich man in his castle,
The poor man at his gate,
GOD made them, high or lowly,
And ordered their estate.
(Mrs C.F. Alexander, 1848)

Nor was "paternalism" a charge that most missionaries could easily escape. The mission movement eventually learnt its lessons, and its place, but this was a gradual process over decades.

The authorities moved to put Prempeh even farther out of reach in 1900, following a serious revolt. This was inspired and led by Yaa Asantewaa, the queen mother of

Edweso (Ejisu), a nation of the confederacy. The fort at Kumase was besieged for three months. The deposed asante-hene and his party were sent to the remote Seychelles islands, to be joined there by Yaa Asantewaa and her party.

The trigger for the uprising was Governor Sir Frederick Hodgson's insensitive demand for the return of the hidden Golden Stool. In words that sound both vainglorious and plaintive, he harangued his hearers:

> Let me tell you once and for all that Prempeh will never again rule over this country of Ashanti ... The paramount authority of Ashanti is now under the great Queen of England whose representative I am at this moment ... Under the Governor the Resident at Kumasi exercises the powers of the King para-mount ... *Where is the golden stool? Why am I not sitting on the golden stool at this moment? I am the representative of the paramount power; why have you relegated me to this chair?* (Emphasis added.) (Quoted by Kimble: *A Political History of Ghana, 1850-1928*)

Hodgson continued to sit on chairs and his successor, Sir Matthew Nathan, had the good sense to disclaim any interest in the whereabouts of the Golden Stool. This helped to reconcile Asante to British rule when the country was incorporated into the Gold Coast colony in 1902.

The Asante exiles, numbering 74 in 1901, were settled on a 27-acre (10.9-ha) estate near the Seychelles capital, Victoria. Prempeh and his family occupied an imposing two-storey villa while roomy single wooden storey houses were built close by for the other chiefs, their families and dependants.

This account of Prempeh in exile was given by Professor. Albert Adu Boahen for a souvenir booklet published in 1985.*

> In this estate, which became known as the Asante Camp, the Asante political prisoners were allowed freedom of movement and led normal lives [writes Boahen]. They made farms and gardens on which they cultivated such crops as plantain, rice, sweet potato, pawpaw and vegetables. Nana Prempeh I him-self had a large farm in which he cultivated rubber, vanilla, vine, coconuts etc. Some of the wives also reared hens and pigs for consumption as well as for sale. The inmates could go the

---

* Republished on the official Asante website www.manhyiaonline.org

market and shops in Victoria for the purchase of their daily needs.

Like Kabalega, also in the Seychelles, Prempeh learnt to read and write, and became a Christian. He, his mother and others were baptised into the Anglican Church. Nana Yaa Asantewaa also became a Christian. Prempeh's son, John, became an Anglican priest, working in Kumase and other places.

For all the relative comfort of their surroundings, the group were political prisoners. Prempeh made frequent applications for repatriation. These were all turned down until 1924 when he was finally allowed to return to Kumase as a private citizen. Two years later – disproving Sir Francis Hodgson's prediction in the affair of the Golden Stool – he was reinstated as king of Kumase (but not asantehene), this time under British oversight. He filled the role until his death in 1931.

His nephew succeeded Prempeh under the title Nana Osei Tutu Agyeman Prempeh II. By popular demand he became asantehene in 1935.

For Prempeh's fellow exile, Kabalega, there was to be no happy ending – rather, there was a burgeoning happy ending that was sadly cut short.

The Banyoro came face to face with the past in 1923. It was announced that the former mukama would return to the country, at the request of his son, Duhaga, the current mukama. The old man, now aged around 70, had spent more than two decades in exile, but had not been forgotten by the Banyoro.

Kabalega reached Jinja, in Busoga, in February but got no farther, dying there two months later. The place where he died, Mpumudde Hill, is now an honoured historical site. (Mpumudde is a Runyoro word for "resting".) The mukama's tomb is at Mparo, outside Hoima. Mparo is said to have been his favourite capital.

"To all intents and purposes Kabalega remained the spiritual king of the Banyoro until his death," S.R. Karugire says in *A Political History of Uganda*. He adds that with Kabalega's death the spirit of passive resistance in Bunyoro came to an end.

15 Mission field

On the heels of the British conquest of Bunyoro came Ganda Christian evangelists. Kabalega had had earlier brushes with Christianity but nothing came of them. He sheltered Christians fleeing Mwanga's persecution and from that invited the CMS missionary Alexander Mackay to visit his court. He wanted Mackay to "to come and teach him the white man's book, as he had tried the Arab book and could make nothing of it". Mackay, however, did not take up the offer.

The Uganda historian Sir John Gray observes that Kabalega wanted the practical benefits that Europeans brought, but adds that "he might well have allowed Mackay and other missionaries to sow the seeds amongst his subjects, which, as happened in Buganda, would in due season have yielded a bountiful harvest".*

As it was, Christianity had to wait for two decades after it reached Buganda. The (Anglican) CMS was established in Bunyoro in 1896 and the (Roman Catholic) White Fathers in 1900. The CMS developed the written form of Runyoro, publishing the bible in the Nyoro language in 1913. The White Fathers created orthographies for the related languages, Runyankore and Rukiga.

Mika Fataki, who was baptised in July 1898, considered himself the first Nyoro convert to Christianity (although he was of Soga origin). The breakthrough came in 1900, when the leading chief, Byabacwezi, was baptised. After the death that year of his rival, Rwabadongo, Byabacwezi was the leading figure in Bunyoro alongside the mukama, Duhaga. The king was a keen Anglican – described by Louise Pirouet in *Black Evangelists* as the most deeply committed of all Uganda's traditional rulers of the time.

Many of the first Christians in Bunyoro were barusura or sons of barusura. This noteworthy circumstance Pirouet

---

* "Kabarega and the CMS", Uganda Journal, vol 35 pt 1 (1971)

attributes to barusura being "adventurers, more willing than most people to try out something new".

A strong attraction of the Christian churches was the literacy classes they ran – indeed insisted upon. It had become obvious that to prosper in the colonial state reading and writing were needed.

Ruth Fisher was a missionary and the wife of a missionary who spent several years in Bunyoro after her husband, Arthur, developed mission activities there. As Mrs A. Fisher she was the author of a book about Bunyoro, *Twilight Tales of the Black Baganda*. The author was furious about the title. With sublime disregard for accuracy, the publisher chose it because the Baganda were well known to readers and the Banyoro were not. In his view, one tribe was much the same as another.

Published in 1911, *Twilight Tales* is one of the earliest books in the region to give an African viewpoint, in this case of Bunyoro-Kitara's history. Fisher edited the accounts provided for her by Daudi Kasagama and Andereya Duhaga, the bakama of Toro and Bunyoro respectively. The kings, who as she explained "were only just learning to wield the pen", clearly took the task seriously.

> The work was a novel and laborious task to these two dusky potentates [wrote Fisher], who, day after day, sat in their crude studies, writing as rapidly as they could, while the quaint, withered up, skin-clad ancients squatted on the floor, and related the legends that had been handed down by the generations of sages before them.

The tradition of royal authorship was maintained when years later another mukama of Bunyoro, Tito Winyi IV, wrote a series of articles about the history of the country for the Uganda Journal. They appeared under the initials KW, the K standing for the author's father, Kabalega.

The missionary enterprise was justified in the eyes of its practitioners by the belief that Africans, like all human beings, contained within them the divine spark but needed rescue from the forces of superstition and false religion. Mrs Fisher was appalled by what she called "fetishism" among the Banyoro and what she saw as their moral laxity.

Possessing no moral law, no standard of righteousness or justice, no thought of retribution or punishment hereafter, there is nothing to check these people from giving full reign to their unbridled instincts [she wrote]. Present comfort and prosperity are the only considerations of their life. This has made the African a savage, and almost crushed in him any God-given instinct with which he must at one time have been endowed.

The view is very much of its time, and is partly contradicted by the author's observations on the safety of travel in Africa. This implies a moral sense of not robbing or killing even when it could be done with impunity.

Here let me say that firearms are not needed in Africa as a protection against the natives [Fisher added]. We have journeyed and stayed among the wildest, and even cannibal tribes, and have only met with friendly curiosity and crude courtesy. I will not say that one has always felt quite comfortable at heart, but that was the fault of our suspicions, and not of their behaviour.

For Ruth Fisher the Banyoro as a people compared poorly with the Baganda. This was partly because of the "disintegration" of Bunyoro (although it is not clear whether the author meant the recent British conquest or the earlier erosion of the kingdom to Buganda):

The Baganda are undoubtedly the dominating tribe of Central Africa; patriotism and cohesion have characterised them as a race, whereas its (sic) neighbour nation of Bunyoro has become shattered by its spirit of disintegration. The Banyoro and Batoro* are suspicious and sensitive to a degree, and their racial pride will be the greatest hindrance to their progress. The Baganda are made of harder stuff; they are an aggressive people, and fearless to step out – almost impudent in the cool way they make themselves instantly master of any situation: possessing keen business instincts, a Muganda will turn his hand to anything that promises reward, whether it is calligraphy, languages, money, sums, building, tailoring, cotton growing – nothing comes amiss to him.

---

* The people of Toro, of the same racial stock

On this view the relative progress of the Baganda and the
Banyoro has not come from colonial policy and investment
favouring Buganda but from the character of the two peoples.

The evangelisation of Uganda by Ganda and European
missionaries was to bear strange fruit among the Acholi.
Kabalega's traditional allies found themselves supporting
another rebellion against central authority almost a century later. This was the Holy Spirit Movement (HSM), which
formed in 1986 around the prophetess, Alice Lakwena.

The movement sought to rid Acholiland, and the whole
of Uganda, of witchcraft. The 20 "holy spirit safety precau-
tions" included much to please the missionaries of old,
including no charms, no adultery or fornication, no smoking and no drinking. Heike Behrend comments in *Alice
Lakwena and the Holy Spirits*:

> The HSM, which carried on a discourse against the Catholic
> and Protestant Churches, must nonetheless be seen as a
> movement which ultimately and radically fulfilled the goals of
> the missionaries (though not necessarily in the way the mis-
> sionaries might have wished).

Many people, Behrend reports, deserted the established
churches and gathered in yards (ritual centres) to hear the
Holy Spirit preachers. They burnt their magic charms and
visited ajwaka (spirit mediums) and diviners less frequently. Alice declared that elaborate funeral rites were
useless: since all the dead would be resurrected on
Judgment Day there was no need to take particular care of
the mortal remains.

Alice's time was short. Her army began a march on
Kampala by a peripheral route. It gathered strength as it
passed through Lango and Teso, but after crossing into
Busoga its numbers dwindled from more than 7,000 to
around 2,500. The HSM warriors were defeated by
President Museveni's troops at Jinja in October 1987, and
Alice fled to Kenya. She died there in January 2007.

The movement subsequently degraded into the long-
running rebellion of the Lord's Resistance Army, headed
by Joseph Kony, which became notorious for child abduc-
tions and brutality.

While Alice and her Holy Spirit Mobile Forces could still claim to be fighting for labi, a just cause, the successor movements were caught up in the logic of violence and counterviolence and became increasingly unjust [Behrend comments] ... Driven into isolation, they have degenerated into ever more brutal bands of brigands.

In 2005, evangelism flowed in the reverse direction, from Africa to Britain. A Ugandan, Bishop John Tucker Mugabi Sentamu, was consecrated Archbishop of York, second only to the Archbishop of Canterbury in the Anglican hierarchy in England – a unique achievement in modern times for a foreign-born churchman.

Sentamu stoutly proclaimed the faith in a way that mainstream church leaders in Britain had forgotten about for years. His outspokenness recalled the holy firebrands of old.

In late 2006, for example, he warned how draconian terror laws threatened British citizens' freedoms. He found time to berate a city council, Plymouth, for a decision to end free parking for church attenders. The council had argued it should not discriminate in favour of one religion.

Muslim women who wore the veil were not conforming to "norms of decency" in a British context, said Sentamu. He described as a "nonsense" based on "flawed reasoning" a decision by British Airways to stop an employee wearing a small cross. It emerged that the airline permitted Muslims and Sikhs to wear head-scarves and turbans respectively. Sentamu gave voice to wide public anger at the cross affair, leaving the Archbishop of Canterbury, Rowan Williams, supposedly the nation's chief spiritual leader, trailing in his wake.

16 Land revolution

For Buganda it was like the Norman Conquest without the Battle of Hastings. Mwanga had signed Lugard's piece of paper, the implications of which he and the chiefs cannot have known. The Europeans quickly re-made the country, and the other kingdoms and nations of the Uganda Protectorate – usually with the best of intentions but without of course asking the "natives" whether they wanted it re-made. The question would not have occurred to the Uganda incomers; only the most extreme of radicals in England thought such a thing at the time!

D.A. Low wondered why the Ganda elites seemed to accept British rule so readily. His *Buganda in Modern History*, in the language of its time – it was published in 1971, in the first glow of African independence – asks who were the collaborators and who were the resisters. His answer is that they were often the same people. The politically adroit Baganda had "a dual concern to preserve one's own cultural and political integrity while seeking to ensure that the advantages which could be gained from contact with the wider world were secured as well: a brilliantly constructed ideology, which has the chief claim to being Buganda's greatest achievement". Apolo Kaggwa, for instance, was the katikiro of Buganda from 1889, before the coming of the British, until 1926, which was 32 years after the declaration of the Uganda protectorate.

Colonialism impinged less heavily in Buganda than it did in other British African territories. The "native administration" (in the contemporary phrase) enjoyed substantial autonomy formalised by treaty relations, and was willing to take on the colonial government when it needed to. Low believes Buganda was in this relatively favourable position not for the most immediately obvious reasons: because there were few white settlers or because it had been a powerful traditional kingdom; it was because the country "made a quite unusually positive response to the western impact when it came, which earned it a quite unusual reward". This meant among other things that the British rulers saw working with the chiefs and local administrations as the best way to develop the country.

Low's rather comfortable thesis that the Ganda elites willingly embraced colonialism would be unlikely to appeal to an African writer like Kiwanuka. In his *History of Buganda*, published in the same year (1971) as Low's book, he argues it was specifically the Protestant elite that co-operated with the British, for the purpose of entrenching the victory of their faction. Kiwanuka brands the ba-Ingleza chiefs as collaborators, no-one more so than the Protestant katikiro, Apolo Kaggwa.

For Kiwanuka, Lugard's victory at the Battle of Mengo – which he believes was provoked by Lugard – was the defining moment for all that came after in Buganda and Uganda as a whole. It meant that Buganda was to be not only a British colony but also an emphatically Protestant state. The events of 1892 intertwined politics and religion to the destruction of former structures of the Buganda state. Kiwanuka points out: "Families had been divided and clans were no longer a source of protection." These processes are sadly common in history, as for example with family members finding themselves on opposite sides in the American Civil War and the forced dispersal of the Scottish clans after the 1745 Jacobite rebellion.

For the people of Buganda, Catholicism was the French party and Protestantism was the English party. Now that Britain had taken over Uganda, this association was very damaging to the Catholic cause. Nor were the terms wa-Fransa and wa-Ingleza, as used in the world beyond, at all helpful. The obvious solution for Catholicism was to send missionaries who were both Catholic and English. This was the inspiration behind the arrival of the Mill Hill Fathers in 1895. The fathers were named after the head-quarters of their order, St Joseph's Foreign Missionary Society of the Sacred Heart, at Mill Hill, at that time a village to the north of (now a suburb of) London.

The Vatican agreed to split up the vast Nyanza Vicariate. The north-eastern part was renamed the Vicariate of the Upper Nile and was given to the Mill Hill Fathers. It comprised the eastern part of Uganda and part of Kenya. An Italian missionary group, the Verona

Fathers, took the north-western portion, including a small
part of Uganda above Lake Albert and much of the Sudan.
The name Nyanza Vicariate was kept for the area including western Uganda and German territory south and west
of Lake Victoria. The White Fathers retrenched their
activities to this vicariate.

After some disputes between the Catholic brethren, the
boundary in the Mengo area between the Nyanza and the
Upper Nile vicariates was drawn between Rubaga and
Namirembe hills – through the Battle of Mengo fighting
ground, in fact. This kept the White Fathers in possession
of their Rubaga headquarters while leaving the town of
Kampala, growing to the east of Lugard's fort, to the Mill
Hill Fathers. They were allocated land and built their
headquarters on Nsambya hill.

The first party of Mill Hill missionaries consisted of
Bishop Henry Hanlon and four other priests. After a diffi-
cult trek up-country they arrived at Kampala on
September 6, 1895. They found themselves caught up with
much ceremony among the Catholic faithful and the small
European community. Among their visitors were
Archdeacon Walker of the Church Missionary Society and
two colleagues, the fathers' neighbours-to-be at
Namirembe.

Under the Uganda protectorate, the Roman Catholic
missionaries knuckled down to the new order and concentrated on education. The CMS missionaries with Bishop
Tucker at their head were another matter. They were
proud of the fact that the CMS had been the first in the
field in Buganda, and proud too that the society's campaigning had produced the money for the British to stay on
in 1892. CMS personnel continued to be highly involved in
the politics of the new protectorate, not always to the
pleasure of the administration.

"Difficult to satisfy, the CMS developed an extraordinary capacity for generating unpleasantness [says
Kiwanuka] by writing direct to the Foreign Office, by
appealing to their headquarters for support, by writing to
influential friends and to newspapers." Bishop Tucker was
to be remembered "for claiming a special position for his
co-religionists, although the issue had really been decided
long before by Lugard's actions".

Land-holding was one of the most fundamental changes introduced by colonialism. It was Buganda's turn first. The Uganda Agreement of 1900, despite its name, applied only to Buganda. It replaced the traditional African system of land held under the patronage of chiefs with tenure similar to English freeholds. Land allocations were measured in square miles, hence the term "mailo" land from the word "mile".

Of Buganda's 19,600 square miles (50,760 sq km), 10,500 square miles (27,200 sq km) was to be held by the government and 8,958 square miles (23,200 sq km) by the kabaka, chiefs and other land occupiers. The balance was made up of allocations to the three regents ruling Buganda on behalf of the child kabaka, Daudi Chwa (Mwanga's son), and the three religious missions. The Church Missionary Society received 40 square miles (104 sq km), the White Fathers 35 square miles (91 sq km) and the Mill Hill Fathers (who had been in the country only since 1895) 17 square miles (44 sq km).

By now Buganda had new forms of land control, the Muslims had been neutralised and the Catholics had seen the king sidelined and then removed. Uganda was ruled by the British and a largely Protestant indigenous elite. It was only a quarter of a century since Henry Morton Stanley visited the unknown and exotic country beyond the Great Lake ruled by the famous prince, Mutesa.

The Uganda Agreement was negotiated by the British commissioner, Sir Harry Johnston, and the regents. It confirmed the Ganda occupancy of Bunyoro's Lost Counties, and stipulated that the northern Buganda boundary would continue to be the Kafu and Nkusi rivers. This together with the county of Kabula taken from Ankole and the island of Buvuma from Busoga doubled the size of Buganda.

Johnston agreed this in exchange for the Ganda chiefs giving up traditional forms of primacy: they agreed to renounce tribute from other tribes, merge Buganda's revenue into protectorate revenue, enforce protectorate laws in Buganda and accept Buganda's equality of status within the protectorate. The last mentioned inevitably became the equality of the elephant and the mouse.

In the run-up to independence more than half a century
later Buganda had 16 per cent of the Uganda population,
52 per cent of the country's gross national product, 54 per
cent of secondary school enrolments and most of the students at Makerere university college. (Jean-Pierre
Chretien: *The Great Lakes of Africa*)

Similar agreements were made with two other traditional kingdoms, Ankole and Toro, but Bunyoro was
excluded for many years. Johnston added to the European
narrative of Kabalega by describing the king, like his
father, as "evil-tempered". This was a judgment made sec-
ond-hand for Johnston apparently never saw fit to visit
Bunyoro. (Roland Oliver: *Sir Harry Johnston and the
Scramble for Africa*)

The Baganda had much to thank Johnston for, and duly
did so. After his death in 1927 his tombstone at Poling,
Sussex, was inscribed with a tribute in Luganda from the
kabaka and people of Buganda: "Amazimage ku Buganda
galago nti Bungereza eya-gala bona bekuma babere ne
dembe" (His faithfulness to Buganda shows that England
wishes all whom she protects to be free).

Johnston's Uganda Agreement entrenched the superiority of Buganda within the protectorate. As the new century progressed, Bunyoro continued to be treated like occupied territory by a partnership of the British and the
Baganda.

In 1901, Jemusi (James) Miti, a Ganda chief who
became famous as an historian, reorganised the government of Bunyoro on the Buganda model. Of the 10 saza
(county) chiefs only four were Banyoro, including
Kabalega's former general, Byabacwezi. (Edward I.
Steinhart: *Conflict and Collaboration: The Kingdoms of
Western Uganda 1890-1907*) Within a few years the total
of Ganda chiefs had risen to about 20 at various levels of
the administration.

The Baganda were all over Bunyoro, as teachers, tax
collectors, clerks and senior administrators, adding fuel to
the flames of resentment by insisting on the use of
Luganda. They were prominent as missionaries. They
ostentatiously proclaimed bananas as a superior food
(these were eaten more widely in Buganda than in
Bunyoro).

For Yoga Adhola, throughout the protectorate "perhaps the most determined resistance to the use of Ganda agents in administration came from Bunyoro". (www. upcparty.net)

By 1907 the Nyoro chiefs had had enough. They revolted under the banner of Nyangira Abaganda (I Refuse the Baganda). The Baganda were driven out of the countryside and fled to Hoima. The revolt, which lasted several months, spilled over into Toro, Ankole and Busoga.

After a stand-off with the authorities 54 Nyoro chiefs were arrested. All were removed from Bunyoro, and 12 were deported from Uganda. The Ganda chiefs were reinstated, but were eventually retired. It was a long-term victory for the Banyoro, in the classic British governmental manner: no new Ganda chiefs were ever appointed.

Even so sympathetic a character as the missionary, Arthur Fisher, showed short-sightedness towards the Banyoro. He had entered Bunyoro in 1896, when the country was in disarray, and had worked there and in Toro ever since. He did not join in the general European denigration of Kabalega, stating: "I have never yet heard an old man speak unkindly of the old king and am now convinced he was not as bad as painted."*

But in 1907 Fisher was urging Luganda rather than Runyoro as the language for the Old Testament of the Bible to be used in Bunyoro, on the grounds that the use of the Ganda language had become common. Fortunately for generations of Nyoro Christians, the view did not prevail.

Johnston had dismissively called Kabalega "the so-called king of Bunyoro"; now another official, George Wilson, stated: "Bunyoro must clearly understand that it is a conquered country, and more than in any other the disposal of authority lies with His Majesty's Government." Remarkably, even in 1931 the authors of a report on land tenure were driven to say: "(W)e think the time is come when reference to Bunyoro and the Banyoro as a conquered country and people should cease." *

---

* A.D. Roberts: "The 'Lost Counties' of Bunyoro", Uganda Journal, vol 26 pt 2 (1962)

It was in an only slowly improving political environment that Mukama Tito Winyi IV reigned from 1924 to 1967. He was served for the first part of his reign (to 1939) by Petero Bikunya as katikiro. In 1927 Bikunya published *Ky'Abakama ba Bunyoro*, the earliest account in Runyoro of the history and customs of Bunyoro.

Bunyoro finally got its political agreement with the Uganda Protectorate in 1933, more than three decades after not only Buganda but also the other traditional kingdoms of Toro and Ankole. It left Bunyoro's land area unchanged – that is, it did not address the issue of the Lost Counties.

The principal Nyoro signatory, Tito Winyi, made a public statement reiterating his claim to the counties. The agreement at least gave a guarantee against further land loss: Article 2 provided that "there shall be no contraction of the existing boundaries without the consent of the Mukama".

The mukama gained the right to appoint the katikiro and county and sub-county chiefs. This was subject to the governor's approval, but nevertheless it was a significant new power – or rather an old power retrieved from pre-colonial days.

All land in Bunyoro was to be held by the governor of the protectorate "for the occupation and use of the natives of the Obukama bwa Bunyoro-Kitara (the Nyoro people)". This provision, Article 25, contrasted sharply with that in the 1900 agreement with Buganda. There, barely more than half the land was held by the government with the rest owned by the kabaka, chiefs and religious missions.

For the Nyoro elite this was yet another sign of discrimination. However, as John Beattie makes clear in *The Nyoro State*, the colonial administration felt there was a better way to address land problems in Bunyoro than by recreating the Buganda mailo system.

Shane Doyle, in his 2006 study, *Crisis & Decline in Bunyoro*, acknowledges that by the 1930s estates of the mailo pattern had acquired "a thoroughly bad name". The success of peasant agriculture in eastern Uganda had demonstrated the advantages of a "peasant-focused land policy".

And that was what the Bunyoro's kibanja land reforms sought to provide. The problem was one of a non-productive landlord class and of tenants without security. In pre-colonial times office holders were traditionally landed magnates, supported by the produce of the estates and tribute of the tenants. Official (bwesengeze) estates continued in that role, although tribute had been commuted to cash payments. In the colonial period many private (kibanja) estates had arisen. These were formed by chopping parts off the bwesengeze estates to give retired chiefs an income in lieu of pensions.

The trouble was that this represented a massive transfer of funding away from the public sector, threatening the government's ability to support its officials. The 1933 agreement, drawing on a survey of two years earlier, abolished the official estates and turned the Nyoro territorial chiefs into salaried officials. Land was supposed to be opened up to small farmers with "certificates of occupancy", which were conditional on the holder cultivating the land or occupying it. The certificates could be bequeathed, but could not be sold. Despite the latter condition, a "brisk trade" in the certificates developed. (Jan Jelmert Jorgensen, *Uganda, a Modern History*)

Somehow the kibanja estates, with a bit of tactful adaptation, survived. Meanwhile, the territorial chiefs seethed at the loss of the bwesengeze estates, fuelling antagonism with the colonial authorities. Cultivators found that a certificate of occupancy was not good enough title to serve as collateral security for loans and equipment purchase.

For Doyle the land programme was "a total failure ... a disastrous, incompetent administrative reform".

Nor was Buganda's mailo system the failure it was held to be at the time. The huge landholdings at the start had given way through inheritance and purchase to thousands of smaller plots, many measured in tens of acres. The 3,700 landholdings in 1905 had become 20,000 in 1935 and 58,000 in 1953. Mailo as it worked out had encouraged peasant farming and was driving Buganda's economy.

The land reform episode is an example of how hostility over the years led the Banyoro to see mistreatment where none was intended. In this case the British had identified a problem and tried to solve it according to the beliefs at the time.

For all its shortcomings, the Bunyoro Agreement marked the country's transition from occupied territory to a state with defined relations with the protectorate government. Nevertheless, it reinforced the feeling among the Banyoro that they were still discriminated against because it was held to be less favourable than Buganda's agreement.

Shane Doyle's *Crisis and Decline in Bunyoro* provides a valuable close-up of environmental conditions during the colonial years. For him, British rule brought few advantages to set against the negatives. There were education and modern medicine; and the roots of Bunyoro's rapid population growth since the 1950s, after decades of damaging decline and stagnation, lay in colonial developments. But colonialism upset traditional social structures and environmental practices. Estates created at the expense of peasant farmers and tsetse fly infestation were two of the consequences.

Colonialism, Doyle argues, could be "at its most destructive" when it was the unwitting agent of pests and pestilence. These ecological effects of the conquest were long lasting, and traditional practices well adapted to local disease environments were discarded.

Doyle appears to idealise the age of Kabalega, despite a disclaimer in the dying sentences of the book that pre-colonial government could be "brutal, arbitrary and discriminatory".

The effects of the conquest arguably were felt throughout the colonial period. The Banyoro were apathetic and listless. Many feared government hospitals because they thought the British wanted to kill off the Nyoro people. With the cattle driven away in the war of the 1890s, this was "a cattle culture *sans* cattle". (F. Burke, *Local Government and Politics in Uganda*) In the 1950s Bunyoro still had the fewest cattle per head of population in colonial Uganda.

The population crisis had its origin in pre-colonial times – Doyle thinks the prolonged 19th-century struggle between Bunyoro and Buganda is the source – but the British did little to put the situation right. And because

Bunyoro was underpopulated it missed out on developments that benefited other parts of the protectorate, notably transport links.

To those that have shall be given: officially until 1926 and unofficially afterwards, "non-productive" areas like Bunyoro were seen as less deserving of capital resources than east and central Uganda, notably Buganda. Bunyoro thus became a reservoir for migrant labour.

From census returns, Bunyoro's population in 1911 was 126,275 and in 1921 it had fallen to 95,928. Even by 1959 the population had barely recovered to its 1911 level. With the population explosion all over Africa in recent decades, the population reached around 800,000 in the early 2000s (including the part of the Lost Counties returned in 1965).

Emigration to elsewhere in the protectorate was one factor in Bunyoro's population problem. Other factors were sexually transmitted diseases and diseases that were able to establish themselves after Colvile's invasion. The abandonment of grass burning in the disrupted areas opened the way to East Coast fever and bovine trypanosomiasis, the latter carried by the tsetse fly.

Country abandoned to the bush was ideal for the tsetse fly; as people returned to these areas the human form of "tryps" spread with them. Loss of control over nature also exposed Banyoro to malaria, river blindness and sleeping sickness. Bunyoro in common with much of East Africa was afflicted in the 1890s with rinderpest and the jigger. The country suffered a long-lasting epidemic of sleeping sickness from the first decade of the new century.

Early colonial conditions, according to Doyle, were ideal for the spread of the tsetse fly – a countryside of bush and swamps with much game. Regulations in 1906 doubled the size of the Budongo forest game reserve.

The game question, above all, illustrated Bunyoro's secondary status in Uganda [writes Doyle]. The creation of an immense game reserve reflected a disregard for Bunyoro's land rights, its traditional economy and its commercial future.

That traditional economy was symbolised by Nyoro ironwork and by the high-quality salt produced at Kibiro. Both manufactures collapsed in the colonial economy. Poor

Banyoro could not afford to buy locally made hoes – that
vital tool of agricultural production – and wealthy Banyoro
preferred imported German hoes. Kibiro salt production
dived under the weight of imports from India and Aden,
and heavy taxation. The population of Kibiro in 1928 was
just 353 compared with 5,000 in pre-colonial times.

The Banyoro might well have wondered what they got
out of the new order. They were heavily taxed, forcibly
resettled for disease control, made to grow unpopular or
undesirable crops and compelled to supply labour for road-
building. Malnutrition was common and child mortality
high. In some villages almost half of children did not survive to adulthood.

The malnutrition was caused by a lack of beef – after the
war of the 1890s, cattle herds had been all but wiped out a
second time in a rinderpest epidemic between 1939 and
1946 – as well as cultural prohibitions for some people of
meats like chicken and goat.

Doyle – always ready to blame the colonial administration with anything he can lay his hand to – complains
about the enforced cultivation of "famine foods". These
were intended to avoid starvation during famines, but
growing them meant people did not have time to cultivate
nutritious traditional foods. Thus groundnuts replaced
simsim, maize replaced millet and cabbage replaced traditional greens. The unpopular introduced crop, cassava,
became a staple despite being known as "nyamira ntyo" (I
will just swallow).

Bunyoro had been gripped by a vicious circle of underdevelopment leading to lack of incentive for investment leading to continued underdevelopment, and so on.

> Bunyoro's development potential [Doyle writes] was ignored
> in the early colonial period because districts nearer Lake
> Victoria already enjoyed good communications and were con-
> sidered more deserving. Later, Bunyoro's low population den-
> sities, combined with its continued lack of railways or first-
> class roads, meant that postwar development here would be
> unusually expensive and lacking in democratic equity. As
> colonial time progressed, active discrimination tended to give
> way to passive neglect.

Not everyone in Bunyoro was suffering, however. It was marked by extreme differences in wealth. It became the main tobacco-growing area in Uganda, and towards the end of the colonial period was one of the richest districts in Uganda. Cotton, unprofitable in the early days because of the lack of a ginnery and poor access to markets, later became a lucrative cash crop.

Like the rest of Uganda, Bunyoro was spared the white settler class that dominated Kenya, where in the 1950s the Mau Mau revolt protested at inequitable land distribution. Britain encouraged settlers in Kenya to produce cash crops on a large scale to help pay for the operating costs of the Uganda Railway. The land troubles of Kenya therefore had their origin north of the Great Lake since the railway was built to serve Uganda.

This dramatic line, opened in 1901, ran from Mombasa to Port Florence (later Kisumu) on the southern side of Lake Victoria, traversing the Rift Valley. From Kisumu goods and passengers crossed the lake to Uganda. The Uganda Railway finally lived up to its name as a railway *in* Uganda, not merely *for* Uganda, by reaching Jinja in 1928 and Kampala in 1931.

The city of Nairobi, Kenya's capital, was previously nothing more than a collection of huts at a river crossing. It was chosen as the railway headquarters because it was halfway along the 600-mile (970-km) line.

Unlike in Kenya, Uganda's cash crops were in the hands of Africans. Trade in cotton grew rapidly. In 1905 baled cotton exports were valued at £200; in 1906 £1,000; in 1907 £11,000; in 1908 £52,000. By 1915 cotton exports had climbed to £369,000, and Britain was able to end its subsidy of the colonial administration in Uganda.

The policy of indirect rule meant the continuation of the traditional kingdoms – Buganda, Bunyoro, Ankole and Toro – and the other constituent parts of Uganda. For Onyango Odongo the absence of a unitary state in the colonial years created the conditions that tyrants later exploited. (*A Political History of Uganda: Yoweri Museveni's Referendum 2000*) Tribal governments – variously called kingdoms, territories and districts – had separate relations with the central government, he says. There were no socio-political or economic networks linking them.

Uganda, once called "the Pearl of Africa", is now best known in the West for the tyrannical regime of Idi Amin in the 1970s. The country's troubled post-independence history has included two periods of government by Milton Obote, who was overthrown both times, the flight into exile of the kabaka of Buganda as troops stormed his palace, a guerrilla war that brought Yoweri Museveni to power in 1986 and the long-running rebellion of the Lord's Resistance Army in the north of the country.

Whatever the arguments for and against unitary government in a Ugandan setting, Britain managed the worst of both worlds by exiling Sir Edward Mutesa II, the kabaka of Buganda, in 1953 because of his opposition to a unitary state, then allowing him back in triumph two years later. The deportation caused uproar with Baganda donning the pre-colonial garb of bark cloth in symbolic protest, as Mutesa, who was dubbed "King Freddie", recalls in his memoirs, *Desecration of My Kingdom*.

The governor, Sir Andrew Cohen, was seemingly not a man to tread carefully.

> He began, as he continued, in a whirl of energy [writes Mutesa] ... he was incessantly promising new jails, laying foundation-stones, travelling about the country, or simply giving parties. There he would continue to speak, halting conversation for a moment to beckon an official and say, "I think we can have a new school-house in Mbale, don't you? Make a note of it".

Owen Griffith, who served in the Uganda administration from 1944 to 1963, suggests that Cohen threw away one of the brightest colonial legacies in Africa. ("What went wrong?" in *Looking Back at the Uganda Protectorate*, edited by Douglas Brown) To deport the kabaka was a mistake; to allow him back was an "even greater mistake". This entrenched his authority in Buganda and set the scene for a clash with politicians from elsewhere in the protectorate.

> On the surface, all seemed set fair [writes Griffith]. Thanks largely to Andrew Cohen, Uganda was better prepared for independence than any territory in East and Central Africa.

Africanization of the civil service had proceeded apace; education and medical services were of a high standard; the economy was sound with the African share in it steadily increasing; finances were strong; there were no serious problems, for example arising from large-scale alienation of land to foreigners or chronic land hunger, which might have driven the government off course.

All was not what it seemed, however.

Though no-one paid much attention to it at the time, there was clearly an ominous gap between the newly entrenched feudalism of Buganda and nationalist politicians resentful of the privileged position of the Kingdom. The gap had been hastily and thinly papered over to provide a basis for independence. The British, in the spirit of the times, were all too anxious to get out.

In 1966 Obote decided to break the kabaka's power. Troops attacked the palace. Mutesa II slipped out of a back door and into permanent exile.

"From the day of the Kabaka's final downfall, there began the cycle of conspiracy, repression and coup which made Uganda one of the most wretched countries in Africa, and all but destroyed orderly government," Griffith comments.

A personal postscript gives an insight into cultural differences between Uganda's ethnic groups. Griffith was in Teso, a north-eastern district, awaiting the kabaka on a triumphal tour after his first exile. He recalls:

The Kabaka arrived about four hours late. He was perfectly courteous and friendly towards me, but he ignored almost completely the Iteso leaders. Such conduct was in accordance with the seigniorial traditions of his Kingdom, but it just did not do with the more egalitarian nilotic and nilo-hamitic people of northern Uganda.

The Baganda's love of their country was matched by the Banyoro's for theirs. Walter Bazley, a colonial officer in Bunyoro during the closing years of British rule, notes the intensity of feelings:

> A combination of the Russian love of their land which they call
> Holy Russia; the French concern for their language, the lan-
> guage of princes and lovers whose purity is a national obses-
> sion; the American mania surrounding their political system;
> and finally the British admiration of their royalty combined
> with their sense of history". (Bunyoro, Tropical Paradise)

Bunyoro was, however, a backwater. Bazley, a Canadian,
found it made even Canada seem lively. Kabalega was
remembered as a Robin Hood figure – "a fugitive in the
forests, a hunted man, yet he was the true Mukama, the
chief milkman of his tribe, an aristocrat whose place was
the open grassland among his pure white cattle". But for
Bazley the parallel with Robin Hood broke down.

> Robin Hood, according to improbable legend, had at least
> stolen from the rich and given to the poor, but the Banyoro
> adulation of Kabarega possessed no salutary overtones. He
> was pictured only as a fugitive surrounded by enemies, an ani-
> mal eluding pursuit. As a hero figure he did not point in any
> discernable direction or express any values.

This comment is informative yet unfair. To a beleaguered
people the idea of a leader offering dogged resistance to the
invader is surely enough in itself.

Today, Bunyoro does not feature on maps of Uganda. In
its place are the districts of Masindi, Hoima and Kibale.
Uganda's four kingdoms were abolished in 1967 by
President Obote. In 1993 they were restored by President
Museveni as cultural but not political entities. Bunyoro
therefore lives on in the hearts and minds of its people and
in the person of the mukama.

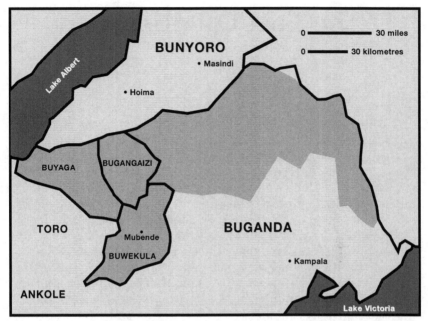

Map 8: Bunyoro's Lost Counties. Areas claimed by the mukama (shaded).
Source: Cmd 1717, HMSO 1962

17 The 'Lost Counties'

The land annexed to Buganda after Colvile's invasion of 1893-95 comprised all of Bunyoro south and east of the Kafu and Nkusi rivers. The area, which included the counties of Buyaga, Bugangaizi and Buwekula, contained 40 per cent of the Nyoro population. These were the "Lost Counties" of Bunyoro – an issue that festered during more than six decades of colonial rule.

The area includes historic royal tombs near Mubende, in Buwekula. Nearby is Mubende Hill, an ancient ritual site soaring 700 ft (213 m) above the surrounding plateau. This was the home until the early 20th century of a line of priestesses each known as Nakaima. The priestess was consulted for smallpox and infertility; the spirits were encouraged by sacrifices of cows, sheep and sometimes youths.*

Bunyoro's kings down to Kabalega were crowned on Mubende Hill. The coronation tree, which became known as the Witch Tree, by the 1960s towered 50 ft (15 m) above the grove of the last priestess. Not long before his capture in 1899 Kabalega is reputed to have returned to Mubende Hill. If this is so it was a long, extraordinary journey, across enemy-held territory, from Lango in the east to Mubende in the west – a sign of the importance of the place and its ceremonies to him. It is also remarkable that news of the trip did not leak out to the British.

Colvile took the decision to annexe the territory that became known as the Lost Counties on his own authority. Much of this had, in fact, fallen to the Baganda years before the British invasion. Colvile did not report his action to the Foreign Office in London. The apportionment was confirmed by the British government, but it cannot have been pleased with the fait accompli.

---

* E.C. Lanning: "Excavations at Mubende Hill", Uganda Journal, vol 30 pt 2 (1966)

In his book, *The Land of the Nile Springs*, Colvile fails to mention this single most controversial action of his time in Uganda. We may wonder whether this silence was because of the political sensitiveness of the case or a simple lack of concern about what the annexation meant to the Banyoro.

The annexed area was divided into Catholic and Protestant parts. Estates were handed over to Baganda so that many Banyoro found themselves landless in their own country.

Two courageous British officials tried to improve the condition of the Banyoro in the Catholic part of the Lost Counties. The land issue was acute there because of immigration: the Ganda Catholics were overcrowded in their own country, where the land settlement favoured the Protestants.

William Pulteney (who became a prominent general in the First World War) appointed Rwabadongo, the former leading chief with Kabalega, as senior chief. He was to be assisted by two other Nyoro chiefs. All were Banyoro. The local people were also allowed to cultivate land again.

The moves brought protests from the Baganda. Colvile's successor as commissioner, Ernest Berkeley, rescinded Pulteney's policy, and Pulteney resigned.

Berkeley even had a plan to absorb the rest of Bunyoro, and Toro, into Buganda. He won Foreign Office approval but the plan was never proceeded with.

Pulteney's place was taken by an official named Forster, who also realised how unfair the annexation was to the Banyoro. Although Rwabadongo and his assistants had been replaced, Forster persuaded the local population to accept the supremacy of Baganda chiefs on the basis that their own property and persons would not be molested.

Berkeley's successor on the fast-moving conveyor belt that was the commissionership of Uganda, Trevor Ternan, authorised Baganda to take over some land and villages. This went plainly against Forster's settlement, and he asked to be transferred. J.W. Gregory commented: "(H)e resigned his post, rather than be the instrument for the enslavement of the Wanyoro by their hereditary foes." Ternan later had the grace to admit that southern Bunyoro had been annexed "contrary to the wishes of its owners".

Principled actions like Pulteney's and Forster's give the lie to the idea that colonial rule was simply about exploitation. They show that the Europeans took the natives (in the term of the period) seriously. So too in another context does an incident recounted by Colvile.

A Muganda fell into a dangerous river during an expedition. James Macdonald (whom we met earlier at the siege of Luba's) bravely jumped in after him. He was unable to find the body, and was fished out thoroughly exhausted.

A number of later British administrators were sympathetic to the Banyoro, but the Uganda Agreement of 1900 had set the land alienation in stone. To redraw the boundaries of Buganda without the consent of the Baganda would destroy the inviolability of Britain's word on a treaty.

A typical view of these Banyoro sympathisers was expressed by J.R.P. Postlethwaite, the district commissioner for Mubende in the 1920s:

> The inclusion of this area (the Lost Counties) in Buganda kingdom is considered by many to have been one of the greatest blunders we committed in the past [wrote Postlethwaite], but its correction, if it is to be corrected, could only come with the consent of the Kabaka and the native government of Buganda. I most emphatically opposed the idea of insisting upon a forcible alteration of the Uganda Agreement to right this wrong. (*I Look Back*)

A submission by the long-established Mubende Banyoro Committee* cited practical difficulties faced by Banyoro in the Lost Counties:

— Saza chiefs Auguste Kibuka (Buyaga, 1933), Yonna Yakuza (Buyaga, 1940s) and S. Kiruruta (Bugangaizi, 1960) prohibited the use of the Runyoro language in all official and religious places.

— A woman was imprisoned and later fined (June 1960) for failing to speak Luganda in a court.

— Three Buyaga representatives were expelled from the Buganda lukiko (parliament) in 1956 for expressing

---

* Reprinted by S.R. Karugire: *A Political History of Uganda*

Bunyoro's demands for the return of the Lost Counties.

— Several Banyoro were imprisoned for between six months and one year for demonstrating in support of the mukama of Bunyoro when he toured Mubende district around 1960.

— A headmaster at Kikoma junior secondary school (Buwekula), Mr Sajjabi-Ssemouuze, was alleged to have destroyed application forms from his own pupils to block their way to secondary school or training college.

After declining to act over the Lost Counties for decades, Britain in the twilight of its rule set up not one but two commissions to report on the issue. Both recommended that the counties of Buyaga and Bugangaizi should be returned to Bunyoro, in the case of the first commission subject to approval in referendums. These counties, in Mubende district, were the only parts of the territory claimed by Bunyoro where Banyoro were in a majority, according to a pre-independence census.

Buwekula, described by the Mubende Banyoro Committee as Bunyoro's "most important territory" because of its royal associations, was excluded from the proposals. At this time the Baganda outnumbered the Banyoro in Buwekula by four to one.

As with most long-running territorial disputes, the arguments were not all one way. Banyoro were in a minority over most of the area of the Lost Counties. Some of this, including Buwekula, had been overrun by the Baganda long before the British arrived, and they understandably saw it as the spoils of war.

Referendums in Buyaga and Bugangaizi were duly held after independence, despite fears in some quarters that the new government would not go ahead with them. The man entrusted with running the referendums after independence in 1962 was Eric Norris. He was a British member of the Uganda administration who had previously organised a referendum for the pre-independence legislative council. Voting day was November 4, 1964.

Looking back after three decades, Norris reflected that "obduracy, not vacillation, had marked the British approach to the Lost Counties question". (In *Looking Back at the Uganda Protectorate*)

Because of the highly charged feelings surrounding the referendums, it was decided to use polling staff who were neither Baganda nor Banyoro. At the same time, the staff had to be intelligible to voters in their own languages. Norris found a sufficient number – 64 – from among civil servants and retired chiefs.

Some 14,000 leaflets and posters were produced in Runyoro, a similar number in Luganda and about 5,000 in English – saturation coverage in territories with a total population of about 60,000.

The government had to see off an apparent attempt to boost the Ganda electorate in Buyaga with thousands of settlers at Ndaiga. The move was defeated in court when it was ruled that they had arrived too late to qualify as voters. From the Ganda point of view, however, the settlers were working land that was unused. The kabaka, Mutesa II, was personally associated with the scheme. The land, he wrote in his memoirs, *Desecration of My Kingdom*, was "empty and fertile"; the "resources should not be wasted".

The referendum campaign was largely peaceful although "it had its moments", Norris remembers.* He gives credit to the Buganda authorities in the two counties for not trying to stop people voting although "they expected to lose". There was civil unrest before the campaign and after the result, but during the campaign and the vote no lives were lost. Neither was the result or the conduct of the poll challenged by the losing side. Both were achievements for Norris and his staff.

"I believed in talking to both sides and keeping them informed. I tried not to tread on toes," he says. "There was also tight security for the ballot papers, and arrangements for observers from both sides."

Voting was by marking a cross on the ballot paper or by making a thumbprint – the latter producing a large number of spoilt papers because ink smudges often "rendered the voters' intentions unclear". Voters in each county had

---

* Interview with author

three choices: to stay with Buganda (symbol a shield), to rejoin Bunyoro (symbol a drum) or to become a separate district of Uganda (symbol a lamp).

The referendum result broadly reflected ethnic origins. In Buyaga 8,327 voted for Bunyoro against 1,289 for Buganda (87:13% in favour); in Bugangaizi 5,275 to 2,253 (70:30%). Support for a separate district failed to reach three figures in each case.

On January 1, 1965, Buyaga and Bugangaizi returned to Bunyoro.

Even so, more than half of the territory claimed by the mukama remained in Buganda. This included Mubende town and the royal tombs. In the first sunlight of independence, Bunyoro was poor and underdeveloped. It was progress of a kind, but it was not living happily ever after.

Nor has history been forgotten by many Banyoro. In 2004 the mukama, Solomon Iguru I – Kabalega's grandson – announced a plan to sue Britain for at least £3 billion for alleged war crimes committed during Colonel Colvile's 1894 expedition and the five-year war that followed.

Another claim was launched by the Mubende Banyoro committee concerning land titles in Kibale district, part of the Lost Counties returned to Bunyoro in 1965.

The mukama's suit alleged torture, pillage, destruction of food crops and theft. Sudanese soldiers under British command were said to have killed and raped civilians.

Field reports of British officers were seen as key exhibits. Major Thruston's *African Incidents*, referred to above, may be a rare book, but it is well known in Bunyoro. The claimants hoped its candid observations would support their cause.

The claimants faced many difficulties. One was that the Geneva and Hague Conventions, which embody the international laws of war, were not in force at the time.

Another was money. When the case was announced, Adrian Blomfield of the (London) *Daily Telegraph* wrote from Hoima of the air of poverty surrounding the Nyoro court:

The modern palace, constructed in the 1960s, is a dilapidated white building with garish purple tiles and the heirlooms of the kingdom lie rusting on the floors of damp rooms. There is

no money for the 10th anniversary celebrations of King
Solomon's coronation ... Kabalega's tomb itself receives only
cursory upkeep.

For the losers, history always casts a long shadow.

.

18 Expatriates at home

For the ordinary people of Uganda, especially in the rural areas, the change of rulers was not too noticeable except at taxation time. The British ruled Africa indirectly through the local chiefs. They had to, because men and resources were too few to do otherwise. As an old hand told Charles Allen for a BBC radio series later made into the book, *Tales from the Dark Continent*:

> We couldn't possibly administer all these people and these vast territories closely. So our policy always was to leave as much as possible to the people themselves and not to interfere with their lives unless it was obvious that what they were doing was wrong. If they could settle their own quarrels, so much the better.

The situation in one district of Nyasaland (now Malawi) was typical of Britain's African colonies: four Europeans (the district commissioner [DC], his two assistants and a policeman), an African sub-inspector, two sergeants and a dozen police administered a population of 100,000.

The white officials were visible from time to time throughout their districts through the hallowed institution of "the tour". An officer might spend as much as half his time in the rural areas for the purposes of collecting taxes, hearing complaints or just showing the flag. Former African administrators and their wives who talked to Allen for the programmes made clear that for many these tours were what Africa was all about. Safaris into some of the world's most exotic areas, or the Sanders of the River-style of venturing forth into the interior, all underpinned with the comfort of being in command of the country, could hardly fail to enter the bloodstream.

Uganda-born Mavis Stone, who returned to live there for 14 years up to 1962, was among those who shared her memories in *Tales from the Dark Continent*. She wove vivid word pictures of expatriate Africa:

... long khaki-coloured plains with the flat-topped thorn trees
and scrub bushes ... the rather attractive little villages with
woven fences ... chicken houses made up like little mud huts
with thatched roofs and stuck up on stilts ... the children that
were half-grown, all legs and smiles ... the women always
graceful, always carrying loads on their heads – even a match-
box I've seen them carrying on their heads – never anything
in their hands ... [the camp fire] was usually lit at sunset
which we would sit and watch and there was supposed to be a
blue flash which you did just see as the sun disappeared ...
you had to swat at the mosquitoes while you were having your
bath ... then you got into your trousers and mosquito boots
and a long-sleeved shirt and you went and sat by the camp fire
and had your drink.

Mavis Stone's husband, Richard, who spent his Colonial
Service career in Uganda, retiring in 1962 as the Resident
of Buganda, remembered the baraza, that institution
taken over from the African chiefs, as the main way for the
touring official to meet the people. It was an opportunity
both to explain government policies and to hear complaints. Mutual leg-pulling was often the style. Villagers
would try to bait the bwana by saying something outrageous.

If they succeeded in making the DC turn a little pink in the
face or stutter with rage then this was their day and they all
roared with laughter [Richard Stone recalled]. But of course
the DC was also able to pull their legs a bit, and so we carried
on these proceedings with the greatest of friendship and
enjoyment.

The picture was painted in darker colours by Patrick
Mullins, who served in Nyasaland from 1952 to 1964:

It was a tradition of the country that they were hospitable to
visitors and this went for the white bwana as much as it did
for anyone else. Much of what the DC was always on about
cannot have been particularly welcome to them, particularly
the enforcement of agricultural rules or the collection of taxes,
and I think behind it all most of the village Africans rather
wanted to be left alone and not bothered on these subjects.
But there was no active resentment; I think this was mostly
town-bred. The villagers were polite and attentive and one

always felt a little that they weren't too sorry when you went away again.

As late as the 1930s, even at the topmost level, touring parties in Uganda operated very much as the caravans from the coast of half a century before. Violet Bourdillon, wife of the then-governor, recalled: "I marched every bit of Uganda; we had two fly-tents that we slept under and everything was portered and done on the march."

Yet timelessness was an illusion: already in that decade it was possible to fly from Britain to Uganda. A flying boat service starting from Poole in Dorset made several night-stops on its way to Lake Victoria. After the Second World War two other innovations changed Africa forever for the Europeans. The drug Paludrine removed the risk of malaria while the four-wheel-drive Land Rover meant for the administrator that "your people were always accessible", as one official told Charles Allen, adding: "You might have an exciting time getting to them, but you did get there. And it really altered things for us." As it did for the Africans being visited.

Those caravans from the coast became redundant in 1901, when the journey to Kampala took a few days sitting down rather than three months walking. What brought about this transformation was the Uganda Railway.

The line was driven across almost 600 miles (970 km) of often fearsome terrain in the quick time of five years. The chief engineer, George Whitehead, with his railhead chief Ronald Preston, directed an indentured Indian labour force which over the duration of the project totalled more than 30,000. Many of these coolies did not go home after the line was completed; they were the founders, with imported Indian troops, of today's East African Asian population.

The death toll on the Uganda Railway would be quite unacceptable by modern standards (a single death was news when the Channel Tunnel was being built); nevertheless, Whitehead and his force successfully bridged the strait between Mombasa Island and the mainland, crossed the Taru Desert, spanned the River Tsavo, crossed the Athi Swamps, found a way onto the floor of the Great Rift Valley and out again, cut a way over the mountains on the far side of the valley before bringing the 1-m (3.3-ft) gauge rails to a place beside Lake Victoria that the engineer named Port Florence (later Kisumu). From here steamers crossed the lake to the port for Kampala. From sea level at Mombasa the line climbed to 8,300 ft (2,550 m) at the Mau Summit (beyond the Rift) before dropping more than 5,000 ft (1,500 m) to the lake.

Driving a great railway forward mile by determined mile is a romatic undertaking anywhere, but seldom can builders have had such an inspiring goal as that legendary inland sea. Ronald Hardy in *The Iron Snake* imagines Whitehead's feelings when, from far away atop the Mau Escarpment, he glimpsed Lake Victoria for the first time:

> On the crest of the hill they waited for the light to strengthen, for the sun to suck mists from the plateau and the plains of the west. It was very cold. Below, the forest ended abruptly and the grass, greening now in sunlight, ran in immense meadows, into purple, into distance. There, behind the mist and perhaps one hundred miles (160 km) distant, Rashedi said, lay the north-east tip of the Lake. The mist dissolved. Something bright at the limit of vision, like a platter of translucent white glass, spread undefined between land and sky. It was a radiance; no more than that. But this was the Nyanza. "I could have wept," Whitehouse wrote later. "It was as if it had never really existed until then" ...

> Five years had passed since he had learned that his was to be the task of bringing rail to the greatest of the African lakes. During those years his mind had encompassed nothing else. The Lake was too large, too steeped in history and the myth of exploration to admit of other things. The Lake occupied him, overflowed, it seemed, from the spring of his own ambition. He was of course in bondage to it. Failure of the railroad meant failure as a man: for him nothing would lie beyond. He, and others, would drown in the enormity of the failure. Conversely, success meant professional and public honour.

The city of Nairobi, Kenya's capital, was born out of Whitehead's decision to site the headquarters of the railway at a midway point along the line. The colonial administration, which had been nearby at Machakos, could not afford to be off the line of rail and so the new capital was decided upon.

In building the Uganda Railway, many coolies lost their lives to man-eating lions, stealing into the fragile tents at nights. Lieutenant-Colonel John Patterson, who worked on the railway project, produced the 1907 best-seller *The Man-eaters of Tsavo*. He originally laid at least 28 deaths to the lions' door, later dramatically upping the figure to 135. Modern research puts the likely toll at around 35.

More deaths occurred from hostile tribesmen. With smallpox and other diseases that ran through the coolie camps, the overall death toll was 2,493 Asians – a fearful eight per cent of all who built the railway – and five Europeans. Tribal resistance came not from the Masai despite their ferocious reputation. Although the line ran right across their territory, they had enough sense not to run onto the guns of the work parties. It was the Nandi who put up the stiffest resistance to the railway line and the British rule that came with it. They continued to resist until 1905 when they were broken by the authorities' over-whelming firepower.

From the start it was realised that effective administration in Uganda, and the opening up of its trade, depended on the railway and the telegraph. Railway activity was present from the start: Captain James Macdonald was conducting a railway survey even while Captain Frederick Lugard was conquering Buganda on behalf of the Imperial British East Africa Company. The railway was an intensely political creation. Whitehead had to have one eye on the construction and the other on the British House of Commons. He was under constant pressure to cut costs. His problems were compounded by attacks from the radicals led by Henry Labouchere, for whom the project was an exercise in colonial adventurism. Macdonald's projected route over the mountains beyond the Rift was abandoned when one of Whitehead's engineers discovered a lower – and shorter – route to the lake. The saving was many miles, although shallow Port Florence (now Kisumu) was arguably less suitable than Port Victoria where Macdonald's line would have ended.

The telegraph was laid along the railway track but went ahead of the track-laying (it was a favourite target of the Nandi). It also went to Kampala, not just to Port Florence. When any point on the globe's surface can be reached by satellite-linked mobile phones, it is hard for us to imagine the effect this end of isolation must have had on the European residents of Kampala. Where before it took several months to send a message and get a reply (the time needed to take a message to the nearest telegraph station and bring back the answer), the same could now be accomplished in minutes. The world was becoming a global village even then. The railway also abolished time and distance, or so it seemed to those used to the trek to the coast taking three months: that journey could now be done in comfort in easily less than a week, including the steamer crossing.

All glory fades. Despite the hard-won triumph of making a way to the lake, despite the elation of bringing the rails to the water's edge, the last part of Whitehead's route, including some of the most challenging engineering on the line, was to become a branch when the railway was extended around the lake. An extension to Jinja was completed in 1928, and the opening of the Nile railway bridge in 1931 finally brought the railway to the Uganda capital.

The European presence in Uganda was strongly felt with schools and medicine. The Christian missions founded the formal education system in Uganda, especially after the declaration of the protectorate in 1894. Bishop Tucker reported that in 1898 enrolment in Church Missionary Society (CMS) schools was still only a few hundred but by 1903 the number had grown to 22,000. Growth continued to be rapid: the total primary school enrolment in 1911-12 for all Christian missions in the country was 80,482.

The religious make-up of Uganda changed, reflecting the fact that it was ruled by a Protestant power. Although the Roman Catholics had been more numerous than the Protestants in pre-colonial times, the (Anglican) CMS became the chief beneficiary of government policy. Of those 80,482 primary school pupils in 1911-12 (according to figures cited by Ado K. Tiberondwa in *Missionary Teachers As Agents of Colonialism*), the CMS accounted for 56,482, dwarfing the efforts of the (Roman Catholic) White Fathers and Mill Hill Fathers. In the early 1920s, government financial support for CMS mission activities was broadly the same as for the Roman Catholic missions combined. But the Protestants' success also came from their own efforts. The government stated in 1909 that they had been quicker than the Catholics to recognise that the growth of the educational system depended on the supply of trained African teachers.

An official analysis of Buganda (not the whole of Uganda) by faith illustrated how Protestantism over-hauled Catholicism in the early years of the 20th century:

	CMS missions	RC missions	Muslims	Animists*
1911	140,144	181,141	58,401	325,929
1915	186,672	187,592	55,262	252,267
1916	200,308	186,298	51,783	238,544

(The Handbook of Uganda 1920, cited by Tiberondwa)
*The actual term used was "non-readers"

The policy of the British Empire was religious toleration and neutrality, but inevitably much of the African elite took on the religious colouration of the rulers. Mwanga's son, Daudi Chwa, who was declared kabaka of Buganda as a child, was baptised a Protestant. By 1924, 38 out of the 50 senior chiefs in the country were Protestant. Only in Buganda, the scene of the original Protestant-Roman Catholic competition, did the numbers approach parity: 10 Protestants and eight Catholics, with two Muslims.

Until the end of the colonial administration in the 1960s, it was common for the main Protestant church in each district to place a reserved chair for the British district commissioner, with next to that a chair for the chief. For Tiberondwa, this tended to lock the chiefs into the religion of the rulers. The point need not be pressed too far, however, because some DCs were not Protestant. The Empire was officially secular and did not recruit only Protestants.

The irrelevance of much missionary teaching to African daily experience even shocked secular observers at the time. Simple village children who could barely read and write their own language were taught to worship in the Roman Catholic Church using meaningless Latin; other

children learnt exhaustively about the Rivers Thames and
Severn or how the Vikings invaded England and Hannibal
crossed the Alps.

The Phelps-Stokes Commission, which reported in 1922
and 1924 on Ugandan education, commented eloquently:

> The music you hear will not be a native song but the parody of
> a familiar European hymn. None of the acute problems of vil-
> lage housing, sanitation, water or food preparation are pres-
> ent either in theory or practice ... The chorus of unintelligible
> sounds is the sing-song of the syllables as they follow one
> another in meaningless succession. You will hear reading, but
> it will not describe, explain or appreciate any of the hundred
> and one real things and actions of the village ... In fact you
> will wonder if the schools belong to the village world at all.
> (Quoted by Tiberondwa)

Writing in 1978, Tiberondwa offers a mixed assessment of
missionary-based education in colonial Uganda:

> Missionaries have been praised and praised again for bringing
> education and Christianity to Africa. Indeed the missionaries
> deserve these praises because, despite its limitations and fail-
> ures here and there, Western education definitely contibuted
> to African development ... When education enslaves one to
> foreign values as colonial education has done to the Africans,
> then that education cannot be regarded as successful because,
> instead of providing freedom to the Africans, that education
> has taken African freedom away.

In the immediate sense pinpointed by the Phelps-Stokes
Commission, that concentration on foreign values was
plainly wrong. Colonialism also produced the "cultural
cringe" whereby the foreign values were simply assumed
to be superior. Perhaps we should say colonialism accelerated the cultural cringe. In any situation human beings
tend to copy the leaders, whether countries, cultures, products or personal role models. However, a further question
lies beyond Tiberondwa's valid remarks: was it ever possible to have the pluses of missionary education without the
minuses? Everyone, after all, teaches out of his or her own
background. Indeed, in a Christian context what are foreign values and what are universal ones?

Three generations of expatriates give us snapshots of the European impact on colonial and post-colonial Uganda. These sketches are from the earlier part of the 20th century, the 1950s and the 1990s.

Medical missionary Albert Cook came out with a Church Missionary Society party in 1896 and 37 years later was still working in the country at the CMS hospital in Kampala. He did not die until 1951, by which time the simple mission doctor was Sir Albert Cook KCMG. His life has been described in *The Church Missionary Society and Modern Medicine in Uganda*, written and privately published in 1978 by Professor W.D. Foster of Makerere University, Kampala.

Cook's party reached Uganda by the established caravan safari route from Mombasa except that the first seven miles (11km) were accomplished along the fledgling Uganda Railway in a truck pushed by the engine. Then the railway ran out, and it was for three months to cover more than 600 miles (970 km) to Mengo.

In the Buganda capital Cook was given a typical missionary house, made of muli (bundles of bamboo) with the windows and doorways also framed with muli. Curtains of bark cloth gave privacy. At night shutters also made of bamboo were used. A "certain Spartan level of comfort", in Professor Foster's phrase, could be achieved; an 1898 photo shows an interior with pictures hanging from the muli walls and serviceable camp furniture. The simplicity of this housing contrasts with the solidity of Alexander Mackay's mission station at Usambiro several years earlier, which had 2ft (0.6m) thick clay walls. But by the mid-Nineties there were many CMS missionaries in Uganda. The count in 1897 was 38 throughout the protectorate – far more men than women – which was almost the same number of Europeans as were in the government (40).

Cook was a capable as well as enthusiastic doctor. He performed an appendectomy a year before that on King Edward VII, which was itself hailed as a pioneering operation. He also removed a disfiguring growth from a patient's face against the advice of a medical colleague. That patient became a dedicated hospital assistant at a time when it was hard to persuade local people to do the work.

The CMS soon found there was a culture clash between
its desire to recruit hospital assistants and the willingness
of the Baganda to take these jobs. A vital practical consideration was that hospital work meant soiling hands. For a
people who ate with their fingers, that meant they could
not use the communal bowl of matoke – cooked, unripe
bananas, producing a staple food with the texture of
mashed potato – at home. It was like being a leper in one's
own house.

Mengo Hospital, where Cook was based, charged fees to
those who could afford to pay. The scale of charges was:

OUT-PATIENTS. One to five cents or if wearing
European coats, 10 cents; chiefs and Indians, one rupee
including four days' supply of medicine; Europeans and
Goanese, three rupees, or five rupees for a home visit.

IN-PATIENTS. Five rupees a day. Operation fees
ranged from five to 300 rupees. Africans were not charged
fees as in-patients except for circumcision operations in
venereal cases.

Cook was often called away from the hospital, sometimes over many miles, to treat sick colleagues or their
families, which meant disregarding his African patients
with their endless burden of ailments big and small. As
well as the problem of allocating time between colleagues
and local people, the medical missionary was part-doctor
and part-evangelist, and had to decide what the proportions were. Care of the body was a way of winning the soul
for Christ, but should medicine become the missionary's
preoccupation?

Mengo Hospital was open to all but attendance at religious instruction was a condition of treatment. Cook
recorded:

> (A)t first this led to some little demur on the part of the
> Roman Catholics, who came and protested, but I said they
> must either have our Gospel-preaching and medicine, or go
> without the latter. They chose to attend.

Matters of religion were fraught in other ways. In 1904 a
CMS caravan was heading for Acholi in the north of the
protectorate, beyond the Blue Nile. En route it discharged
three porters – two Muslims and a Catholic – to avoid the

risk of competing doctrines in the mission field. Cook, who was with the party, reported that the terrifying Acholi, who were naked and villainous-looking to European eyes, were most friendly; "not a spear has been raised, or a bow bent against us and we are to all intents and purposes as safe here as say, on Hampstead Heath (in London)".

Cook's facility with languages meant he was often given assignments away from the hospital. He could pick up in a few weeks enough of a language to preach and be understoood when many of his colleagues struggled for years with Luganda or Swahili. In 1905 Cook was chosen to lead a caravan into the southern Sudan to link up with missionaries sent from Khartoum by the British governor there. The caravan had more than 50 porters – and a bicycle, which Cook was able to use some of the way. He intended to ride from Hoima in Bunyoro back to Mengo in two days. This was more than 120 miles (190km), which if achieved is an interesting illustration of the improving condition of the roads.

The outward journey took the party through or close to places that proclaimed the memory of vanished Equatoria: Dufile, Rejaf, Gondokoro itself, the former headquarters of Sir Samuel Baker, General Gordon, Emin Pasha ... Crossing into the Sudan (the border was later moved back to near Dufile), the party at first based itself in Mongalla where the local tribe was the Bari, sparse in numbers, unsophisticated and reputedly hostile. Remarkably, Cook did not have any firearms in his caravan.

He did "not feel naturally drawn to" the Bari but he remembered they had "souls which are just as precious to God as our own" and he was sure "God will implant in my heart a real desire for their salvation". Their time was not yet, however, because the party moved downriver to Bor, still within the borders of Emin Pasha's old province. This was decided by the Khartoum group because the Dinka around Bor were seen as more promising mission subjects than the Bari. In only four months Cook learnt the Dinka language well enough to translate the Anglican morning and evening services (leaving out the prayers for the Royal Family) and 12 hymns.

Professor Foster remarks: "The rapid growth of the

Anglican Church in Buganda owed much to the conviction
of the pioneer missionaries that the translation of the
Bible was a necessary part of their proclamation of the
gospel." Among Cook's language contributions in Luganda
was a book of Ganda proverbs with Christian parallels, a
medical phrase book and a revision of George Pilkington's
Luganda-English grammar. Pilkington, who was responsi-
ble for completing the translation of the entire bible, had
previously worked with Alexander Mackay on the New
Testament, and Mackay alone had even earlier translated
St Matthew's gospel. The United Bible Societies still follow
this sequence of book (known as a portion), testament and
bible in their ongoing work among the world's languages.

In 1931, three years before he retired from Mengo
Hospital although not completely from medical work, Cook
met one of the historic figures in the Uganda story. This
was Lord Lugard, who in 1891-92 had secured the country
for Britain with a handful of soldiers and who went on to
become Britain's greatest African pro-consul. Cook and his
wife Katharine were on furlough in England. Lugard, by
then in his seventies, invited them to his house in Surrey.
Cook commented:

> Lord Lugard was *charming* (original emphasis), with his deli-
> cate clear-cut voice, his old-fashioned courtesy, his scholarly
> habits and penetrating mind. It was an education to be in his
> company and learn from him.

The final years of the widowed Albert Cook were shadowed
by increasing dependence on morphine. What had started
as mild therapeutic doses turned into addiction to a drug
that as a doctor he had only too easy access to. A disappointment was that the world seemed uninterested in the
memoirs that summed up his life of work and worship.
Professor Foster acknowledges that Cook's *Forty Years in
Uganda* is "dull". Failing to find a commercial publisher
who would issue it in the form he wanted, Cook offered the
manuscript to the CMS editorial department. "We have, as
it were, laid it at His feet to be used in His service as He
thinks best," said Cook. The CMS too found they could
manage without it. Eventually it was published by the
Uganda Society as *Uganda Memories.*

When Tommy Gee was in Bunyoro, from 1951 to 1954, he found a low level of political consciousness compared with Buganda. The Lost Counties – land claimed by Bunyoro and lost to Buganda – were, he said (speaking half a century later*), not a live issue; Kabalega was "an historical figure", not the folk hero he has become in modern Uganda.

The Gee family were typical of colonial administrators, who saw themselves not as conquistadores but as promoters of development among their other roles – the Oxfam and Christian Aid workers of their day. Tommy was first assistant district commissioner and then district commissioner. He was only in his twenties. Looking back, he felt it was a measure of the lack of importance attached to Bunyoro that a more senior officer was not appointed as DC. He explained:

> Bunyoro was a kingdom defeated by the Baganda so it was greatly impoverished and a far cry from its former glory, but it had its pride, and remembered when they'd won their fights against the Baganda.

He and his wife, Anne spent 17 years in Uganda. "We were privileged to be sent to undertake the work," said Tommy. "Some of the colonial powers were exploitative, for example, Belgium in the Congo. I believe that one day Britain's overall record will be recognised despite the bad things."

Tommy showed he was no flag-wagging imperialist by being asked to stay on after independence in 1962. He was among the five per cent of expatriates "on the side of the angels", as the local people put it. He became permanent secretary for education charged with securing a massive increase in secondary schools.

The Gees left Uganda in 1965, with Tommy later pursuing a career in international development. "We said we'd never go back because we didn't want to interfere. We'd handed over and we felt it was wrong to go back." It all remained vivid, however, and 50 years later the Gees were still following events in Uganda.

---

* Interview with author

Life in Bunyoro certainly was not luxurious for Tommy, Anne and their children. The family had no meat, milk or butter because of trypanosomiasis (tryps), as well as rinderpest, East Coast fever and occasionally anthrax. Water was scarce and had to be carried on mules to the house. Malarial mosquitoes were a constant hazard. One of the children died of pneumonia soon after birth.

Tommy shot guinea fowl and brought them home for a meal. He contracted typhoid fever but survived. One colleague died of blackwater fever. Another was eaten by a lion. He went after it in the bush following a close hit, and it took him.

Tito Winyi, the mukama, his wife (the omugu) and many of the Nyoro chiefs lacked the sophistication of their opposite numbers in Buganda, Tommy remembered. Leading Baganda had access to the best schools, and some sent their children to England for education.

Kabalega's hostility to Britain had not been passed down in the Gees' everyday experience.

We found no hostility towards the British. On the contrary, expatriates were made use of. We weren't dealing with the big things for the most part. We were practically useful.

Anne's dinner party was an example. This was to be a grand affair including the kabaka of Buganda and other kings on the occasion of their biennial rulers' conference. There would be no problem with crockery and cutlery for the big numbers; "we have all that", the palace said.

Stored in a large hut, Anne found, was an "Aladdin's cave" of items presented as gifts to the bakama over the years, unused and many of them in the original packing and wrapping. A blue vase known to have been presented by Sir Samuel Baker was not to be found, however.

The dinner was a great success. The guests tucked into a three-course western meal with the ever-popular steak.

Another case in point that Tommy recalled was an ex-servicemen's resettlement scheme at Kigumba, where bush was cleared to grow tobacco and other cash crops under the guidance of an agriculturalist.

Broader issues like representative government, our sense of

justice, and law and order, did penetrate, though [Tommy added].

I remember some anxious occasions when we had to enforce law and order, but on the whole our administration was peaceful, just, respected and accepted. People knew that we were there to protect them, and to provide access to the West's education, medicine, agriculture, technology, democracy and so on.

Milton Obote's political war-cry was that the Uganda Peoples' Congress would combat poverty, ignorance and disease. He was continuing our policies, but was more succinct and connected with the people.

Tommy was very aware that the truncated Bunyoro was not well endowed agriculturally unlike the enlarged Buganda. The only serious cash crop was tobacco while Buganda grew rich on coffee and cotton.

This and the small population put the Banyoro "at a serious disadvantage", he says. Large herds of cattle were kept outside Bunyoro. Anne's fillet steaks came from slaughter of royal cattle kept outside the kingdom.

A census in 1959 gave the population of Bunyoro as 128,198 and Buganda as 1,881,149. Buganda's land area at that time was about $3^{1}/2$ times that of Bunyoro, but the population was more than 14 times greater. Yet before the coming of the British the two kingdoms were able to engage each other militarily on level terms. With colonialism development became focused on Buganda. It is a dramatic illustration of the adage "To the victor the spoils".

Politics entered Bunyoro in a big way when, with independence in view, the governor, Sir Andrew Cohen, was promoting a unitary state in Uganda. This had implications for the historic kingdoms, and required a revision of the Bunyoro Agreement.

Guided by Tommy, the mukama and his chiefs signed the changes. "The kabaka of Buganda wouldn't sign – and you know what happened to him (he was deported to Britain)."

Tommy was very young. Looking back, he admitted to doubts about the wisdom of a unitary state in Uganda. "We had promised indirect rule from first contact, and a federal state was the logical conclusion. A unitary western democracy has been at the root of misuse of power and led to the collapse of good government."

The Rev Stephen Coulson was a Church Mission Society "mission partner" in 1998, working as the principal of a Church of Uganda theological college at Namugongo, scene of the 1886 massacre. He said, speaking at the time:*

> They stopped calling us missionaries a few years ago and called us mission partners. There wasn't any embarrassment about the word "missionary", but they felt the new term "mission partner" more clearly reflected what we are – working in partnership with and under the authority of the church here. They would say our contribution to the church is not in big donations but in personnel, in the interchange of sending people here and bringing people from Uganda to Britain.

> The CMS role has changed from pioneering and a sort of authoritative controlling work to just humbly being in partnership. You can't find a CMS office in Kampala because it's not an NGO (non-governmental organisation) functioning as an independent society. It's just here to feed into and be a partner under the church. The other side of that is that over the years CMS has brought Ugandans to Britain for study or sometimes for ministry in the Church of England. Occasionally it has been able to provide bursaries for Ugandan clergy to go somewhere else.

Students at Namugongo included five from Sudan and three from Rwanda as well as Ugandans. Among the 50 or so CMS personnel in the country, including partners and dependants,was a family working with Sudanese Christians at Arua, near the borders with Sudan and Congo.

> They (the CMS personnel) are working at the Bishop Allison Theological College, where students – pastors and lay people – come from southern Sudan really as refugees. An office for the Church of Sudan is being set up in Kampala. A CMS lady is helping in the logistics of that, and in the future she wants to go up to Arua to be of service to the churches in southern Sudan.

* Personal interview

One of CMS's concerns in the last few years has been particularly to try and see how they can help in the whole work of refugees. I think they would like to be doing more at Arua. Here in Uganda we also have quite a lot to do with the mission partners in the neighbouring countries, particularly in Congo. Twice in the last two years they have all had to be evacuated, and they have come to Uganda as the first stop.

The Namugongo college is an offshoot of the former Bishop Tucker Theological College at Mukono, now renamed the Uganda Christian University. Stephen explained: "Many of the churches here have a university. There's a Catholic university, an Adventist university, a Muslim university. The Anglican Church felt for a number of years that it ought to have its own university, and so Bishop Tucker became a university offering degrees particularly in education and social sciences as well as teaching theology."

He listed other CMS personnel at work in Uganda at that time – a woman with the education department in Kampala, a couple at a hospital in Luwero, an architect at Fort Portal, a husband and wife team of occupational therapist and hospital engineer in Kampala and a medical family due to take up Aids prevention in Kampala.

Before moving to Namugongo with his wife and four children, Stephen worked for four years with churches serving slum areas at the base of Namirembe hill, near the original CMS mission site, where the cathedral now stands. Here he saw Aids at first hand:

> In the slum areas where I was working the incidence of HIV-positive would be even higher than the official one in three figure, I think. That's the sexually active adult population, say 15 to 30 in particular. It's the future and it's the useful workforce. Old people are not dying of AIDS. Babies are dying of AIDS, being born with HIV from their parents.

> When I was in Britain I worked for three years as a curate in Birmingham, and only one time did I bury anyone younger than me. Since I came to Uganda I rarely bury people older than me, aged 38.

> The HIV rate in the slum areas seems to me more devastating, but even out here in the villages what I have noticed real-

ly is the loss of children. We baptised my daughter with 22 other children one memorable Sunday last year. I've buried five or six of her baptismal classmates, which has been very poignant for me remembering that great day when they were baptised together. Children whose mothers have HIV have a 40-50 per cent chance of being infected.

Against this background, one of his worries about Uganda's booming Pentecostal churches was the practice of all-night prayer meetings – "fairly irresponsible in terms of the freedom and opportunity it gives young people to be promiscuous".

His job as the CMS representative in Uganda was "very low key":

It's just helping out other mission partners, particularly when they arrive, and occasionally acting as a representative of the society at great events like the consecration of a new bishop. Each mission partner is under the individual diocese or institution with which they're working, but on the rare occasion when the church here needs to communicate something to all mission partners they might come to me and say you're the representative, it's your job to tell the others.

Stephen acknowledged the "huge history of polarisation" between Protestants and Roman Catholics in Uganda, which continued for many years after the hoped-for settlement of the issue with the Uganda Agreement of 1900. He insisted that "things have got so much better" in the last few years.

Many of Uganda's leading politicians and officials went to CMS-founded schools, particularly Gayaza for girls and Budo, mainly for boys. At Gayaza, three women teachers notched up more than 100 years' service between them.

When I meet top Ugandan ladies, I can almost guarantee half of them have gone to Gayaza and they'll say what about Miss Warren, what about Miss Hobday, what about Miss Cutler? They'll say how much they owe to those ladies and their input.

I preached at Budo at one of their founder's days. Several members of the cabinet who had been through that school were there listening to me preach, which took me aback a bit. Many of their teachers were from Britain and many were CMS.

Not only at Namugongo but throughout Uganda the spirit of the Christian martyrs is ever-present. Just outside Kampala, at Natete, "Mackay's church" was built by the pioneer missionary. Nearby is a cave where Protestants used to hide during the religious troubles.

> There are people alive today who remember Namugongo survivors, who obviously knew the boys who were murdered. It's only been a generation or so ago, and that's why it continues to be celebrated. Their witness gave such life to the church.

The martyrs include Bishop Hannington on the Buganda road. Hannington is a popular Christian name in Uganda. "There's a lot of looking back to those first missionaries, and also a great affection for missionaries in living memory – people like Roy Billington at Mengo Hospital," said Stephen. Dr Billington served in Uganda from 1939 until his retirement in 1971.

The finite resources of the Church Mission Society have to be shared among several mission fields around the world. It is up to individual church leaders to put in their requests for help. The CMS sees itself as a responding organisation – just as it so famously responded to Stanley's call of 1875 for "practical Christian tutors". Stephen said:

> Partnership is a key word of CMS's whole philosophy of what it's doing. Each mission partner has come to Uganda because a bishop has made a request to CMS. It sees itself very much as responding to requests from the church in Uganda.

One of the priorities of the early missionaries was to provide Scripture in the local language. Alexander Mackay translated St Matthew's gospel into Luganda, and the entire bible was completed by George Pilkington. Stephen was delighted that the Luganda bible published by the Bible Society of Uganda was "probably the cheapest book you can buy as a big hardback ... when people get to sixth form, they have to buy a number of textbooks and the equivalent size is far more expensive".

Even so, the bible cost almost one week's earnings based

on the average national per capita income. All is not what
it seems, however. Villagers who are largely outside the
cash economy (and depress the national income statistics)
can do things in another way.

> Villagers are basically self-sufficient for all they need to eat.
> They haven't got money to spend on a bicycle or a car or fine
> clothes, but in this part of central Uganda you can't imagine
> them starving if they're willing to dig the land. The climate
> and the ground are good. The villagers have a very small
> income on paper, but they may get a few harvests of matoke
> (cooking bananas). If I go to a village to preach and I come
> back with a pick-up loaded with matoke and chicken and
> pineapples, I'm very grateful. But while I really appreciate it,
> it hasn't actually cost them so much in money terms.

> You can't buy bibles this way, but if you want the cost of a
> bible, you might put two bunches of matoke on the bicycle and
> cycle them to the road (to sell). You wouldn't be able to raise
> your annual income fivefold that way, but for a one-off thing
> you would be able to make it.

Stephen said: "CMS has been a huge influence in Uganda
not just in the church but in schools and hospitals. (As he
spoke, a current mission partner was the engineer at
Mengo Hospital, founded by the CMS in the 1890s.)
Probably a dozen or more big hospitals around the country
were church-founded or CMS-founded."

In fact, the CMS is so well known in Uganda that many
older people describe themselves as "CMS" rather than
Anglican. Stephen added: "I think all primary school children would know what CMS stands for because it's one of
the questions they quite often get in history lessons. In
exam papers asking what do the following initials stand
for, CMS is often there."

19 Mindset of the masters

David Livingstone's vision of a benign coming together of "commerce and Christianity" was only half-realised. That half is Christianity, which whatever the false turns along the way has mutated into an indigenous religion in equal partnerships with churches around the world. Commerce in Africa, on the other hand, quickly turned into colonialism, which in all but name has lasted to this day. Western nations continue to make their own rules for trade and aid with Africa.

Perhaps the flaw in the vision was that commerce between continents of such unequal power and development as Europe and Africa could be separated from political control and the arrogance of power that comes with it. Racial attitudes became entrenched among the whites. F. Spencer Chapman (in another setting a Second World War hero and the author of a famous war book, *The Jungle Is Neutral*) took his family on a motor tour of southern and central Africa in 1953. He wrote about the journey in *Lightest Africa*.

Spencer Chapman's chapter Into Uganda, which is 12 pages long, uses the term "native" 15 times. Among the references are "native villages" and "natives (who) paddled dugout canoes" – as if anyone else might be expected in the heart of Africa! At a resthouse a "native" did the family's washing, and other "natives" tried to dig the author's vehicle out of a swamp. While the N-word did not carry today's perjorative meaning, Spencer Chapman nevertheless reveals himself as a man who does not see just human beings but people in racial categories.

The same chapter describes his excitement at getting permission "to go to remote Karamoja, which is not normally opened to tourists, to see the really primitive African" – language which half a century later we might use about the Rwanda gorillas.

European attitudes to Africans in the colonial period ranged from the bone-headed to the humane. After marching into Kumase (Asante) in 1896, Colonel Scott, the commander of the British expeditionary force, was asked to rescue eight captives awaiting execution. He replied that "he was sure the black people did not mind or care much about their fate". Colonel F.J. Kempster angrily objected that all human beings cared about their lives. Reluctantly, Scott agreed to free the captives.*

Colonialism bred a sense of inferiority among the Africans to which religious organisations were party. The church-run Mengo Hospital, admittedly with the best intentions as noted previously, charged fees based on race. Missionary schools taught children about the Thames and the Seine, the Alps and the Pyrennees, rather than the Nile and the Ruwenzori.

In 19th century Africa, however, the alternatives were not stable indigenous rule or European colonialism. Indigenous rule was rarely stable. The introduction of firearms escalated the constant warfare that plagued the continent, creating more opportunities for one African people to colonise another. It was not a foregone conclusion that Britain would take over Buganda from the IBEA Company, but if it had not another European power would have stepped in.

British colonisation became inevitable in Uganda partly because a section of the missionary community, the Anglicans, came to believe that externally imposed order and stability provided the best soil for Christianity to grow in, and had the political clout to promote its ends. The White Fathers wanted to leave indigenous rule untouched, but Lugard made the realistic point that this would have produced an arms free-for-all and continued turmoil.

Despite the Church Missionary Society's formidable lobbying abilities, it would be fanciful to think that religious groups could single-handedly determine major political outcomes. The other factor that made colonisation inevitable was trade. The Great Lakes region was rich in elephants. Stanley's *In Darkest Africa* acknowledged the importance of ivory when it spoke of "every tusk, piece and scrap" being "steeped and dyed in blood", of "the rich heart of Africa" laid waste for ornaments and billiard games.

---

* The incident is described by Robert B. Edgerton in *The Fall of the Asante Empire*, quoting an eye-witness.

Uganda from the start was perceived as worth trading with, provided it could be reached by railway; Kenya initially was not, although the fact of the Uganda Railway passing through it triggered trade and development. The railway proved to be so expensive to build – more than twice the projected costs of the first surveyor, Captain James Macdonald – that trade had to be found quickly to justify the outlay. This forced the emergence of cash crops in Uganda and Kenya, and with the plantations, particularly in Kenya, came white settlers. The Uganda Railway offers a curious circularity: it was built to allow trade, and trade had to be created to allow the railway. Cotton, coffee, tea, sugar, maize, wheat and livestock were among the commodities to emerge.

Colonisation is as old as the human experience, with both Bunyoro and Buganda being colonial powers in their day. Buganda when the Europeans arrived was an expansionary power surrounded by tributary states.

The distinctive elements in European colonialism were its global nature and its all-pervasiveness on the ground. Where earlier imperialisms were intermittent, perhaps requiring nothing more than the annual payment of tribute, European colonial administrations were never far away from the administered.

We can glimpse from the few non-western states around the world that were never colonised what might have happened in Uganda. These include Thailand, Afghanistan, northern Yemen, Liberia and Ethiopia (disregarding the late and short period of Italian occupation). These now are not so very different from adjacent ex-colonies. They are not strikingly more advanced; in fact, the opposite is true. On the positive side, the non-colonies are proud of having kept their independence, and this at some level must rub off on individual psyches.

Although they stumbled in Bunyoro, Britain's colonial administrators believed they were taking part in the development of the countries in their charge. The words of Sir Harry Johnston, the architect of the Uganda Agreement, as expressed in *A History and Description of the British Empire in Africa* (undated but around 1910), can serve as the credo of generations of imperial civil servants:

> It is only by maintaining [Johnston wrote] a perfectly honest administration of these lands assigned – perhaps only temporarily – to our control, that we shall merit the distinguished position in which we have been placed by circumstances, and that without recourse to mere force we may be able to maintain ourselves as rulers in Africa, with the full consent and fraternal co-operation of the Negroes, negroids, and other backward coloured peoples, for whom we are doing what the Romans and the Normans did for us.

It is easy today to mock the idea of Britain doing for Africa "what the Romans and the Normans did for us", but the cynicism belongs to a later age – our own.

Johnston – also a naturalist who was the first to identify the okapi – returned a few years later to the theme of the equality of races through progress. In 1920 he published *The Backward Peoples and Our Relations with Them*. (This includes a map of Africa shaded to show perceived degrees of backwardness!)

The closing words of Johnston's book were cited approvingly by Roland Oliver in 1957 as "a passage which belongs in sentiment nearer to 1950 than to 1920". (*Sir Harry Johnston and the Scramble for Africa*)

> The Coloured man on the other hand must remember [Johnston wrote] that his lands cannot properly be developed without railways and without the White man's capital; and the White man in Europe and North America is not going to risk his money where there is no security and where he runs the danger of losing his capital and the investment of his energy. Without the tapping of wealth in rock and soil and desert sand, the Coloured man will always remain poor and futile.

> But the White peoples must try to realize that the still Backward races, the still-decrepit nations, have travelled far in intellectuality since the middle of the nineteenth century, and that the continuance of an insulting policy towards them will join them some day in a vast league against Europe and America, which will set back the millennium and perhaps even ruin humanity in general. Nature will have conquered by setting one half of mankind against the other.

In the 21st century, the leading industrial nations still dictate the conditions of trade to the Majority World, which becomes increasingly restive. It progressively acts as a voting bloc in trade fora, underlining the pertinence of Johnston's warning.

For westerners of the late 19th and early 20th centuries it was usual to believe that nations evolve towards the highest forms of civilisation. When Apolo Kaggwa, the katikiro of Buganda, visited England, an official told him: "We were like you once or even worse, and you too if you work hard will be like we are now." (Quoted by D.A. Low: *Fabrication of Empire*)

Few dare to express evolutionary beliefs today, but behind the lip-service to relativism the reality is much the same. This is tacitly accepted by leaders in the Majority World, who welcome experts from the First World and generally embrace the idea of development. Favoured concepts like *good governance* and *civil society* require the evolution of political and social structures, while the growth of economies depends on changes to fiscal, credit and trading practices.

The separation of executive and judiciary, elected governments, individual titles in land and freedom of association, expression and religion can hardly be called specifically western. They are characteristics of the developed nations, most of which happen to be western, but upon examination they emerge as the universal desires of humanity. We no longer use the word, at least without inverted commas, but a society that has these characteristics is more *civilised* than one that does not.

What colonialism suppressed, in Africa and elsewhere, was the emergence of an indigenous First World sector amid Third World conditions. This might have been a driver for faster development. Every country in the world, no matter how underdeveloped, has a modern sector. It may still be tiny today, but its fortunate inhabitants not only live to a First World standard (or better) but also think in First World terms.

As late as 1963, Margery Perham, the doyenne of British Africanists and the biographer of Lord Lugard, felt able to express this evolutionary perspective in plain words when she described the European impact on African society. In spite of the apparently settled conditions of the colonial years, "two acids were eating into the healthy cells

of family and tribal life". (*The Colonial Reckoning*) They
were the Western money economy and Christian education. These forces weakened old cultures before they could
build new ones.

Through the money economy young men were drawn
away from the village, and the cash they earned "bit into
the authority of status". Old men sat outside their huts in
"otiose bewilderment" as the younger ones "broke off from
the clustered group and became units floating hither and
thither in the open restless currents of the fluctuating
exchange economy".

Christian education elevated the book-learned child
above the illiterate parent. The child "would lose respect
for the ancestors and perhaps regard the religious or mag-
ical powers of the chief and the medicine man as heathen
superstition and polygamy as a sin". The Christian school-
boy might find himself in "a mental no-man's-land".

Perham pointed out that many peoples of the world had
been through such a process. In Africa, however, the
impact had been sudden and came from outside.

For Gardner Thompson, in *Governing Uganda*, the colonial government was anything but all powerful. Change
was as much managed by Africans as by the government.
The colonial state was marked by "limited power, minimal
cost, and modest pretension". It had its eccentric touches.
Governor Andrew Cohen, for example, was well known for
visiting peasant households on his bicycle.

Even as independence drew near the mass of the population made little reaction against colonial rule, because in
Thompson's view there was little to react against. Britain
showed an absence of bad intentions. A case in point is
when the Colonial Office in London decided against a close
association between Kenya and Uganda for fear that white
settlers in Kenya would dominate. (This was the issue that
bedevilled and then destroyed the Central African
Federation of Southern Rhodesia [Zimbabwe], Northern
Rhodesia [Zambia] and Nyasaland [Malawi].)

While *Governing Uganda* is in no sense an apologia for
colonialism, it presents a softer view of British rule than
we have been used to reading since independence. By contrast, Anthony Low, the doyen of Uganda historians,

bringing together much of his lifetime's work with the con-
spectus volume, *Fabrication of Empire*, ends the book with
a savage conclusion. Imperialism, he says, was "a state of
being to be endured as well as one could, prior to the
means of getting rid of it".

Thompson's book is refreshingly off-message, perhaps
because it is published in Kampala, the Uganda capital,
far away from the groves of Academe in Europe and North
America, and its author at the time of publication (2003)
was a secondary school teacher, not a university don.

A special headache for relativists is when the colonised
take the part of the colonisers. The Ugandan-born Dr John
Sentamu, who became Archbishop of York and the second-
ranking bishop in the Church of England, told Sarah
Sands of the (London) Daily Mail in an interview
(November 2006):

> While the empire was there, the British thought they were
> doing some good in the world. For me, the vision was what
> made the missionaries go out, made the empire what it was:
> the sense of education, better roads, infrastructure, the sepa-
> ration of the executive from the legislature. All these fantas-
> tic values which, as someone who was a recipient of them, I
> can look back on and say: what a vision!

David Rieff, one of the few modern US writers able to tran-
scend his nation's fixation with colonialism, points out in *A
Bed for the Night* (2002) the similarity between the
European imperialism in the 19th century and the West's
developmentalism in the 21st century. Today's development and relief agencies are seen as the successors of
Victorian missionary societies, driven by many of the same
impulses. Rieff writes of the earlier period:

> (F)or Europeans of the time, not only was there no moral
> incompatability between the antislavery project and the impe-
> rial enterprise, but the latter was seen widely as the guaran-
> tor of the former.

He adds:

> Particularly striking is the similarity in the way the invoca-
> tion of a higher moral norm led, in practice, to an alliance
> between activists intent on relieving suffering and great pow-

ers in the era of late-nineteenth-century imperialism, and to twentieth-century humanitarian interventionism.

... And at least some contemporary humanitarians have not shied away from making the connection between their efforts and Western values almost as explicitly as their nineteenth-century forebears would have done."

Here we must enter the reservation that, as argued above, the values referred to are not western but universal.

The American private relief agencies, Rieff points out, generally espouse the same policy goals as the US government – globalisation, free markets, democratic openings and human rights. Most mainline US humanitarian agencies have taken co-operation with government for granted.

The deepest level of explanation for this is to be found in the abiding Wilsonianism* of the American policy establishment, of which the American humanitarian leadership has always been a member in good standing.

Most European humanitarian groups, too, are in bed with officialdom. Of the world's great relief agencies, Rieff sees the French group Médecins sans Frontières (MSF) as the least involved with governments. The price of this is to be taken as the perpetual "naysayer".

The organisation went through a civil war on the issue. Bernard Kouchner, one of its founders, broke with MSF after he failed in his insistence that humanitarianism should be at the service of governments.

The implication of Rieff's important book is that development suffers when great aid agencies give up their independence and become arms of governments. For all the similarity in beliefs, development is best served by the two staying separate from each other.

---

* Woodrow Wilson, internationalist US president who was the driving force behind the creation of the League of Nations after the First World War

20 Conclusion

The Uganda story is part of a massive historical process in which western powers took on sometimes advanced African states and subdued them through superior technology. Two other examples – Barotseland in what is now Zambia and Asante in modern-day Ghana – have been examined in this book to place Uganda in a comparative perspective.

Comparative but far from the same. Barotseland was taken over in short order by Cecil John Rhodes and his associates in pursuit of mineral riches. Asante fell for political reasons only after decades of coexistence with the British and Dutch authorities on the coast.

In Uganda, however, Christianity triggered the sequence of events that led to colonialism. Explorers paved the way for missionaries, who in turn paved the way for administrators and colonial conquest. Each phase seems to have made the next inevitable without anyone willing it to be so.

Stanley did not appeal for missionaries to go to Buganda because he saw them as a means of Britain seizing the country. Buganda was a victim of its own success: as an advanced state it was especially worth evangelising.

The Anglican missionaries did not head out into the unknown with a political agenda in their pockets. The Catholic missionaries followed them at least partly because they did not want to leave the field clear for their rivals in God. Yet the conflict between these groups magnified the existing instability in Buganda, which in turn opened the way for British political control.

However, an overstretched Britain was not eager to assume control. It did so only after a change of government in London and after the national controversy known as the Uganda Question. Meanwhile, the Buganda conflict spilled over into Bunyoro, and Kabalega was drawn into the net.

The three Europeans who feature most prominently in this book – Henry Morton Stanley, explorer; Alexander Mackay, missionary; Frederick Lugard, soldier – all pos-

sessed exceptional commitment and drive. So too did
Kabalega, the mukama of Bunyoro.

Stanley three times crossed the fearsome Ituri Forest
where his colleagues of the rear column managed a single
journey of less than 100 miles (160km). Mackay was 14
years in Africa without a break while colleagues came and
went, sometimes alone and often with the activity hostility of Mwanga, the kabaka of Buganda. Lugard, with just
50 soldiers, imposed his settlement on the Ganda state
after an earlier representative of the Imperial British East
Africa Company, Frederick Jackson, had left empty-handed despite his 400 soldiers.

This toughness is most visible in Stanley. Practically
every contemporary and subsequent writer has remarked
on his iron will. This willpower was forged in the Welsh
workhouse of his childhood and the America of his young
manhood, where he survived as a solitary runaway. But
tough circumstances by themselves do not produce tough
people: there has to be innate material to work with.

It was the same will that took Stanley across the Ituri
Forest and enabled him to produce his massive two-volume *In Darkest Africa* in just 50 days while sitting in a
Cairo hotel room. To produce a book of that scale – it is
about 400,000 words, or three to four times the length of a
typical modern book – in that time is above all a feat of
willpower and physical energy. No matter what documents
or diary entries were tipped into the book wholesale to
bulk it out, it is a staggering achievement.

Beyond his most obvious quality, Stanley has puzzled
biographers because he was a bundle of opposing characteristics. The Bible-quoting Christian who knew the Good
Book well enough to satisfy Kabaka Mutesa on the subject
of angels is also the person whose brutal methods were
remembered two generations later by the ba-Mbuti pigmies, who hanged several men for punishment and as
examples and who abducted women in order to ransom
them for food.

Few other African travellers carried on in this violent
way. A.J. Mounteney-Jephson, one of Stanley's officers on
the Emin Pasha expedition, gave an example of the
leader's methods when obtaining a canoe:

All day long we could see canoes ahead crossing and re-crossing the river, the natives were very much terrified and hardly seemed to know what to do. We harassed them all day long and Stanley pursued a canoe with four men in it, he shot one of the men and the others jumped ashore and got off. We towed the canoe to the other side of the river with the wounded native in it, but he bled to death before we reached the bank and the men threw him overboard ..." (Quoted by Iain R. Smith: *The Emin Pasha Relief Expedition, 1886-1890*)

And yet Alexander Mackay could comment that Stanley only used violence when he had no alternative and was notably considerate towards Africans. The lion at rest is a peaceable creature. Hungry or threatened, he is dangerous. For Stanley the survival of the expedition and the meeting of its objectives justified the actions needed to bring these about. Where the expedition was not threatened, he became the resting lion that Mackay saw at Usambiro.

Emin Pasha's associate, Gaetano Casati, praised Stanley's "brilliant conversation and gentlemanly courtesy". These were rarely on display for European colleagues on his expeditions for he held himself aloof, often taking his meals alone. He felt separateness to be a necessary attribute of leadership. On the Emin Pasha Relief Expedition, his relations with the other officers were poor, except for Mounteney-Jephson. Throughout his travels, he felt he had found only one equal: David Livingstone. One can see in all this the traces of the workhouse boy and auto-didact, born into the lowest social class and illegitimate as an added burden; ultimately unsure of his place in society and the skills and graces that society demands.

Stanley was the only person who did not see the funny side of his most famous remark: "Dr Livingstone, I presume?" What else, after all, did one say when meeting a stranger? Years later Stanley was being invested with an honorary degree. At a key moment in this dignified ceremony an undergraduate called out "Mr Stanley, I presume?" Everyone laughed except Stanley.

Stanley took his opportunities where he found them. He started life British, became American and ended up British again (and a knight of the realm). He fought on both sides of the American Civil War – a portent for his ambiguous position on the Emin Pasha expedition. He remained under contract to King Leopold of Belgium while leading the expedition (although unpaid) for William Mackinnon of the Imperial British East Africa Company. The two men's ambitions in Equatoria were mutually exclusive, yet Stanley had propositions for Emin from both.

Nor was he above being economical with the truth. Stanley may have been one of those people who, not knowingly lying, are so imbued with self-belief that any setback is overwritten and ceases to exist. *In Darkest Africa* presents an account of the disaster of the rear column in which no blame attaches to the leader. It is patently a selective presentation of the facts designed to exonerate Stanley.

For instance, he emphasises that the tragedy occurred because the rear column stayed at Yambuya and rotted away, but on the evidence (actually in Stanley's book) it is clear that he initially expected the rear column to wait for him to come back, and that moving forward was always just one option. Iain R. Smith, in *The Emin Pasha Relief Expedition, 1886-1890*, says Stanley's inability to make good his promises to Tippu Tip, the Arab trader and ruler, was a key reason for Tippu not supplying enough carriers, which in turn was the reason why the rear column could not move.

Writing, lectures and his years with King Leopold of Belgium building the Congo State made Stanley a rich man. He cheated death from fever many times on his travels, although ever afterwards he suffered from shaking spasms, which he described as "the Africa in me". For his closing years he built a handsome house at Pirbright, Surrey. It had been completed just a few weeks when he caught a chill and died, aged 63.

His controversial reputation followed him to the grave. He was refused burial in Westminster Abbey alongside his hero, Livingstone, and rests in St Michael and All Angels churchyard at Pirbright.

Stanley's house, Furze Hill, became a time capsule associated with the great explorer. The Belgians were keener than the British, and Stanley's heirs sold and in some cases donated to the Royal Museum for Central Africa in

Tervuren huge quantities of archival material in 1954, 1982, 2000 and 2002-03. The papers seemed to keep on coming!

In 2002 Christie's auctioned the remaining contents of Furze Hill. They included treasures like a Winchester rifle that Stanley carried when he met Livingstone at Ujiji, a sextant presented to Stanley by Livingstone's daughter Agnes, Stanley's map that he used in his west-east crossing of Africa, complete with water stains and his personal annotated copy of Sir Richard Buton's *The Lake Regions of Central Africa*, as well as spears, knives, axes, paddles and bows and arrows.

Tom Lamb of Christie's told the Daily Telegraph: "Never before has such a large collection of artefacts relating to one explorer been offered at auction." The collection realised £891,711.

Alexander Mackay embodied Stanley's vision of "practical Christian tutors" to serve as missionaries in Buganda. Mackay was an educated and talented engineer, who was never ordained. He was equally at home mending a boat, improvising a coffin without the proper materials, operating a printing press, translating Scripture into Luganda, proclaiming the faith and even unravelling the structure of Ganda theology.

His amazing versatility was the key to his survival for so long in the always wary and often hostile environment of Mengo. He was simply too useful to the kabaka and the chiefs. Most of them were not after his message but his hands, a fact that he recognised himself in his letters. He believed that practical help built friendship and confidence, from which acceptance of the gospel would naturally follow.

He also possessed physical courage and a stern devotion to duty drawn from the Scottish presbyterianism of his upbringing. He rejected repeated appeals from headquarters to return home on leave; with the journeys it would mean a year away, and that time he would not spare. In 1887, during Mwanga's persecution of the Christians, Mackay wrote: "I have not the slightest desire to 'escape', if I can do a particle of good by staying."

If he had wanted to escape Mackay could have done. The mission's boat, the Eleanor, was lying nearby. He was on his own at the Protestant mission and under continual threat of his life. Even he was driven out in the end as the kabaka became increasingly desperate and set in motion a series of events that resulted in his own undoing. He went only as far as Usambiro on the other side of Lake Victoria, where he kept busy preparing scripture texts and other materials for Buganda.

Mackay was lionised in his own time, although he is largely forgotten today by the world at large. Bishop Hannington, when outside Buganda, found that Mackay's was the name that everyone knew – "But of the others I scarce ever hear a word" – and after his premature death in 1890, aged 40, a book by his sister, *Mackay of Uganda*, quickly ran through several editions. Mackay, unlike his colleague, Robert Ashe, did not write any books, but he did not need to. He wrote many articles. His letters are voluminous and often very long. Many are reprinted in *Mackay of Uganda*, which uses so much verbatim material that it is in effect Mackay's autobiography

Frederick Lugard's *The Rise of Our East African Empire* was written, like Stanley's *In Darkest Africa*, partly for self-defence. Lugard had to defend himself and Captain Williams against Catholic charges of atrocities. The book does not reveal much about the man, who presents himself as a steely hero admitting at most to a touch of neuralgia or a spot of fever while all around are dropping. He respects the Baganda, but does not believe in equality between the races. Europeans should "unostentatiously assert" their superiority, while the missionaries Ashe and Pilkington are criticised for listening to complaints by Africans against himself, thus setting off "one Englishman against another". Ashe collects another brickbat for kneeling before the king, as Mackay also did.

In Margery Perham's biography, *Lugard: The Years of Adventure*, her subject comes across as unstuffy among his own people. She knew him when he was deep into his still-active retirement, living as a widower in a cottage at Abinger, Surrey. He demanded to be called "Fred", which she managed to do to his face, but she admitted that privately she was unable to think of the great imperial proconsul as Fred.

Lugard's racial inequality is not that of a conqueror; it is the inequality of the parent and the child. His book has no feeling that Africans are congenitally inferior, or that Europeans are in Africa to rape it. The question is one of social development. In pursuit of this, as Lugard sees it, Europeans are entitled to walk into someone else's country and impose a treaty.

What Lugard managed credibly to promise the African rulers was law and order. The Baganda were tired of civil war. Countries like Ankole and Toro were glad to have protection against their enemies. Defeat in war meant death and enslavement. Lugard himself believed that the most significant part of his work was reducing slavery.

Stanley's 1875 appeal for missionaries in Buganda was one of the most influential letters ever written. It produced an immediate response from the British public and the Church Missionary Society, which one year later had a party on its way to Africa. It was the presence of these missionaries, coupled with public appreciation in Britain of their work and lobbying by the CMS, that drew a reluctant British government into taking over the country. That Uganda today is mainly Christian, significantly Protestant and a member of the Commonwealth speaks of the permanent effects of that letter. With another set of circumstances, it might have become German or Belgian, or part of a greatly enlarged Sudan.

When Stanley took on the Emin Pasha Relief Expedition in 1886 he committed himself to a roundabout route that destroyed the expedition's chances of success. Under threat from the Mahdists to the north, the government of Equatoria might have survived if Stanley had reached the province earlier. Nor did it help that his party arrived in rags after struggling through the Ituri Forest. Emin's soldiers could not believe that the bedraggled band really represented the khedive of Egypt. The collapse of Equatoria created a vacuum that was eventually filled by reincorporating most of it into the Sudan, with the political difficulties that have echoed down the years.

A continuing Equatorial Province might have evolved as a pragmatic Muslim state. More likely, it would have been absorbed into Leopold's Congo or the Uganda Protectorate created by the British in the 1890s. As it is, a small part of

Equatoria, including the last capital, Wadelai, is within the boundaries of Uganda.

The aim of Consul Holmwood in Zanzibar, for the relief expedition to settle the affairs of Buganda as well as Equatoria, was not fulfilled, or even attempted. In 1889 en route to the coast with Emin, Stanley declined to intervene in the Buganda civil war. His decision might have had the widest consequences because soon afterwards Carl Peters reached Mengo and obtained from the kabaka a German protectorate over Buganda. Peters's coup, however, was overtaken by the Anglo-German agreement of 1890, so the country stayed in the British sphere.

Stanley could and did argue that the expedition was a success: Emin had been rescued after all. Yet only a fragment of the province's expatriate population came out with him. The officers and most of the soldiers stayed behind. In an accidental way, the armed bands produced the resolution of the Uganda Question. It was with the help of these troops that Lugard took over the Buganda state and his successors carved out the larger protectorate.

Certainly the expedition was a success in balancing its accounts. In fact, it did better than break even. Income was £32,367 1s 10d (20 shillings [s] = £1 and 12 pence [d] = one shilling) and expenditure was £27,709 9s 5d. The balance of £4,657 12s 5d was distributed to expedition survivors and relatives or owners of the deceased. Thus the philanthropic sponsors found themselves party not only to using slaves on the expedition but also to rewarding slave owners for lending their property.

An extraordinary number of those involved with the Emin Pasha Relief Expedition, and plenty who were not, published books and articles about it. The diaries of the two dead officers, Major Barttelot and James S. Jameson, are a vital counter-balance to Stanley's own account. Even a French priest who joined the expedition on its closing section to the east coast had something to say. Herbert Ward wrote a pleasant and colourful memoir, quoted from earlier, but he barely marched with Stanley. He joined late, left early (not from his choice) and spent much of the time stuck at Yambuya. Many of the accounts are hostile to Stanley and the controversy refused to die. Equatoria and Buganda, those troubled countries, cast a long shadow over the life's work of the great explorer.

The finest testimonial to the work of Alexander Mackay and the other Church Missionary Society pioneers is the fact that modern Uganda constitutes the world's third largest community of Anglicans, with more than nine million adherents. This is behind only England, the birthplace of Anglicanism, and Nigeria, a far bigger country.

Janani Luwum, an Anglican archbishop who was martyred during Idi Amin's rule, tackled head-on the thorny issue of Christianity and indigenous religion. Noting that Europe itself received Christianity from the outside, he said:

> Foreign missionaries have been blamed for undermining traditional religious practices and beliefs, but many of us realise today that they had no option since they were planting and building the Christian Church in what was termed a "dark continent". They had to make sure that a proper foundation was laid and a complete break with evil practices made lest the Master Builder should test their work now and at the end of time and find it lacking in the spirit of Paul's Letter to the Corinthians when he said:

> "According to the commission of God given to me, like a skilled master builder I laid a foundation, and another man is building upon it. For no other foundation can anyone lay than that which is laid, which is Jesus Christ ..."

The archbishop praised the government's land allocation to the three main missions (under the 1900 Uganda Agreement), which helped to quell the "warring spirit" among the missions. The land grants "allowed the religious groups to operate freely and prove their worth. The people were able to choose for themselves without any repressive measures ..."

That "warring spirit", with Protestants and Catholics at each other's throats, greatly impeded the work of the Christian evangelists in Buganda in the early days. A growing awareness of the damage caused by such divisions within Christendom led to the 1910 Edinburgh conference of worldwide Protestant missionary organisations, from which the present ecumenical movement has grown.

The original land settlement, by Frederick Lugard, was the least enduring part of his work in Uganda. The resettlement of the Catholics in Budu was immediately modifed by his successors as unfair. Even though Lugard was specific that the restriction to Budu applied only to Catholics bearing arms, in the unsettled state of the country the possibility of settling elsewhere unarmed was no great attraction. Sir Gerald Portal, encouraged by Captain Williams, enacted the Bishops' Agreement to extend the Catholic area. This in turn was superseded two years later, after the Vatican had assigned to the Mill Hill Fathers the eastern part of Uganda, where many of the Anglican mission stations were located. The Uganda Agreement of 1900 entrenched the missions' ability to evangelise throughout the Protectorate. It was not a case of living together happily ever afterwards, however. Uganda continued to suffer religious polarisation.

Lugard's main achievement was in a short time to construct the framework of the Uganda state. He solved the problem of the large body of Sudanese soldiers marooned in the interior by bringing them out and finding work for them in Uganda. He brought not only Buganda but also Ankole and Toro into treaty relations with the IBEA Company.

It is thanks to Lugard that the traditional rulers kept substantial areas of autonomy. The principle of indirect rule that is so much associated with his name helped the Baganda and the other kingdoms to come to terms with colonialism. Here were no primitive tribes lacking a civic culture. Although the rulers could not forget that the last word was a British one, the colonial administration worked with and through the rulers and chiefs.

Lugard's great failure was his treatment of Bunyoro. He did not make enough effort to win over Kabalega, partly because he listened too much to the Baganda, the traditional enemies of the Banyoro. Lugard's unwillingness to negotiate with the mukama has been criticised both at the time and since. Robert Ashe, a CMS missionary of the period, said Lugard had offered no proof of the king's lack of sincerity.

Kabalega's remains the name that is synonymous with Bunyoro. Yet from the start he was the subject of contradictory narratives. Already in the 1870s the conflicting versions of Bunyoro's first relations with Europeans had become entrenched, and the basis had been laid for further misunderstanding and hostility, John Beattie notes in *Bunyoro, an African Kingdom*.

In the predominant European narrative of the time, Kabalega is an untrustworthy and blood-thirsty tyrant who ruled through fear and preferred to fight than to parley. In doing so he brought misfortune on his country.

In the other narrative he is the hero who fought for the independence of his country against impossible odds. He reversed the long decline of his country until finally he was overcome by superior British arms. He was denied the opportunity of coming to terms with the British because of their hostility, fuelled by that of their Ganda allies.

This narrative was unwritten at the time, but it was evidently widely believed among the Banyoro. Otherwise the mukama could not have avoided capture for so long. It is the prevailing narrative about Kabalega today in Uganda, where the Murchison Falls became Kabalega Falls in his honour.

A case in point of observers finding what they want to find was provided by Wilhelm Junker, a German traveller in the 1880s. Junker praised Kabalega for the full vigour of his manhood, his stately presence and "bright penetrating glance", before adding that this glance "betrayed nothing of the tyrant that he really was". There can be no defence against interpretations that conclude the opposite from the facts presented!

Perhaps Junker was displeased by having to wait for his audience with the mukama, who, as the traveller explained, was closeted for three days with wizards and magicians for the new moon ceremonies. On the other hand, Junker was favoured with a rare glass of milk – used almost exclusively to fatten the royal wives. (Incidents described in Junker's *Travels in Africa during the Years 1882-86*)

European travellers generally showed cultural blindness. They were in effect condemning Kabalega for not behaving like a European, Christian gentleman when he was neither of those things. When he ordered human sacrifices, for instance, Kabalega was conforming to the

ancient traditions of the country, as Gaetano Casati recognised.

Some in today's West are more than ready to atone for
their predecessors' blindness. They are more concerned
with old cultural traditions than the morality of killing, as
with Paul Landau's remarks from the comfort of the
University of Maryland (USA):

> *Tapu**, or ancestor-propitiation, did not fall into neglect
> because of inherent flaws in their (*sic*) host cultures, but
> because of guns, wells, corvée (forced labour), racial thinking,
> and extractive bureaucracies, in a word, imperialism.
> Whether murder and feasting are religions or crimes is always
> a political matter. (Chap 10 in *Missions and Empire*, edited by
> Norman Sterlington)

Murder is always a crime. Yet this passage expresses no
sense that murder in the name of religion is wrong or that
the understanding of human sacrifice in places where it
was practised has moved on. The author's dislike of missionaries and empire has ensnared him in this ultra-rela-
tivistic approach.

Only one side left contemporaneous accounts – the
Europeans got to write the history. An exception is Sir
Apolo Kaggwa, who, remarkably, was katikiro of Buganda
before the British takeover and for more than two decades
afterwards. His several books include *Basekabaka be
Buganda* (The Kings of Buganda). This, however, stops
with Mutesa, and has little to say about Bunyoro.

Both narratives of Kabalega agree that he was a spirit-
ed and tenacious leader. He showed great valour fighting
for his kingdom first against the rising power of Buganda
and then against the British. From Lugard's arrival in
1890 until 1899 he continued to resist, with an unquench-
able optimism. He never won much. The story is of fighting retreats and hit-and-run guerrilla attacks.

Yet from the Battle of Mengo in 1892 to the Sudanese
Mutiny, there was nothing inevitable about Britain's possession and retention of Uganda. As late as 1897, the
mutiny year, Kabalega might have hoped that the junction

---

* Sacred practices

of local Muslims, Sudanese rebels and his own forces would prise Bunyoro from the British grasp. It was not unreasonable: the British too knew how tenuous their grasp was at that point.

From the failure of the mutiny until his capture in 1899, Kabalega's cause was hopeless. A classic military dilemma is whether to continue fighting or to stop. The paradox is that Kabalega the hero brought ruin to his country by keeping up a futile resistance. For its part, Britain refused him the opportunity of surrender on honourable terms and then blamed him for fighting on.

Bunyoro found itself on the wrong end of political processes. It was treated so harshly because of how Britain saw its imperial role. It perceived its empire as founded on treaties made with indigenous rulers. Bunyoro had not made a treaty and had needed to be conquered. Therefore, on this logic, it did not deserve the entitlements of Buganda, Ankole and Toro, all of which had signed treaties.

Because of its armed resistance, Bunyoro was seen by the British as a conquered territory. It suffered decades of discrimination, the effects of which are still felt. It became the Uganda whipping boy. One of the modern meanings of "whipping boy" is a frequent recipient of pain or punishment. That, sadly, is the Bunyoro story.

The treatment of Bunyoro represents one of the greatest failures of imagination in the whole empire experience. The Banyoro suffered because generations of British officials allowed themselves to be stuck in tramlines of a limited vision. Colonial administrators inherited and maintained Sir Samuel Baker's negative perceptions of Bunyoro. The failure was more acute in the 20th century when old wrongs might have been righted.

Although active hostility towards Bunyoro gave way relatively soon in the colonial period to neglect, the antagonism of both sides lasted longer. Even in the 1930s some British officials had to be warned not to keep viewing Bunyoro as a conquered territory, while the Banyoro were defeatist and suspicious of the colonial administration's every move. Thus the land reforms of 1931-33 were seen as a way of denying the Banyoro the entitlements long ago given to Buganda, Ankole and Toro. In fact, British officials were responding to the land problem according to best practice of the period.

The situation was made worse by Britain's enthusiastic preference for the Baganda, and the Baganda's unusual willingness to get alongside the colonialists. This was because that enterprising people perceived advantages for themselves in the British connection, particularly an end to political turmoil, the expansion of trade and the entrenchment of their supremacy in the region.

To cap it all, geography favoured Buganda. Its location bordering Lake Victoria gave it easier access to the export markets that were the focus of the colonial cash economy. Across the lake lay Kisumu, the railhead for the Uganda Railway (later extended to Kampala), which carried goods to the coast. Bunyoro from this point of view was in the remote interior.

Under colonialism, Buganda ran out the clear winner over Bunyoro. Its victory is proclaimed in the name of the whole country, chosen by the British. "Uganda" is merely the Swahili version of "Buganda".

APPENDIX: LIVINGSTONE'S SENATE HOUSE SPEECH

This is the full text of David Livingstone's speech delivered before the University of Cambridge, in the Senate House, on December 4, 1857. The building was described as "crowded to excess with all ranks of the University and their friends"

SOURCE: David Livingstone and Cambridge – A Record of Three Meetings in the Senate House, published by the Universities' Mission to Central Africa, 1908

WHEN I went to Africa about seventeen years ago I resolved to acquire an accurate knowledge of the native tongues; and as I continued, while there, to speak generally in the African languages, the result is that I am not now very fluent in my own ; but if you will excuse my imperfections under that head, I will endeavour to give you as clear an idea of Africa as I can. If you look at the map of Africa you will discover the shortness of the coast-line, which is in consequence of the absence of deep indentations of the sea. This is one reason why the interior of Africa has remained so long unknown to the rest of the world. Another reason is the unhealthiness of the coast,which seems to have reacted upon the disposition of the people, for they are very unkindly, and opposed to Europeans passing through their country. In the southern part of Africa lies the great Kalahari desert which contains no streams, and water is obtained only from deep wells. The people living there, not knowing the physical reasons why they have so little rain, are in the habit of sending to the mountains on the east for rain-makers, in whose power of making rain they have a firm belief. They say the people in those mountains have plenty of rain, and therefore must possess a medicine for making it. This faith in rain-making is a remarkable feature in the people in the country, and they have a good deal to say in favour of it. If you say you do not believe that these medicines have any power upon the clouds, they reply that that is just the way people talk about what they do not understand. They take a bulb, pound it, and administer an infusion of it to a sheep. In a short time the sheep dies in convulsions, and then

they ask : Has not the medicine power ? The common argument
known to all those tribes is this——" God loves you white men better
than us ; He made you first, and did not make us pretty like you ;
He made us afterwards, and does not love us as He loves you. He
gave you clothing, and horses and waggons, and guns and powder,
and that Book which you are always talking about. He gave us
only two things—cattle, and a knowledge of certain medicines by
which we can make rain. We do not despise the things that you
have ; we only wish that we had them too ; we do not despise
that Book of yours, although we do not understand it ; so you
ought not to despise our knowledge of rain-making, although you
do not understand it." You cannot convince them that they have
no power to make rain.

I went into that country for the purpose of teaching the doctrines
of our holy religion, and settled with the tribes on the border of the
Kalahari desert. These tribes were those of the Bakwains, Bush-
men, and Bakalahari. Sechele is the chief of the former. On
the occasion of the first religious service held, he asked me if he
could put some questions on the subject of Christianity, since
such was the custom of their country when any new subject was
introduced to their notice. I said, " By all means." He then
inquired, " If my forefathers knew of a future judgment ? " I said,
" Yes ; " and began to describe the scene of the great white throne,
and Him who should sit on it, from whose face the heavens shall
flee away, and be no more seen ; interrupting he said, " You startle
me, these words make all my bones to shake, I have no more strength
in me. You have been talking about a future judgment, and
many terrible things of which we know nothing," repeating, " Did
your forefathers know of these things ? " I again replied in the affirma-
tive. The chief said, " All my forefathers have passed away into darkness, without knowing anything of what was to befall them ; how is it
that your forefathers, knowing all these things,
did not send word to my forefathers sooner ? "

This was rather a poser ; but I explained the geographical difficulties, and said it was only after we had begun to send the knowledge of Christ to Cape Colony, and other parts of the country to

which we had access, that we came to them ; that it was their
duty to receive what Europeans had now obtained the power to
offer them ; and that the time would come when the whole world
would receive the knowledge of Christ, because Christ had promised
that all the earth should be covered with a knowledge of Himself.
The chief pointed to the Kalahari desert, and said, " Will you ever
get beyond that with your Gospel ? We, who are more accustomed
to thirst than you are, cannot cross that desert ; how can you ? "
I stated my belief in the promise of Christ; and in a few years
afterwards that chief was the man who enabled me to cross that
desert ; and not only so, but he himself preached the Gospel to
tribes beyond it. In some years more rain than usual falls in the
desert, and then there is a large crop of water-melons. When this
occurred, the desert might be crossed. In 1852 a gentleman crossed
it, and his oxen existed on the fluid contained in the melons for
twenty-two days. In crossing the desert, different sorts of country
are met with ; up to 20th south latitude there is a comparatively
dry and arid country; and you might travel for four days, as I
have done, without a single drop of water for the oxen. Water for
the travellers themselves was always carried in the waggons, the
usual mode of travelling south of the 20th degree of latitude being
by ox-waggon. For four days, upon several occasions, we had not
a drop of water for the oxen ; but beyond 20th south latitude,
going to the north, we travelled to Loanda, 1,500 miles [2,400 km],
without carrying water for a single day.

My object in going into the country south of the desert was to
instruct the natives in a knowledge of Christianity, but many
circumstances prevented my living amongst them more than seven
years, amongst which were considerations arising out of the slave
system carried on by the Dutch Boers. I resolved to go into the
country beyond, and soon found that, for the purposes of commerce, it was necessary to have a path to the sea. I might have
gone on instructing the natives in religion, but as civilization and
Christianity must go on together, I was obliged to find a path to
the sea, in order that I should not sink to the level of the natives.
The chief was overjoyed at the suggestion, and furnished me with
twenty-seven men, and canoes and provisions, and presents for the

tribes through whose country we had to pass. We might have
taken a shorter path to the sea than that to the north, and then to
the west, by which we went ; but along the country by the shorter
route there is an insect called the tsetse, whose bite is fatal to horses
oxen, and dogs, but not to men or donkeys.—You seem to think
there is a connexion between the two.—The habitat of that insect
is along the shorter route to the sea. The bite of it is fatal to
domestic animals, not immediately, but certainly in the course of
two or three months ; the animal grows leaner and leaner, and
gradually dies of emaciation : a horse belonging to Gordon Cumming
died of a bite five or six months after it was bitten.

On account of this insect, I resolved to go to the north, and then
westwards to the Portuguese settlement of Loanda. Along the
course of the river which we passed game was so abundant that
there was no difficulty in supplying the wants of my whole party :
antelopes were so tame that they might be shot from the canoe.
But beyond 14 degrees of south latitude the natives had guns, and
had themselves destroyed the game, so that I and my party had to
live on charity. The people, however, in that central region were
friendly and hospitable, but they had nothing but vegetable productions ; the most abundant was the cassava, which, however
nice when made into tapioca pudding, resembles in its more primitive condition nothing so much as a mess of laundress' starch.
There was a desire in the various villages through which we passed
to have intercourse with us, and kindness and hospitality were
shown us ; but when we got near the Portuguese settlement of
Angola the case was changed, and payment was demanded for
everything. But I had nothing to pay with. Now the people
had been in the habit of trading with the slavers, and so they said
I might give one of my men in payment for what I wanted. When
I showed them that I could not do this, they looked upon me as
an interloper, and I was sometimes in danger of being murdered.

As we neared the coast, the name of England was recognised,
and we got on with ease. Upon one occasion, when I was passing
through the parts visited by slave-traders, a chief who wished to
show me some kindness offered me a slave-girl ; upon explaining

that I had a little girl of my own, whom I should not like my own
chief to give to a black man, the chief thought I was displeased with
the size of the girl, and sent me one a head taller. By this and
other means I convinced my men of my opposition to the principle
of slavery ; and when we arrived at Loanda, I took them on board a
British vessel, where I took a pride in showing them that those
countrymen of mine and those guns were there for the purpose of
putting down the slave-trade. They were convinced from what
they saw, of the honesty of Englishmen's intentions ; and the hearty
reception they met with from the sailors made them say to me,
" We see they are your countrymen, for they have hearts like you."
On the journey, the men had always looked forward to reaching
the coast ; they had seen Manchester prints and other articles
imported therefrom, and they could not believe they were made by
mortal hands. On reaching the sea, they thought that they had
come to the end of the world. They said, " We marched along with
our father, thinking the world was a large plain without limit ; but
all at once the land said, ' I am finished, there is no more of me' ; "
and they called themselves the true old men—the true ancientsb-having
gone to the end of the world. On reaching Loanda, they
commenced trading in firewood, and also engaged themselves at
sixpence a day in unloading coals, brought by a steamer for the supply
of the cruiser lying there to watch the slave-vessels. On
their return, they told their people, " we worked for a whole moon,
carrying away the stones that burn." By the time they were ready
to go back to their own country, each had secured a large bundle of
goods. On the way back, however, fever detained them, and their
goods were all gone, leaving them on their return home as poor as
when they started.

I had gone towards the coast for the purpose of finding a direct
path to the sea ; but on going through the country, we found forests
so dense that the sun had not much influence on the ground, which
was covered with yellow mosses, and all the trees with white lichens.
Amongst these forests were little streams, each having its source in
a bog; in fact, nearly all the rivers in that country commence in
bogs. Finding it impossible to travel here in a wheel conveyance,
I left my waggon behind, and I believe it is standing in perfect

safety, where I last saw it, at the present moment. The only
other means of conveyance we had was ox-back, by no means a
comfortable mode of travelling. I therefore came back to discover
another route to the coast by means of the river Zambesi.

Having got down amongst the people in the middle of the country,
and having made known to my friend the chief my desire to have a
path for civilization and commerce on the east, he again furnished
me with means to pursue my researches eastward ; and, to show
how disposed the natives were to aid me in my expedition, I had
114 men to accompany me to the east, whilst those who had travelled
to the west with me only amounted to twenty-seven. I carried
with me thirty tusks of ivory ; and, on leaving my waggon to set
forth on my journey, two warriors of the country offered a heifer
apiece to the man who should slay any one who molested it. Having
proceeded about a hundred miles (160 km), I found myself short of
ammunition, and despatched an emissary back to the chief to procure
more percussion caps from a box I had in my waggon. Not understanding the lock, the chief took a hatchet and split the lid open, to get what
was wanted ; and notwithstanding the insecure state in which it
remained, I found, on returning two years after, that its contents
were precisely as I left them. Such honesty is rare even in civilized
Christian England, as I know from experience ; for I sent a box of
fossils to Dr. Buckland, which, after arriving safely in England,
was stolen from some railway, being probably mistaken for plate.

I could not make my friend the chief understand that I was poor ;
I had a quantity of sugar, and while it lasted the chief would favour
me with his company to coffee ; when it was gone, I told the chief
how it was produced from the cane, which grew in Central Africa,
but as they had no means of extracting the saccharine matter, he
requested me to procure a sugar-mill. When I told him I was poor,
the chief then informed me that all the ivory in the country was at
my disposal, and he accordingly loaded me with tusks, ten of which,
on arriving at the coast, I spent in purchasing clothing for my
followers ; the rest were left at Quilimane, that the impression
should not be produced in the country that they had been stolen,
in case of my non-return.

Englishmen are very apt to form their opinion of Africans from
the elegant figures in tobacconists' shops ; I scarcely think such are
fair specimens of the African, I think, at the same time, that the
African women would be much handsomer than they are if they
would only let themselves alone ; though unfortunately that is a
failing by no means peculiar to African ladies ; but they are, by
nature, not particularly good-looking, and seem to take all the pains at
they can to make themselves worse. The people of one tribe
knock out all their upper front teeth, and when they laugh are
perfectly hideous. Another tribe of the Londa country file all their
front teeth to a point, like cats' teeth, and when they grin, put one
in mind of alligators, Many of the women are comely, but spoil
their beauty by such unnatural means. Another tribe has the
custom of piercing the cartilage of the nose, and inserting a bit of
reed, which spreads it out, and makes them very disagreeable-
looking ; others tie their hair, or rather wool, into basket-work,
resembling the tonsorial decorations of the ancient Egyptians ;
others, again, dress their hair with a hoop around it, so as to resemble
the gloria round the head of the Virgin ; rather a different application of the hoop to that of English ladies !

The people of Central Africa have religious ideas stronger than
those of the Kaffirs and other southern nations, who talk much of
God, but pray seldom. They pray to departed relatives, by whom
they imagine illnesses are sent to punish them for any neglect on
their part. Evidences of the Portuguese Jesuit missionary operations are still extant, and are carefully preserved by the natives.
One tribe can all read and write, which is ascribable to the teaching
of the Jesuits. Their only books are, however, histories of saints,
and miracles effected by the parings of saintly toe-nails, and such-
like nonsense. But surely, if such an impression has once been
produced, it might be hoped that the efforts of other missionaries,
who would leave the Bible with these poor people, would not be
less abiding.

In a commercial point of view, communication with this country
is desirable. Angola is wonderfully fertile, producing every kind of
tropical plant in rank luxuriance. Passing on to the valley of
Quango, the stalk of the grass was as thick as a quill, and towered

above my head, although I was mounted on my ox ; cotton is
produced in great abundance, though merely woven into common
cloth ; bananas and pine-apples grow in great luxuriance ; but the
people having no maritime communication, these advantages are
almost lost. The country on the other side is not quite so fertile,
but, in addition to indigo, cotton, and sugarcane, produces a fibrous
substance which I am assured is stronger than flax.

The Zambesi has not been thought much of as a river by Europeans,
not appearing very large at its mouth ; but on going up it for about
seventy miles it is enormous. The first three hundred miles might
be navigated without obstacle ; then there is a rapid, and near it a
coal-field of large extent. The elevated sides of the basin, which
form the most important feature of the country, are far different
in climate to the country nearer the sea, or even the centre. Here
the grass is short, and the Angola goat, which could not live in the
centre, had been seen on the east highland by Mr. Moffat.

My desire is to open a path to this district, that civilization,
commerce, and Christianity might find their way there. I consider
that we made a great mistake, when we carried commerce into
India, in being ashamed of our Christianity ; as a matter of common
sense and good policy it is always best to appear in one's true
character. In travelling through Africa I might have imitated
certain Portuguese, and have passed for a chief ; but I never attempted
anything of the sort, although endeavouring always to keep to the
lessons of cleanliness rigidly instilled by my mother long ago ; the
consequence was that the natives respected me for that quality,
though remaining dirty themselves.

I had a pass from the Portuguese consul, and on arriving at their
settlement I was asked what I was. I said, " A missionary, and a
doctor too." They asked, "Are you a doctor of medicine ?"—
" Yes." " Are you not a doctor of mathematics, too ? "—" No."—
" And yet you can take longitudes and latitudes."—Then they
asked me about my moustache ; and I simply said I wore it because
men had moustaches to wear, and ladies had not. They could not
understand either why a sacerdote should have a wife and four

children ; and many a joke took place upon that subject. I used to say, " Is it not better to have children with than without a wife ? " Englishmen of education always command respect, without any adventitious aid. A Portuguese governor left for Angola, giving out that he was going to keep a large establishment, and taking with him quantities of crockery, and about five hundred waistcoats ; but when he arrived in Africa he made a " deal " of them. Educated Englishmen seldom descend to that sort of thing.

A prospect is now before us of opening Africa for commerce and the Gospel. Providence has been preparing the way, for even before I proceeded to the Central basin it had been conquered and rendered safe by a chief named Sebituane, and the language of the Bechuanas made the fashionable tongue, and that was one of the languages into which Mr. Moffat had translated the Scriptures. Sebituane also discovered Lake Ngami some time previous to my explorations in that part. In going back to that country my object is to open up traffic along the banks of the Zambesi, and also to preach the Gospel. The natives of Central Africa are very desirous of trading, but their only traffic is at present in slaves, of which the poorer people have an unmitigated horror ; it is therefore most desirable to encourage the former principle, and thus open a way for the consumption of free productions, and the introduction of Christianity and commerce. By encouraging the native propensity for trade, the advantages that might be derived in a commercial point of view are incalculable ; nor should we lose sight of the inestimable blessings it is in our power to bestow upon the unenlightened African, by giving him the light of Christianity. Those two pioneers of civilization—Christianity and commerce—should ever be inseparable ; and Englishmen should be warned by the fruits of neglecting that principle as exemplified in the result of the management of Indian affairs. By trading with Africa also, we should at length be independent of slave-labour, and thus discountenance practices so obnoxious to every Englishman.

Though the natives are not absolutely anxious to receive the Gospel, they are open to Christian influences. Among the Bechuanas the Gospel was well received. These people think it a crime to shed a tear, but I have seen some of them weep at the recollection of

their sins, when God had opened their hearts to Christianity and
repentance. It is true that missionaries have difficulties to encounter ; but what great enterprise was ever accomplished without
difficulty ? It is deplorable to think that one of the noblest of our
missionary societies, the Church Missionary Society, is compelled
to send to Germany for missionaries, whilst other societies are amply
supplied. Let this stain be wiped off.

The sort of men who are wanted for missionaries are such as I
see before me—men of education, standing, enterprise, zeal, and
piety. It is a mistake to suppose that *any one*, as long as he is
pious, will do for this office. Pioneers in every thing should be the
ablest and best qualified men, not those of small ability and education. This remark especially applies to the first teachers of Christian truth in regions which may never have before been blest with
the name and Gospel of Jesus Christ. In the early ages the monasteries were the schools of Europe, and the monks were not ashamed
to hold the plough. The missionaries now take the place of those
noble men, and we should not hesitate to give up the small luxuries
of life in order to carry knowledge and truth to them that are in
darkness. I hope that many of those whom I now address will
embrace that honourable career. Education has been given us
from above for the purpose of bringing to the benighted the knowledge of a Saviour. If you knew the satisfaction of performing
such a duty, as well as the gratitude to God which the missionary
must always feel, in being chosen for so noble, so sacred a calling,
you would have no hesitation in embracing it.

For my own part, I have never ceased to rejoice that God has
appointed me to such an office. People talk of the sacrifice I have
made in spending so much of my life in Africa. Can that be called a
sacrifice which is simply paid back as a small part of a great debt
owing to our God, which we can never repay ?—Is that a sacrifice
which brings its own blest reward in healthful activity, the consciousness of doing good, peace of mind, and a bright hope of a glorious
destiny hereafter ?—Away with the word in such a view, and with
such a thought ! It is emphatically no sacrifice. Say rather it is a
privilege. Anxiety, sickness, suffering, or danger, now and then,

with a foregoing of the common conveniences and charities of this life, may make us pause, and cause the spirit to waver and the soul to sink, but let this only be for a moment. All these are nothing when compared with the glory which shall hereafter be revealed in, and for, us. I never made a sacrifice. Of this we ought not to talk, when we remember the great sacrifice which HE made who left His Father's throne on high to give Himself for us—" Who being the brightness of that Father's glory, and the express image of His person, and upholding all things by the word of His power, when He had by Himself purged our sins, sat down on the right hand of the majesty on high."

English people are treated with respect ; and the missionary can earn his living by his gun—a course not open to a country curate. I would rather be a poor missionary than a poor curate.

Then there is the pleasant prospect of returning home and seeing the agreeable faces of his country-women again. I suppose I present a pretty contrast to you. At Cairo we met a party of young English people, whose faces were quite a contrast to the skinny, withered ones of those who had spent the latter years of their life in a tropical clime. They were the first rosy cheeks I had seen for sixteen years ; you can hardly tell how pleasant it is to see the blooming cheeks of young ladies before me, after an absence of sixteen years from such delightful objects of contemplation. There is also the pleasure of the welcome home, and I heartily thank you for the welcome you have given me on the present occasion ; but there is also the hope of the welcome words of our Lord, " Well done, good and faithful servant."

I beg to direct your attention to Africa ; I know that in a few years I shall be cut off in that country, which is now open ; do not let it be shut again ! I go back to Africa to try to make an open path for commerce and Christianity ; do you carry out the work which I have begun. I LEAVE IT WITH YOU !

BIBLIOGRAPHY

Allen Charles (ed). *Tales from the Dark Continent* (Andre Deutsch/British Broadcasting Corporation, 1979)

Anderson William B. *The Church in East Africa, 1840-1974* (Dodoma, Tanzania: Central Tanganyika Press, 1988; first published 1977)

Anstruther Ian. *I Presume* (Geoffrey Bles, 1956; New English Library, 1974)

Ashe Robert P. *Two Kings of Uganda* (Sampson Low, Marston, Searle and Rivington, 1889)

Austin Major Herbert H. *With Macdonald in Uganda* (1903; reprint by Dawsons of Pall Mall, 1973)

Baker Sir Samuel W. *The Albert Nyanza, Great Basin of the Nile*, vol 2 (Macmillan, 1866)

Baker Sir Samuel W. *Ismailia: a Narrative of the Expedition to Central Africa for the Suppression of the Slave Trade* (Macmillan, 2nd ed 1879)

Bazley Walter. *Bunyoro, Tropical Paradise* (Pentland Press, 1993)

Beattie John. *Bunyoro, an African Kingdom* (Holt Rinehart and Winston, 1966)

Beattie John. *The Nyoro State* (Oxford University Press, 1971)

Behrend Heike. *Alice Lakwena and the Holy Spirits: War in Northern Uganda 1985-97* (James Currey, 1999; translated from the German)

Bourret F.M. *Ghana: The Road to Independence, 1919-1957* (Oxford University Press, 1960)

Brown Douglas and Brown Marcelle V. (editors). *Looking Back at the Uganda Protectorate: Recollections of District Officers* (Douglas Brown, 1966)

Burke Fred G. *Local Government and Politics in Uganda* (Syracuse University Press, 1964)

Caplan Gerald L. *The Elites of Barotseland 1878-1969* (C. Hurst & Co, 1970)

Catholic Union of Great Britain. *Notes on Uganda, or an Analysis* (Waterlow & Sons, 1893)

Casati Major Gaetano. *Ten Years in Equatoria and the Return with Emin Pasha*, vol 2 (Frederick Warne, 1891; translated from the Italian)

Chapman F. Spencer, DSO. *Lightest Africa* (Chatto & Windus, 1955)

Chretien Jean-Pierre. *The Great Lakes of Africa* (Zone Books, 2003; translated from the French)

Claridge W. Walton. *A History of the Gold Coast and Ashanti*, vols I and II (John Murray, 1915 – reprint Frank Cass, 1964)

Clay Gervas. *Your Friend, Lewanika* (Chatto & Windus, 1968)

Coillard Francois. *On the Threshold of Central Africa.* (First published 1897. Original in French. Republished by Frank Cass & Co, 1971)

Colvile Colonel Sir Henry. *The Land of the Nile Springs, being chiefly an account of how we fought Kabarega* (Edward Arnold, 1895)

Comby Jean. *How to Understand the History of Christian Mission* (SCM Press, 1996; French edition 1992). Chaps 7 and 8

Cunningham J.F. *Uganda and Its Peoples* (Hutchinson, 1905)

Doyle Shane. *Crisis & Decline in Bunyoro: Population & Environment in Western Uganda 1860-1955* (British Institute in Eastern Africa in association with James Currey etc, 2006)

Dunbar A.R. *A History of Bunyoro-Kitara* (Oxford University Press [Nairobi], 1968)

Dunbar A.R. *Omukama Chwa II Kabarega* (East African Literature Bureau, 1965)

Edgerton Robert B. *The Fall of the Asante Empire* (The Free Press, 1995)

Fisher Mrs A. *Twilight Tales of the Black Baganda* (1911; reprint by Frank Cass, 1970)

Foster W.D. *The Church Missionary Society and Modern Medicine in Uganda: The Life of Sir Albert Cook, KCMG, 1870-1951.* Published by the author, 1978

Fox Bourne H.R. *The Other Side of the Emin Pasha Relief Expedition* (Chatto & Windus, 1891)

Galbraith John S. *Mackinnon and East Africa, 1878-1895: A Study in the 'New Imperialism'* (Cambridge University Press, 1972)

Gale H.P. *Uganda and the Mill Hill Fathers* (Macmillan, 1959)

Gann. L.H. *The Birth of a Plural Society* (Manchester University Press, 1958)

Gluckman Max. *Economy of the Central Barotse Plain* (Rhodes-Livingstone Institute, Livingstone, 1941)

Greenlee James G., and Johnston Charles M. *Good Citizens: British Missionaries and Imperial States 1870-1918* (McGill-Queen's University Press, 1999)

Gregory Professor J.W. *The Foundation of British East Africa* (Horace Marshall, 1901)

Hall Richard. *Lovers on the Nile* (Collins, 1980)

Hanson Holly. *Landed Obligation* (Heinemann, 2003)

Harding Colonel Colin. *Far Bugles* (Simpkin Marshall, 1933)

Harding Colonel Colin. *In Remotest Barotseland* (Hurst & Blackett, 1905)

Hardy Ronald. *The Iron Snake* [story of the Uganda Railway] (Collins, 1965)

Harlow Vincent, Chilver E.M. and Smith Alison (editors). *History of East Africa*, Vol 2 (Oxford University Press, 1965)

Hayford J.E Casely. *Gold Coast Native Institutions* (Sweet and Maxwell, 1903)

Herbert Eugenia W. *Twilight on the Zambesi* (Palgrave Macmillan, 2002)

Hird Frank. *H.M. Stanley, the Authorized Life* (Stanley Paul, 1935)

Hochschild Adam. *King Leopold's Ghost* (Macmillan 1999; first published in USA 1998 by Houghton Mifflin Company)

Ingham Kenneth. *A History of East Africa* (Longmans, 3rd ed 1965)

Jackson Sir Frederick. *Early Days in East Africa* (1930; reprint by Dawsons of Pall Mall, 1969)

James Lawrence. *The Rise and Fall of the British Empire* (Little, Brown & Co, 1994)

Johnston Sir Harry. *The Backward Peoples and Our Relations with Them* (H. Milford, Oxford University Press, 1920)

Johnston Sir Harry. *A History and Description of the British Empire in Africa* (National Society's Depository, undated – 1910?)

Jorgensen Jan Jelmert. *Uganda, a Modern History* (Croom Helm, 1981)

Junker Dr Wilhelm. *Travels in Africa during the Years 1882-86* (Chapman & Hall, 1892; translated from the German by A.H. Keane)

Kabaka of Buganda, the (Mutesa II). *Desecration of My Kingdom* (Constable, 1967)

Kaggwa Apolo. *Basekabaka be Buganda*, translated and edited by M.S.M. Kiwanuka as The Kings of Buganda (East African Publishing House, 1971)

Karugire Samwiri Rubaraza. *A Political History of Uganda* (Heinemann [Nairobi], 1980)

Kimble David. *A Political History of Ghana, 1850-1928* (Oxford,

Clarendon Press, 1963)

Kingston Vera. *An Army With Banners: The Romance of Missionary Adventure.* (Sampson Low, Marston and Co. Undated, c 1931. Chaps 3 and 7)

Kiwanuka Malumba S.M.S. *A History of Buganda: From the Foundation of the Kingdom to 1900* (Longman, 1971)

Knight Norman. *Memories of a District Officer in Northern Rhodesia and of the War Years* (privately published, 2007)

Lewin Thomas J. *Asante Before the British: The Prempean Years 1875-1900* (Regents Press of Kansas, 1978)

Livingstone David. *Missionary Travels and Researches in South Africa* (John Murray, 1857)

Livingstone David and Charles. *Narrative of an Expedition to the Zambesi and Its Tributaries* (John Murray, 1865)

Low D.A. and Pratt R. Cranford. *Buganda and British Overrule* (Oxford University Press, 1970)

Low D. A. *Buganda in Modern History* (Weidenfeld & Nicolson, 1971)

Low D.A. *Fabrication of Empire* (Cambridge University Press, 2009)

Luck Anne. *African Saint: The Story of Apolo Kivebulaya* (SCM Press, 1963)

Luck Reginald Arthur. *A Visit to Lewanika, King of the Barotse* (Simpkin, Marshall, Hamilton, Kent & Co, 1902)

Lugard Captain F.D. *The Rise of Our East African Empire*, vol 2 (Wm Blackwood and Sons, 1893)

Macdonald Major J.R.L. *Soldiering and Surveying in British East Africa 1891-1894* (1897; reprint, edited by A.T. Matson, by Dawsons of Pall Mall, 1973)

Mackay A.M. *Mackay of Uganda (Mackay, Pioneer Missionary of the Church Missionary Society to Uganda).* By his sister (Hodder & Stoughton, 9th thousand 1891)

Mackintosh C.W. *Coillard of the Zambesi* (T. Fisher Unwin, 1907)

Mackintosh C.W. *Lewanika of the Barotse* (United Society for Christian Literature, 1942)

Marlowe John. *Cecil Rhodes: The Anatomy of Empire* (Paul Elek, 1972)

Matheson Elizabeth Mary. *An Enterprise So Perilous* (history of the White Fathers). (Mellifont, undated; believed 1970s)

Mathews Basil. *Livingstone the Pathfinder.* (Livingstone Press, 1943; first edition 1912)

McLeod M.D. *The Asante* (British Museum Publications, 1981)

McLynn Frank. *Hearts of Darkness: The European Exploration of Africa* (Hutchinson, 1992)

Metcalfe G.E. *Maclean of the Gold Coast* (Oxford University Press. 1962)

Murray Jocelyn. *Proclaim the Good News: A Short History of the Church Missionary Society.* (Hodder & Stoughton, 1985. Partic Chap 7)

Museveni Yoweri Kaguta. *Sowing the Mustard Seed* (Macmillan, 1997)

Neill Stephen. *A History of Christian Missions*, Vol 6 of the Penguin History of the Church) (Penguin Books, second edition revised by Owen Chadwick, 1986; first published 1964. Chaps 10 and 11)

Nothling F.J. *Pre-Colonial Africa: Her Civilisations and Foreign Contacts* (Southern Book Publishers, South Africa, 1989; second impression 1995)

Nyakatura John. *Aspects of Bunyoro Customs and Tradition*, translated by Zebiya Kwamya Rigby (East African Literature Bureau, undated – 1970?)

Odongo Onyango. *A Political History of Uganda: Yoweri Museveni's Referendum 2000* (WiCU Publishing Press, 2000)

Oliver Roland and Mathew Gervase, editors. *History of East Africa*, Vol 1 (Oxford University Press, 1963)

Oliver Roland. *The Missionary Factor in East Africa* (Longmans, Green & Co, 1952)

Oliver Roland. *Sir Harry Johnston and the Scramble for Africa* (Chatto & Windus, 1957)

Omara-Otunnu Amii. *Politics and the Military in Uganda, 1890-1985* (Macmillan Press, 1987)

Padwick C. *Mackay of the Great Lake* (Kingsway, 1948; revised edition)

Pakenham Thomas. *The Scramble for Africa* (Abacus, 1992; first published in UK by Weidenfeld and Nicolson, 1991. Partic Chaps 17, 19 and 23)

Palmer R.H. *Lewanika's Country: Reminiscences of a Pioneer* (privately printed, undated)

Perham Margery. *Lugard: The Years of Adventure, 1858-1898* (Collins, 1956. Partic Part 3)

Perham Margery. *The Colonial Reckoning* (Collins: Fontana Library, 1963)

Pirouet Louise. *Historical Dictionary of Uganda* (Scarecrow Press, 1995)

Pirouet Louise. *Black Evangelists: the Spread of Christianity in Uganda 1891-1914* (Rex Collings, 1978)

Postlethwaite J.R.P. *I Look Back* (Boardman, 1947)

Rieff David. *A Bed for the Night: Humanitarianism in Crisis* (Vintage, 2002)

Roscoe John. *The Bakitara* (Cambridge University Press, 1923)

Schweitzer Georg. *Emin Pasha: His Life and Work*, Vol 1 (Archibald Constable, 1898; translated from the German)

Shorter Aylward. *Cross and Flag in Africa* (Orbis Books, 2006)

Smith Iain R. *The Emin Pasha Relief Expedition, 1886-1890* (Oxford University Press, 1972)

Speke John Hanning. *Journal of the Discovery of the Source of the Nile* (Wm Blackwood & Sons, 1863)

Stanley Henry M. *In Darkest Africa*, Vols 1 and 2 (Sampson Low, Marston, Searle and Rivington, 1890)

Stanley Henry M. *Through the Dark Continent*, Vol 1 (Sampson Low, Marston, Searle and Rivington, 1878)

Steinhart Edward I. *Conflict and Collaboration: The Kingdoms of Western Uganda 1890-1907* (Princeton University Press, 1977)

Sterlington Norman (editor). *Missions and Empire* (Oxford University Press, 2005)

Stigand Major C.H., CBE. *Equatoria: The Lado Enclave* (Constable, 1923. Chap 14)

Stirke D.W. Barotseland: *Eight Years Among the Barotse* (John Bales, Sons & Daniellson, 1922)

Stock Eugene. *The History of the Church Missionary Society* (CMS, 1899 all three volumes; supplementary volume 1916)

Thompson Gardner. *Governing Uganda: British Colonial Rule and Its Legacy* (Fountain Publishers [Kampala], 2003)

Thruston Major A.B. *African Incidents* (John Murray, 1900)

Tiberondwa Ado K. *Missionary Teachers as Agents of Colonialism: A Study of Their Activities in Uganda, 1877-1925* (Kenneth Kaunda Foundation, Lusaka, 1978)

Tuma Tom and Mutibwa Phares (editors). *A Century of Christianity in Uganda, 1877-1977* (Uzima Press, Nairobi, for the Church of Uganda, 1978)

Turnbull Colin. *The Forest People* (Jonathan Cape, 1961; Pimlico edition 1993)

Turner V.W. *The Lozi Peoples of North-Western Rhodesia* (International African Institute, London, 1952)

Twaddle Michael. *Kakungulu and the Creation of Uganda 1868-1928* (James Currey, 1993)

Uzoigwe G.N. *Britain and the Conquest of Africa: The Age of Salisbury* (University of Michigan Press, 1974)

Various authors. *David Livingstone and the Victorian Encounter with Africa* (National Portrait Gallery Publications, London, 1996)

Ward Herbert. *My Life With Stanley's Rear Guard* (Chatto & Windus, 1891)

White Stanhope. *Lost Empire on the Nile* (Robert Hale, 1969)

Wills J.T. *Emin Bey: Gordon's Lieutenant in Africa* (Edward Stanford, 1887; reprinted from the Fortnightly Review)

Wilson Rev C.T., and Felkin R.W. *Uganda and the Egyptian Soudan* (Samson Low, Marston, Searle and Rivington, 1882)

INDEX

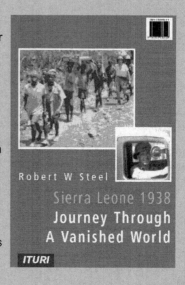